THE
WEAPONS
—THAT—
CHANGED
—THE—
WORLD

THE WEAPONS THAT CHANGED THE WORLD

IAN HOGG

ARBOR HOUSE
New York

Published by Arbor House Publishing Co.
Division, the Hearst Corporation
235 East 45th Street
New York, N.Y. 10017

First impression 1986

Library of Congress Cataloging-in-Publication Data
Hogg, Ian V., 1926-
    The weapons that changed the world.
    Bibliography: p.
    Includes index.
    1. Weapons systems—History—19th century.
2. Weapons systems—History—20th century. I. Title.
UF500.H64 1986   355.8′2′09   86-1120
ISBN 0-87795-809-2

Typeset by Peter MacDonald, Twickenham
Origination by A.G. Coop, Verona, Italy
Printed and bound by Motta, Milan, Italy

This book was designed and produced by
The Paul Press Ltd
22 Bruton Street, London W1X 7DA

CONTENTS

LAND POWER

As nations struggle for dominion, the common man is thrown into conflict

The story of modern warfare begins with Napoleon. His impact on the art of war can be considered in a variety of ways – his innovative genius transformed strategy, tactics, organization and logistics. His mastery of rapid troop movement and his abandonment of the time-honoured seasonal system of warfare were both innovations that disgruntled many professionals of the time; "In my youth", complained an elderly Prussian officer, "we used to march and countermarch all summer without losing or gaining a square league, and then we went into winter quarters. But now comes an ignorant hotheaded young man who flies from Boulogne to Ulm, and from Ulm to the middle of Moravia, and fights battles in December. The whole system of his tactics is monstrously incorrect".

Incorrect or not, it was this system that won Napoleon his greatest successes, plus the fact that he had abandoned the time-honoured practice of relying on a small corpus of professional soldiers and set up a system of a "Citizen Army" – romantically referred to as "the nation in arms" – whose size enabled him to sustain operations in several places simultaneously. His advance into Russia in 1812, for instance, involved almost half a million troops; their fighting quality as a whole may not have been the equal of the professional armies opposed to them, but their sheer numbers and their enthusiasm for their cause made up for any technical shortcomings.

Napoleon, therefore, can be credited with being the progenitor of the concept of the "nation in arms", whereby the conduct of warfare was no longer the prerogative of a small body of professionals but, in one way or another, began to impinge upon the daily life of an entire country. With Napoleon's downfall, most European military leaders breathed a sigh of relief, dispersed the militia and volunteer forces, severely pruned their armies back to the minimum level, and generally looked forward to "getting back to real soldiering". But what Napoleon had set in motion could not be undone, particularly when taken in conjunction with the advances in weaponry made possible by industrialization.

Before the 19th century, the technological and industrial support needed to sustain land warfare – or sea warfare, for that matter – took up a relatively small proportion of a nation's manufacturing capability. Virtually all the specialized equipment necessary consisted of muskets, cannon, swords and lances; anything else was of basically civilian pattern – carts, cooking pots, clothing – and could either be directly purchased on the market or required only a small amount of modification from some essentially similar commercial product. Since the strength of armies was small (Marlborough, for instance, had about 11,000 English troops under his command at Blenheim, in 1704), the weaponry required could be largely supplied by standard stocks, if necessary, and then supplemented by small contractors, whose output sufficed both to replace losses in the field and to furnish equipment for recruits.

The railroad and war

Because of this relatively small demand for equipment, the initial impact of the Industrial Revolution on the military establishment was minimal. The only aspect which immediately interested armies was the prospect of using the new railways to move troops. Within days of the opening of the Liverpool and Manchester Railway, in 1830, a British infantry battalion was conveyed between the two cities in just two hours, a journey which would have meant a two-day march. By 1846, *Regulations Relative to the Conveyance of Her Majesty's Forces, their Baggage and Stores, by Rail* had been promulgated. In 1842, a Prussian writer, Carl Ponitz, published *Die Eisenbahnen als militarische Operationslinien betrachtet und durch Beispiele erlautet* ("The railway exemplified as a military operational line") which, among other observations, pointed out the likelihood of Prussia having to fight on two fronts – Russia and France – and the desirability of siting railway lines, which, in addition to serving the population, could be used as rapid transit channels to move troops to a threatened front or from one front to another. Whether Ponitz's writing had an effect, or whether the Prussian government had already drawn the same conclusions, by 1845 lines were

in construction towards both Prussia's frontiers, and in 1846 the Sixth Army Corps – 12,000 men with their associated horses, guns and stores – was moved from Potsdam to Posen by rail. The Prussian example was not lost on other European powers. In 1851, an Austrian division of 14,500 men, with 2000 horses, 48 guns and 464 assorted vehicles, moved from Krakow to Ungarisch-Hradish on the Hungarian border in two days, a journey which would have taken 15 days if the division had been forced to march.

The first use of railways in actual warfare came with France's Italian campaign of 1859, when Napoleon III crossed the Alps "to set Italy free" from Austrian domination. In 86 days the French railways moved 604,000 men and over 129,000 horses in various directions to concentrate the French army on the Italian border. This was a remarkable feat, and it left the remainder of the administrative system gasping; trainloads of men and horses would arrive at their destinations but would then have to wait for their rations, ammunition and supplies to catch up with them.

By the sword divided

In 1861 the American Civil War broke out; both sides began the war with relatively small professional forces and then augmented them with short-service volunteers. Before it was over both sides were drafting in men to fill the ranks; from an eligible male population of some four million, the Union mobilized over 1.5 million, while the Confederacy mobilized just short of one million from an eligible population of 1.14 million. To sustain these enormous armies, the technology of the Industrial Revolution was mobilized for the first time, and this changed the face of warfare forever.

At the outbreak of the Civil War the Union Army had 30 regiments – about 16,000 men – of whom a proportion were newly-enlisted state militia. The existing armouries and arsenals – Springfield, Harper's Ferry, Watervliet together with some assistance from commercial manufacturers – Colt, Spencer, Remington – could supply the regular army with its needs, but as soon as war loomed, volunteer militia regiments began to blossom, and the demand for weapons and equipment soon outran the existing facilities. It became necessary to throw open

Artillery on rails Union forces in the US Civil War were quick to utilize the mobility railroads provided. As well as using them to move troops from front to front, they developed train-driven armoured batteries of the kind shown here. These could be used for infantry support.

Successful sabotage With a front stretching across half a continent, railroads became vital lines of communication for both North and South in the US Civil War. It soon became clear, however, that the tracks were relatively easy to sabotage; here, a Union pioneer makes his escape after blowing up a railroad line. These pioneers carried a belt containing small charges of guncotton or dynamite, which they used to sabotage strategic targets.

contracts to any manufacturer who cared to bid, so expanding the armaments manufacturing base. At the same time the demand for miscellaneous hardware, uniforms, rations, supplies of every sort, rapidly exceeded the capacity of the normal commercial organizations, and, again, contractors sprang up with small factories to cope with the demand. Within a year of the start of the war it was a rare community which was not directly touched by events, even if only because it contained a small factory turning out powder horns or water bottles. This proliferation of contracts led to gross inefficiency, corruption and downright swindling – unfortunate side-effects which have never been entirely absent from wartime economics.

Armies, of course, need to be moved about in order to confront the enemy. In times past this had been done by marching them, and this still had its value. But with the active fronts spread across half a continent, and with railroads available, movement of troops by train was soon common practice. At the outbreak of war the Northern states had some 22,000 miles of railway and the Southern states about 9000; during the course of the war another 4000 miles were added in the North, but little in the South. The operation of these lines during the war revealed three important factors in railway development vis-à-vis military

operations: firstly, the ability of a railway to permit operations to be mounted some considerable distance from a supply base; secondly, the need for special military organizations to destroy, repair and maintain railways in the forward areas; and thirdly, the need for an understanding between the military staff and the technical staff of the railway system to ensure the proper control and utilization of railways in wartime. It also brought out some rather more basic requirements; for one thing, the railways of the United States did not possess a single standard gauge, which meant expensive and time-consuming transhipment of freight

Stemming the tide Union reinforcements escape from a derailed troop train in August 1863. As the train was thrown increasingly on the defensive, Union and Confederate tactics differed as far as railroads were concerned. In general, the aim of the Union commanders was to capture

strategic Confederate lines; their opponents were thrown back on sabotage to try to hamper Union operations. The great exception was General Sherman's "march to the sea" in December 1864, when the destruction of Confederate rail links made it impossible for the South to counterattack effectively.

wherever two lines connected. For another, many of the small locally financed and built lines were never designed to take the loads and volume of traffic which the requirements of the war placed upon them, with the result that trains were frequently derailed.

The first significant contribution of the railway to the Civil War came with the first major battle, Bull Run or Manassas. The Manassas Gap Railroad was used to transport the Confederate forces of General Johnston and reinforce the army under General Beauregard just in time to repulse the first Union attack and turn what could have been a Confederate rout into a Union defeat. This focused attention on the tactical value of railway lines, and from then on both sides made the railways of the opposite sides their targets. By occupying a point on a line it was possible to deny the enemy use of that stretch, so that his operations would be affected by either the failure of supply lines or the inability to bring up reinforcements. By and large, though, the aim of the two sides differed; the North tried to capture railways with a view to turning them to their own use, while the South merely tried to raid and destroy lines and bridges so as to hamper the North's operations.

Railroad strategy

An example of the cumulative effect of cutting railway communication can be seen by following the sequence of events which formed a chain reaction after General Halleck and the Union forces captured Corinth, Mississippi in May 1862. The capture of this town was facilitated by the fact that General Grant was threatening the length of the Memphis & Charleston Railroad which supplied Corinth. The withdrawal of Confederate forces from Corinth meant that the Memphis & Charleston was lost to them for the rest of the war, depriving the South of the only continuous railway line from the Mississippi River to the Atlantic coast. The bastion of the outer line of Confederate defence now became Chattanooga, Tennessee, which could be supplied from both east and south by rail. When the eastern line was cut by Union troops taking Knoxville, Chattanooga was almost isolated and lost its strategic significance, leaving upper Georgia and western North Carolina almost defenceless. By means of an involved and circuitous route, supplies could still be moved, but the burden imposed almost led to collapse of the entire system.

The struggle continued until Sherman's famous "March to the Sea" in December 1864. For once a Union force was unconcerned with utilizing a railway line, and Sherman's troops tore up lines as they moved forward. All that was left was a single track which was actually extended as the army advanced, allowing supplies to pass forward from a base 494km (360 mi) away and help sustain the 100,000 men and 60,000 horses of Sherman's army. But Sherman was now in a position to strike from behind the Confederate line of defence and finally cut the one tenuous rail link which held the Confederate armies together, the line between Charleston and Savannah.

The final strategic blow came in April 1865, when Union troops raided into Virginia and captured the important junction of Petersburg. This cut the last supply line and was instrumental in bringing about the surrender of General Lee a few days later.

In 1864, the reports of railway operations in America led the Prussian General Staff to form a Railway Section, which found its first employment in the same year during the short Prusso-Danish War. The hostilities were so short and took place in such a concentrated area that the railways did little more than deliver troops to the vicinity of the front and supply them for a short time – so short, that few difficulties appeared. The Section then had two years to consider the lessons of that experience and perfect their technique before Prussia's next campaign – the Austro-Prussian War of 1866.

THE INDUSTRIAL REVOLUTION

The impact of the change in manufacturing technology upon weapons and warfare

While the railways had been making their slow mark on the consciousness of the military, the Industrial Revolution had been finding other ways to impinge upon warfare. In the 1840s, the flintlock had given way to the percussion-fired musket in military use and the rifled musket had begun to appear. This meant that the humble infantryman, firing his rifled musket, could send a moderately accurate ball further than could an artillery piece opposing him, so that the foot soldier was able to pick off the enemy's gunners before they could bring down effective counter fire. This completely upset contemporary tactics, so, in order to redress the balance and put the artillery back into its position of supremacy, rifled guns had to be developed.

By the 1850s, a number of "systems" of rifling had been suggested, of which the most practical was a French design in which three deep spiral grooves were cut into the interior of the gun barrel. These corresponded with three rows of soft metal studs set into the body of the projectile, their alignment being angled to match the angle of the grooves. The gunner loaded a gunpowder cartridge from the muzzle and followed it by placing the bottom of the shell into the gun and engaging the first of the studs with their grooves. He eased the shell in, made sure the remaining studs engaged, and then rammed it down on top of the powder cartridge. As it went down, so it turned, and when the gun was fired and the shell was blown out, so, once again, it turned, deriving spin from the studs being forced along the spiral grooves.

Apart from the innovation of the grooves, which was found only in a few French guns, the artillery of the day was much as it had been for centuries. Basically, the mid-19th century cannon consisted of a cast iron tube, closed at the back except for a narrow "vent" which was primed with powder before applying ignition. The mass of metal required to make a sound cast-iron gun capable of withstanding the explosion of several pounds of gunpowder inside it meant that the ratio of weapon weight to shell weight was enormous; it also meant that the wooden carriage, which served to move the gun about and support it when firing, had to be equally massive. As a result the entire gun, except for the very small calibres, which were used by horse artillery, was a heavy piece of equipment which moved slowly into action.

Origins of the rifle

It was this aspect which caught the eye of William Armstrong, a British solicitor from Newcastle-upon-Tyne, who had an interest in an engineering works. In addition to his legal abilities, Armstrong was an ingenious engineering designer, who had made himself a respectable fortune by devising and building hydraulic machinery. Armstrong had his attention drawn to a newspaper report of the battle of Inkerman, in the Crimea, in November 1854. A crucial factor in this battle was the firepower of a British 18-pounder gun which had to be dragged into place to silence a Russian battery. The difficulties encountered in manhandling this weapon, which weighed 3 tons, through the mud and up the slopes on the battlefield were graphically described, and Armstrong's imagination was seized by the disparity of weights – a three-ton gun of five-inch calibre firing a projectile weighing only eighteen pounds appeared to him to be ridiculous.

Armstrong therefore designed a totally new type of gun based on the best engineering knowledge available at that time. The significant features were, firstly, that instead of being a solid mass of cast metal with a hole bored in it, the gun was built up from a number of closely-fitted tubes, heated and shrunk one upon the other, so as to build up the requisite strength in the place it was needed – the chamber of the gun where the explosion took place

Forging the future An Armstrong cannon during construction at the Woolwich Arsenal, near London. Armstrong's significant innovations were the way in which his guns' barrels were cast as a series of closely fitting tubes, which saved weight; the introduction of a rifled barrel, which meant that the shells his guns fired could be heavier and stable in flight; and the substitution of breechloading for muzzle-loading.

Victorian innovator British engineer William Armstrong (1810-1900) was one of the leading armament manufacturers of the Victorian age. His "built-up" system of gun construction, in which a thin rifled barrel was surrounded by a succession of shrunken hoops, was the standard method of artillery construction by the end of the 19th century.

– but to save weight in places where bulk was not necessary. Secondly, the inner surface of the bore was rifled with several fine spiral grooves, and the projectile was coated with lead; on firing, the lead engaged with the grooves to spin the shell. Thirdly, the gun was loaded from the breech rather than from the muzzle. Comparison between an old-style muzzle-loading gun and an Armstrong gun of similar calibre showed a reduction in weight and the ability to throw a heavier shell for much greater distances.

The significant feature of the rifle gun was not so much that it was more accurate or fired to a longer range, but that it fired a heavier and more effective projectile. This was due to simple geometrical facts: a round ball fired from a smoothbore gun could be of only one size and weight, which is why these weapons were always called "XX-pounders". Smoothbore guns had to use round balls because this was the only shape which permitted anything resembling accuracy. But the advent of rifled guns meant that the projectile was gyroscopically stabilized in its flight due to its spin, and thus the projectile could be a long cylinder, heavier and with greater capacity than a plain ball. Moreover, since the shell was stabilized, it landed point first, thus making it feasible to devise fuzes which fired the explosive content upon impact; hitherto the only effective way to fuze a shell had been a burning time fuze, and arranging this to burst the shell at the correct place was an art in itself.

Other countries arrived at other solutions. The most significant was the design developed by the German gunmaker Krupp. This was a gun bored from a solid block of steel and fitted with a sliding breechblock. Other gunmakers looked askance, since at that time steel was a dubious substance, prone to be cast with flaws inside the block, flaws which either made themselves apparent during the boring, which meant the block was wasted, or which concealed themselves until the gun was fired, whereupon it burst asunder and killed the crew. Krupp persevered, however, and eventually made his reputation on his steel guns.

The needle gun

Breechloading had also appeared in small arms by this time; the first breechloader to see significant adoption was the Dreyse Needle Gun, taken into use by the Prussian Army in December 1840. Breechloaders had been seen before this, but in very small numbers, and the Dreyse design represented the first attempt to arm a complete force with breechloading weapons. The needle gun also introduced the concept of the bolt-action method of breech closure, together with a firing pin (the "needle") which passed through the bolt, propelled by a spring, to fire a percussion cap on the base of the bullet. It is interesting to note that it was officially called the "Model 1841 Percussion Rifle" on introduction, a security measure intended to conceal the method of operation; not until 1855 was it officially re-named the "Needle Gun".

The next significant step was the introduction by the French Army in 1866 of the "Chassepot" rifle, named

after its inventor Antoine Alfonse Chassepot. This copied the general idea of the needle gun but improved the cartridge, placing the percussion cap at the base of the propelling charge. The Chassepot was introduced with the intention of providing the French Army with a weapon comparable to the needle gun. In order to give themselves a further advantage, the French also adopted the "Mitrailleuse", invented by Joseph Montigny, a Belgian engineer. A "volley gun" which consisted of a cluster of 25 rifle barrels contained in a cannon-like casing, the Mitrailleuse was loaded by inserting a plate carrying 25 cartridges, and fired by rotating a crank to release 25 firing pins in succession. Manufacture began in 1859, under conditions of the most intense secrecy.

Weapons development during the American Civil War had pre-empted

The Chassepot The Chassepot, the French Army's standard infantry rifle from 1866 onwards, was a development of the Prussian needle gun. In common with its predecessor, it used bolt action to close the breech and a firing pin to ignite a percussion cap on the base of the bullet.

The bolt is withdrawn to allow a bullet to be inserted in the rifle's breech and then cocked, ready for firing.

The firing pin is propelled by a spring, which is compressed when the bolt is cocked and released by the pulling of the trigger.

When the pin strikes the base of the cartridge, it ignites a percussion cap at the base of the propelling charge.

The Chassepot cartridge The French cartridge improved on the one devised for the needle gun. The percussion cap was now placed at the base of a propelling charge, rather than relying on the cap alone to power the bullet.

much of this European inventiveness;
Gatling had produced his mechanical
machine gun in 1862 and offered it to
the Union Army, but political enmity
prevented it being adopted in any
numbers until the war was over.
Breechloading rifles such as the
Spencer and Henry, using metallic
cartridges, were also in fairly common
use. But Europe largely ignored the
American Civil War; it was, so far as
many of the professional soldiers were
concerned, little more than tribal
infighting, a type of warfare entirely
at variance with European practice and
therefore not to be taken as any sort of
an example.

Prusso-Danish war

Europe preferred to take its examples
from Europe; and the first exemplar
was the Prusso-Danish war of 1864,
fought around Prussia's complex claim
to the two quasi-independent Duchies
of Schleswig and Holstein. By various
political stratagems, Bismarck, the
German Chancellor, had ensured that
the Prussian action had a semblance of
legality and that no other nation would
come to Denmark's aid – in fact, he
enlisted Austrian military support –
with the result that the entire campaign
was over in five months. What it did was

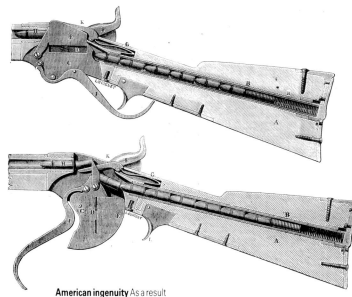

American ingenuity As a result
of the US Civil War, American rifle
developments had surpassed European
ones. The breech-loading Spencer
repeating rifle, seen loaded *(top)* and
during reloading *(above)*, was a
considerable advance on the standard
infantry weapons of its time. Instead of
relying on single-cartridge loading, the
butt of the gun formed a magazine. The
action of snapping open the breech
forced a new cartridge into
the firing position.

Chassepot in action French
sharpshooters exercise with their
new rifle. In the Franco-Prussian
War of 1870-1, the rifle proved
itself superior to its Prussian rival,
forcing the Prussians to modify
their infantry tactics in the field.

Secret weapon The Mitrailleuse
was France's secret weapon in the
Franco-Prussian War. A forerunner
of the machine gun, it consisted of
a cluster of 25 rifle barrels, which
fired 25 cartridges in rapid
succession as the gun was
cranked.

to give the Prussians the chance to prove their needle guns and Krupp artillery in actual warfare, brief though the contact was. It also gave the Austrians an opportunity to evaluate the Prussian training and equipment, an opportunity which they appear to have neglected except for adopting rifled muzzle loading guns for their artillery.

The principal, and almost unrecognized, lesson which emerged from the Danish war was that extemporized earthwork fortifications were as valuable as, if not more valuable than, formal stone fortresses; the Danes, at Duppel, held up a considerable force of Prussian troops for 65 days. That this happened was as much a fault of the besieging force as due to any virtues on the part of the garrison. The Prussian forces had every advantage; they were in full control of the direct railway lines leading from Berlin to their battlefront, and the requisite heavy siege guns were removed from the defences of eastern Prussia and shipped across to Duppel within ten days. The siege began on 12 February 1864, and the besieging artillery, some 54 guns of which 36 were Krupp breechloading rifles, opened fire on 14th March. A month later the investing artillery had risen to 122 guns, of which 78 were Krupp. After a severe bombardment on 17th April, on the following day 18,000 infantry assaulted the position, carrying it with a loss of 1188 men.

And what was this position assaulted so formidably and for so long? It was a line some 3000 yards long containing ten small redoubts, fronted by palisaded ditches, backed by small blockhouses, which were, in fact, visible from the besieging batteries. The redoubts were connected by a rifle trench, and a few weapon pits and outposts had been established in front. The armament consisted of 92 smoothbore guns firing through cramped embrasures and a handful of mortars. The infantry were firing muzzle-loading muskets. The garrison was no more than 6000 strong. By comparison with some of the enormous fortresses on the Franco-German border the defences of Duppel added up to little more than a corporal's guard, and yet it held off the Prussians and soaked up an enormous amount of artillery bombardment, eventually being carried more by luck than good judgment. The Danish commander,

fearful of attack by night or at dawn, as was customary, would garrison the outposts every evening. Equally fearful of losses from the incessant artillery bombardment, he would withdraw his troops to the rear once the danger of a dawn attack had passed. And so when the Prussians attacked at the unheard-of hour of 10 a.m., the redoubts were practically empty and it became a race to see who got there first, the attacking Prussians or the defending garrison. The Prussians won the race and thus the battle.

The significant point about Duppel was that earthworks simply absorbed artillery fire, whereas masonry works would have been splintered and shattered. But when the experts came to review the performance, all they could see was that it had held out for 65 days and, had it been built in accordance with the classical tenets of fortification theory, then it would probably have held out for twice as long. The point that a formidable force had been delayed for two months by a handful of men in an extemporized defensive line was entirely lost upon the pundits. The whole affair is illustrative of the formality into which warfare in Europe had descended. Duppel was, by formal definition, a fortified place; therefore it had to be besieged in accordance with the rules. Siege batteries had to be deployed, besieging lines dug, parallel trenches opened, saps excavated forward, all with the precision and punctilio of a game of chess. Yet with 18,000 troops and 144 guns the Prussian commander should have been able to storm it on the first day. There is an interesting parallel here with some of the British actions during the 1914-18 war; in analyzing the Danish war in later years, a Prussian commander admitted that one reason for the slow performance at Duppel was simply that the Prussians were unprepared for the destructive effects of their new rifled guns firing explosive shells, and that had they had sufficient troops available at the outset it would have been possible to take the defensive line on the second day, while the Danes were still reeling from the initial bombardment. Unfortunately, however, so were the Prussians, and they were unable to take advantage of their success.

The victors of the Danish war soon fell out over the division of the spoils, with the result that in 1866 the Prussians and Austrians were at

The rise of Prussia Prussian infantry storms an Austrian position at bayonet point during the key battle of Königgratz/Sadowa in the Austro-Prussian War of 1866. Although victorious, their losses in action brought home to the Prussian commanders the need for a revolution in tactics to cope with the increased firepower of modern weaponry. The infantry abandoned the old close-order line of advance in favour of a loose, open-order formation, while the artillery was reorganized to provide the infantry with front-line heavy gun support.

each others' throats.

The result of the war was victory for Prussia, but it could very well have gone the other way, since the Prussian army showed some serious organizational defects during the course of the campaign and there were a few occasions when the Austrians, with a little more discipline and dash, might have won some of the more important battles. But the significant point about the Seven Weeks' War is that it represented the meeting point of traditional mass-manoeuvre tactics and modern weapons, and demonstrated that the two were incompatible.

Tactical lessons

Königgratz/Sadowa was not the only battle of the war, but it was the significant one and it showed what sort of results might be expected when two mass armies met. The Prussian losses were 1935 killed and 7237 wounded, mostly by Austrian artillery fire; the Austrians suffered 13,000 killed and

Siege warfare A Prussian battery in action at Duppel during the Prusso-Danish War of 1865. The Danes' success in resisting a vastly superior Prussian force, equipped with the latest Krupp siege guns, for 65 days showed that earthworks could absorb even the most ferocious artillery bombardment, whereas the stonework and masonry of a conventional fortress would have been shattered.

over 18,000 wounded.

Much of this carnage can be attributed to the tactics the Prussian and Austrian generals employed. Both armies adhered to the mass formations, advances in column, advances in line, wheels and similar evolutions which had been in vogue since the Seven Years' War, and found that these tactics were suicidal in the face of modern weapons. Prussian troops fell before the onslaught of improved projectiles from Austrian rifled guns, even though these were relatively primitive, while the Austrians suffered from concentrated rifle fire from the breechloading needle gun. The Prussian infantry were particularly voluble about the effect of the Austrian guns and the poor showing of their own artillery; in both numbers and technical quality, the Prussian artillery outstripped the Austrian, but its handling was inept, it frequently arrived on the battlefield late or in the wrong place to have the best effect, and its state of training was poor. As one Prussian artilleryman said afterwards, "Where, indeed, during the whole of the war of 1866, have we succeeded in hitting a target which was worth the trouble of hitting?"

As a result there was a thorough overhaul of both equipment and tactics within the Prussian artillery. While the infantry looked to their systems of tactical manoeuvre, the artillery improved its shooting, improved various technical points about its guns and ammunition, and, in particular, made it a point to be as close to the line of battle as possible. Their tactics had previously been constrained because of the organizational system which placed the artillery under the hand of brigade commanders with no artillery training. This was now changed and responsible artillery commanders were attached to formations, so that they could direct the guns to the best and most effective locations. The infantry, for their part, began experimenting with loose and open formations, calculated to reduce their vulnerability to rifles and short-range artillery fire.

The proof of the pudding came in the Franco-Prussian War of 1870, in which the Prussian artillery outshone every other arm in its dash and efficiency. Time after time it was the guns which opened the battle and did the most damage to the French. The Prussian infantry made a rather ragged start, since several of their commanders were unconvinced of the need to abandon the old close-order formations, but exposure to the French Chassepot rifle and the Mitrailleuse soon convinced them that open tactics were the best. The French troops fought to the the best of their ability but were abominably commanded by men who were easily outmanoeuvred and outfought by the Prussians. The Chassepot proved to be technically superior to the needle rifle, but the Mitrailleuse, though effective in some instances, was generally wrongly handled and badly sited so that its benefits were never realized. In a nutshell, it was handled as if it were artillery, at artillery ranges, and was shot to pieces by the Prussian artillery before it could have much effect.

Affair at Plevna

While the Prussians counted their gains and the French licked their wounds, the next significant combat took place between the Russians and the Turks in 1877. This had begun as a Serbo-Turkish affair, but the Serbs got the worst of it, and by various pretexts the Russians took up their quarrel. In simple terms, the theatre of war was situated in what is now Bulgaria and the Russian advance was on two fronts, one army moving south from Romania and the other north from the Balkans. The latter had already moved far enough to besiege Adrianople (now Edirne) and the other had come from Bucharest and crossed into Bulgaria at Svistov. The obvious strategy was to prevent the two forces from joining, and an astute garrison commander called Osman Pasha scraped together what troops he could find and force-marched them to take up a position around Plevna.

Plevna was a small country town with no previous military importance, and no form of defence. Osman Pasha set his 14,000 men to digging fieldworks around the town and prepared for the Russian attack by issuing every man with two rifles; a single-shot Ma tini-Peabody with 100 cartridges for long-range fire, and a repeating Winchester carbine with 500 cartridges for close-range work. Both these weapons were of American origin, purchased by Turkey in order to bring their infantry equipment into the breechloading era. Osman Pasha's position threatened the flank of the invading Russian army, who had to detach a force to deal with it. This they did in a somewhat half-hearted manner and were smartly seen

off by the defenders. After a delay of several days, on 30 July 1877, the Russians launched their first major attack to be met with a storm of bullets which cut down 8000 men. This discomfited them and they settled down to a siege, though one without much scientific application. Seeing that little was to be achieved, the Russians called on the Romanian Army for assistance, and on 11 September a massive attack was launched which resulted in no less than 18,000 casualties to the Russian force. In late October, the Russians managed to surround Plevna entirely, thus cutting Osman Pasha off from any supplies or reinforcements. These had been getting through and had built his force up to a maximum of 30,000. By this time, too, the Russian Army had sent for Todleben, the military engineer who had conducted the defence of Sebastopol, and under his supervision the siege began to take on a more serious form. Disease and shortage of rations began to affect the Plevna garrison, and eventually, after an intrepid but foredoomed attempt to break out, Osman Pasha was forced to surrender on 10 December. In the end, the Russians were victorious, but the defence of Plevna had virtually paralyzed their army for six months and was instrumental in turning opinion in Europe against the Russians, thus modifying their political aspirations and any possible gains.

The secret of Plevna's remarkable performance was twofold; firstly, the adequacy of field fortifications in absorbing artillery bombardment – something which, for those who could see it, had been apparent since Duppel – and, secondly, the fearsome ability of modern repeating rifles to slaughter troops making a frontal assault. This was the first time that a magazine breechloader using metallic cartridges – the Winchester 1873 carbine, in 44 rimfire calibre – had been used in quantity, and its appalling firepower was a revelation. Unfortunately, it was a revelation which was rapidly forgotten, and the lesson had to be relearned several times before it was finally driven home.

Centre of resistance The Battle of Plevna in the Russo-Turkish War of 1877 again demonstrated that well-handled modern weaponry could frustrate the most determined of attackers. The Russian artillery failed to smash the Turkish earthworks, while the Turks' repeating Winchester carbines made short work of the Russian infantry's full-scale frontal assaults. The position only fell as a result of the Russian command's return to old-fashion siege tactics, which eventually forced Plevna's surrender.

NEW ARTILLERY

International developments in gun design make rapid firepower possible

Artillery design had, by this time, become an amalgam of the best ideas from Britain, France and Germany. So far as the gun's barrel was concerned there were two methods of construction, the "built-up" system pioneered by Armstrong or the solid steel barrel developed by Krupp. The latter was satisfactory for small guns but as artillery became more powerful, the solid steel gun had to become larger and larger in girth in order to withstand the internal pressure. The Armstrong system used a thin rifled barrel and then by shrinking successive "hoops" around it, allowed the thickness to be precisely calculated to withstand the pressure and, by compressing the inner hoops, gave the gun great resistance to the force of the explosion; this became the universal method of making guns.

Breechloading was by now the only conceivable way of making a gun, and two basic systems evolved. The easiest to manufacture was the sliding block developed by Krupp, simply a square block of steel which slid across the rear of the gun barrel. The drawback was that this did nothing to seal the escape of gas from the rear of the weapon and it was necessary to place the propelling charge inside a metal cartridge case. This expanded under the explosion pressure and sealed the rear of the gun, the breechblock merely serving to stop the cartridge case being blown out.

This was satisfactory, but when guns became larger so did the cartridge case,

and as it became larger it became heavier and more cumbersome for the gun's crew to handle. The French developed a totally different method of breech closure; they formed the rear of the gun into a threaded receptacle and then made a threaded plug, the breechblock, which could be screwed into this aperture. In order to make its insertion quicker and easier they then machined away six slots in the gun's threaded opening and six in the threads of the breechblock. By entering the block's remaining threads into the slots of the gun, forcing the block home, and then rotating it one-sixth of a turn, the block and gun threads engaged with far less effort than that of screwing the solid thread into the gun. Sealing was done by a resilient pad of asbestos on the front of the block, and thus the cartridge was simply a charge of powder, which was contained in a cloth bag and then placed inside the gun's chamber after the shell had been inserted.

Guns of all countries, therefore, adopted these three basic systems. The built-up gun became the normal method of construction throughout the world. Broadly speaking, the Krupp sliding block and the metal cartridge case were adopted for light weapons up to about 12cm calibre – and the French interrupted-screw breech and the bagged charge above that calibre. But this was not an immutable law, and, indeed, the German Army preferred to stay with the simplicity of the sliding block and the drawbacks of the metal cartridge case even to their largest calibres.

In the early 1890s, smokeless powder was adopted as a propellant, replacing gunpowder, and high explosives were adopted for filling shells. These improvements had an undesirable effect in that they increased the recoil force of the weapon when it was fired, and it became imperative to do something about this. A conventional field gun was simply a barrel attached to a carriage, and when

Larger and larger As guns became heavier and heavier, the problems associated with their construction increased. Chief of these was the need to find a means of dealing with increased internal pressures and the gun's recoil. This Armstrong 400-lb cannon, nicknamed "Big Will", attempted to deal with both these problems.

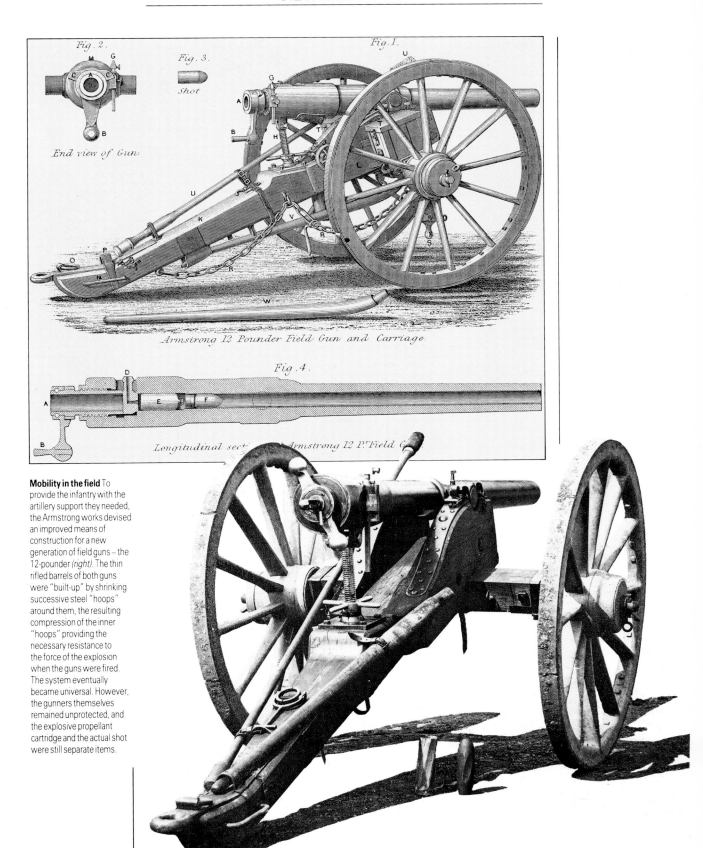

Fig.2.

G

M

C   A   D

B

End view of Gun.

Fig.3.

Shot

Fig.1.

Armstrong 12 Pounder Field Gun and Carriage.

Fig.4.

D

A   E   F

B

Longitudinal sect___ ___ Armstrong 12 P.ʳ Field G___

Mobility in the field To provide the infantry with the artillery support they needed, the Armstrong works devised an improved means of construction for a new generation of field guns – the 12-pounder *(right)*. The thin rifled barrels of both guns were "built-up" by shrinking successive steel "hoops" around them, the resulting compression of the inner "hoops" providing the necessary resistance to the force of the explosion when the guns were fired. The system eventually became universal. However, the gunners themselves remained unprotected, and the explosive propellant cartridge and the actual shot were still separate items.

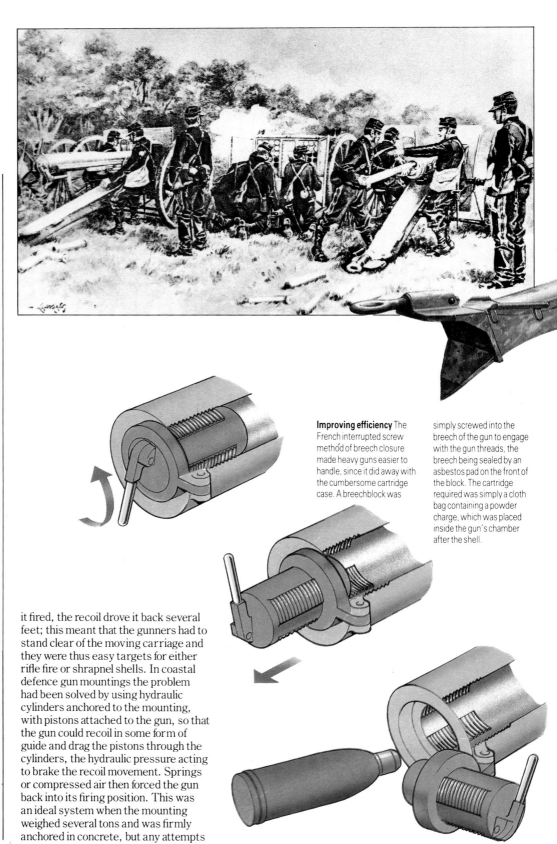

Quick-firing revolution
A battery of French 75mm field guns in action during the 1910 army manoeuvres. The phenomenal rate of fire of these field-pieces – the gun could be loaded and fired as quickly as a magazine rifle – led to a new arms race, as every nation strove to introduce its own variant of the design.

Improving efficiency The French interrupted screw method of breech closure made heavy guns easier to handle, since it did away with the cumbersome cartridge case. A breechblock was simply screwed into the breech of the gun to engage with the gun threads, the breech being sealed by an asbestos pad on the front of the block. The cartridge required was simply a cloth bag containing a powder charge, which was placed inside the gun's chamber after the shell.

it fired, the recoil drove it back several feet; this meant that the gunners had to stand clear of the moving carriage and they were thus easy targets for either rifle fire or shrapnel shells. In coastal defence gun mountings the problem had been solved by using hydraulic cylinders anchored to the mounting, with pistons attached to the gun, so that the gun could recoil in some form of guide and drag the pistons through the cylinders, the hydraulic pressure acting to brake the recoil movement. Springs or compressed air then forced the gun back into its firing position. This was an ideal system when the mounting weighed several tons and was firmly anchored in concrete, but any attempts

Anatomy of the 75 Although construction details of the 75 were one of France's topmost secrets, some of the innovations the French made soon became obvious. They did away with the separate cartridge and shell, devising a single all-purpose round of ammunition, while they also solved the problem of recoil, so that the gun-carriage remained stationary. The bullet-proof shield sheltered the gunners from enemy fire.

The breech's secret The 75's rapid rate of fire owed much to the breech mechanism devised for it. The French built on the idea of the quick-action sliding block mechanism devised by Krupp, the great difference being that now the propelling charge and the shot were combined in a single shell.

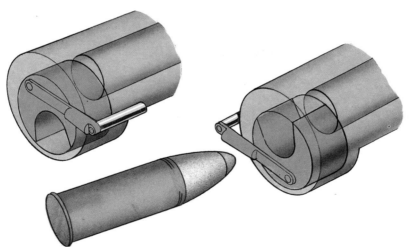

to apply its principles to mobile artillery were not very successful.

It was the French who eventually solved the problem and, into the bargain, introduced an entirely new concept in artillery which became known simply as the "quick-firing (QF) gun". In 1897, surrounded by the usual leaky clouds of secrecy, the French Army introduced a 75mm field piece which was to become a legend. Designed by a Captain Deport, an ordnance engineer at the Puteaux Artillery Arsenal, it was manufactured by Schneider-Creusot. Rumours abounded, but the salient facts seemed to be clear enough; it fired a fixed round of ammunition – one in which the shell

and cartridge were joined together like an oversized rifle cartridge; it had a recoil system which allowed the gun to move backwards under control in the carriage while the carriage remained perfectly stationary; it had a bulletproof shield, so that the gunners could cluster behind it, safe now that the carriage did not move and protected from enemy fire; and it had a quick-acting breech mechanism so that it could be loaded and fired as rapidly as a magazine rifle. With one bound the French artillery had placed themselves ahead of the rest of the world and, moreover, had begun an arms race, since every army now had to adopt a QF field gun or be relegated to second place.

THE MACHINE GUN

*The firepower of a platoon in the hands
of one man*

Dealing out death The Gardener gun was a US invention of the 1870s. In this version, two barrels were placed side-by-side. The crankshaft trigger, powered by a handle, opened and closed the breechblocks in very quick succession, the arrangement allowing the barrels to cool between shots. The vertical gravity feed meant that new rounds of ammunition literally fell into place as the previous ones were fired.

Not everyone was convinced that the French had got it right; after all, in 1870 they had put their faith in the Mitrailleuse, with disastrous results. This, though, was a short-sighted view; because even if the Mitrailleuse itself had failed, the general idea of a multiple-firing infantry weapon had certainly prospered.

International advances

After the Mitrailleuse had come the Gatling, Gardner, Lowell and Nordenfelt mechanical machine guns. The first three came from the United States, the Civil War providing the catalyst which led to their invention, though none actually appeared in any numbers until that war was over. The Gatling, introduced in the late 1860s, used a system of revolving barrels, rotated by a hand-crank, which distributed the process of loading, firing, and extracting the spent cartridge case throughout the cycle of rotation. Thus a particular barrel would collect a cartridge from the overhead supply hopper and gradually insert it into the chamber as it rotated downwards, fire it at the bottommost position, then gradually extract and eject it as it ascended once more. The advantage was that using six barrels gave a continuous fire and allowed the barrels time to cool between shots.

The Gardner gun, the invention of American soldier William Gardner, appeared in the 1870s, was another hand-cranked weapon, having two or more barrels side-by-side. The rotating handle drove a crankshaft which thrust the breechblocks of the barrels open and shut in succession, so that again the barrels fired in turn and had time to cool between shots.

The Lowell gun took its name from Lowell, Massachusetts, where De Witt Farrington invented it in 1875. It looked rather like a Gatling, in that it had four barrels arranged in a circular frame, and it had a crank-driven bolt mechanism similar to the Gardner, but delivered all its shots through only one barrel; when

this became too hot the frame carrying the barrels was rotated and a fresh barrel was brought into use.

The Nordenfelt had been invented in 1879 by Helge Palmkrantz, a Swedish engineer who went to banker Torsten Nordenfelt for financial aid; part of the aid was the change of name. This gun had anything from two to 12 barrels side-by-side and worked by pushing a lever back and forth, each forward stroke loading all the barrels and then firing them in a volley, each backward stroke ejecting the empty cases.

These guns were all more or less effective but, unfortunately, also cumbersome, needing to be taken into action on wheeled carriages. This, as much as anything else, tended to lead to their being employed as a species of artillery and for some years they were really a solution in search of a problem. But experience, particularly British experience in colonial wars, showed that if the machine gun could be placed on a flank so as to "enfilade" – i.e. fire down the length of an advancing line – it could decimate any attacking fire. The problem lay in getting such a ponderous device into place without the enemy seeing it and taking action.

The Maxim

In 1883, the American inventor Hiram Maxim came to Europe to attend an electrical exhibition in Paris. According to legend he was accosted by a friend who said "Hang your electricity! If you want to make your fortune, invent something which will enable these fool Europeans to kill each other more quickly!" Maxim took him at his word and, renting a workshop in Hatton Garden, London, set about developing the first automatic machine gun, a weapon which utilized the energy generated by firing a shot to load and cock the weapon for the next shot. By 1885 he had perfected his design and began touring Europe demonstrating how his weapon could fire 600 shots a minute with no more effort than a finger on the trigger; no handles to turn or

Swedish development The multi-barrelled Nordenfelt machine gun was invented in 1879. Its operator simply pushed a lever forwards to load and fire a volley and backwards to eject the spent cases.

levers to pull. The Maxim Gun Company was formed and production began. In 1888, the first Maxim gun was used in action, in Africa.

The success of the Maxim gun led other inventors to seek methods of self-powering a machine gun. In rapid succession John Browning in the USA developed his first gas-operated gun (Maxim's gun was driven by the recoil force), while in Europe the Skoda, Hotchkiss and Madsen designs appeared. The Skoda pioneered the "delayed blowback" system of operation in which a heavy breechblock, backed up by a powerful spring, kept the breech closed long enough for the bullet to leave the barrel before it began to move backwards and extract the empty case. The Hotchkiss, made in France, was actually designed by Baron von Odkolek of the Austro-Hungarian army, and used a gas piston to operate the bolt. The Madsen, the invention of Captain Madsen of the Danish Artillery, used recoil to operate a swinging breech block and was the first machine gun to be fed from an overhead box magazine. All these weapons were assiduously studied by European armies, but the majority

Two pioneers The Gatling gun *(above)* consisted of a number of revolving barrels, turned by a hand-crank. Cartridges from the overhead supply hopper were fed into each barrel in turn at the top of the gun and gradually inserted into the chamber as the barrel rotated downward. Firing took place at the lowest position, with the spent cartridge being ejected as the barrel rotated back to the top. The Gardener gun *(below)* was a multi-barelled, immobile version of the two-barelled model.

ONE OF THE "MAXIMS" OF CIVILISATION!

OLD AND NEW.

"THINK of the glorious Mottoes," said a Major of the old school. "'Nil Desperandum,' 'Death or Victory,' 'England Expects,' and so forth!" Replied his friend, the modern Captain, "Bother your Mottoes! Give us the Maxims'!"

The mighty Maxim
American inventor Hiram Maxim *(right)* perfected the first automatic machine gun (1896 model above) in 1885. He utilized the recoil generated by the firing of the bullets to load and cock the gun for the next shot. The result was a weapon that could fire 600 rounds a minute – to achieve this, Maxim also developed a belt feed – by simple finger pressure on the gun's trigger. The British Army was quick to adopt the Maxim for its colonial wars and the name "Maxim" passed into common language *(above right)*.

could see no tactical use for them and retained their faith in the heavy Maxim gun. Only the Japanese, in 1899, bought the Hotchkiss, and the Russians, in 1902, the Madsen. The rest of the world was content to wait before taking a decision.

The Pom-pom
Maxim also made improvements, notably by increasing the calibre to 37mm (the first Maxims were .45in calibre) so that it could fire an explosive shell. Nobody was quite sure where this sort of weapon fitted into the current tactical systems and so the European armies looked but didn't buy.

Less inhibited military forces did, however, and when the British Army confronted the rebellious Boers in South Africa in 1900 they discovered just what the 37mm Maxim could do; it could launch a string of very unpleasant explosive shells into a formation of troops at a range too long for them to fire back with small arms. The rapid explosions of the one-pound shells gave the gun its nickname – the "Pom-Pom".

The machine gun, in its automatic form, received its first major application in an unexpected war on the far side of the world, the Russo-Japanese War of 1904. The Japanese, exerting themselves to equip their newly-formed army and bring it up to European standards, had bought quantities of Hotchkiss machine guns

from France. The Russians were equipped with the universal Maxim gun; it was the first time that two major powers, each with machine guns, had come face to face, and the rest of the military world watched with interest. The Russians first used their Maxims at the Yalu River, where eight guns employed in a supporting role beat off several Japanese attacks. The Japanese, attacking en masse in their customary manner, were cut to pieces by the concentrated fire.

They, in their turn, employed their Hotchkiss guns with great boldness in later operations; instead of emplacing them for defence, as was the general tactic at that time, they carried them forward in their attacks so that they

·were available to give supporting or covering fire whenever the advancing infantry were checked. They became particularly adept at giving support to an assault by firing over the heads of their attacking troops so as to keep down the defenders. The Russians, learning from this, acquired a number of Danish Madsen guns, the first light machine gun, magazine fed and with a bipod so that it could be fired from the shoulder of a prone soldier.

Foreign observations

As was customary in those easy-going days, foreign armies had sent official "observers" to both sides of the Russo-Japanese War, to report upon the course of the war and, in passing, to note any technical or tactical innovations. But it is sometimes difficult to see an innovation, even when it is under your nose, and the significance of the machine gun was lost on many of the observers. While it was seen that the machine guns were vastly effective, the general consensus was that they showed up well because the accompanying rifle fire was poor; neither side had trained its conscripts to any high degree of accuracy or skill in rifle firing, and in consequence they rarely hit what they were aiming at. From this, opposite conclusions were reached; the British decided that additional instruction in rifle fire would be beneficial and set about musketry training, while the Germans decided that it was hopeless to attempt to make marksmen out of conscripts, and therefore it would be better to increase the number of machine guns since with the greater volume of fire the conscripts would be more likely to hit something.

The other lesson which came out of Manchuria was the difficulty of seeing and shooting an enemy once he dug himself into the ground, a practice which both sides followed. This, though, was thought to be an aberrant piece of tactics and not necessarily to be taken as an omen for the future. The future war would be in similar vein to previous wars, a matter of movement, of skirmishers followed by lines of advancing infantry, all following on the heels of a brief artillery bombardment. The French army, indeed, after carefully analyzing their defeats in 1870, had concluded that the attack was the secret of everything, and their doctrine now was one of rapidity and dash. Even their artillery was almost

The French answer The success of the Maxim gun spurred other inventors to produce their own variants. The bolt of the French-manufactured Hotchkiss was operated by a gas piston to produce continuous fire.

entirely composed of light 75mm guns intended to pour a devastating 20 rounds per minute into the enemy ranks before the infantry ran forward with their bayonets to finish off the battle. For most soldiers the quick-firing gun was the weapon which would decide the next war; relatively few had much faith in the machine gun.

However, it would be wrong to perpetuate the legend that only the German army saw the machine gun as a decisive weapon and that the British dismissed it with contempt. This is totally inaccurate. The British army had used the Maxim in considerable numbers in South Africa, although they were not particularly impressive in their performance against an enemy who was rarely seen and spread thinly across the veldt. There was little doubt of their efficacy; what troubled the British military mind was their tactical application. The general view, perpetuated in '*Field Service Regulations*' was that they should be used in pairs, since a single gun was of little use and more than two would be likely to attract enemy artillery fire. *Cavalry Training*, though, advocated their use en masse, under the hand of a single commander so as to give an overwhelming torrent of fire against mass cavalry opposition, which, as much as anything, reflected the different tactical viewpoints of the infantry and the cavalry.

The argument is often advanced that the British must have deprecated the machine gun since they had so few of them on the outbreak of war in 1914. This is a simplification in the absence of the facts. The principal fact which affected the machine gun strength on the eve of war was, strangely enough, the question of the service rifle.

THE NEW RIFLES

*Design refinements lead to weapons
of incredible accuracy*

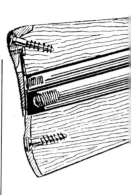

In 1889 the British Army had adopted a new rifle, the Lee-Metford magazine rifle in .303in calibre. This was a considerable step; hitherto military rifles had been of .577, then .45 calibre, and dropping to such a minuscule bullet was received with some scepticism. It was, however, a universal trend (just as the swing to a 5.56mm bullet was in the 1890s) with the Germans adopting 7.92mm and the French 8mm as their service calibres at about the same time. The Lee-Metford took its name from the bolt action and magazine of James Paris Lee, and the barrel which was rifled to a pattern devised by William Metford, an engineer and rifle enthusiast. This rifling was designed so as to resist the accumulation of fouling from the compressed gunpowder propelling charge used in the .303 cartridge.

The Lee-Enfield

In 1891, the first British smokeless powder, Cordite, was developed, a mixture of nitrocellulose (guncotton) and nitroglycerine (Dynamite) formed into a colloid. This was a vast improvement on gunpowder but it was highly erosive and wore out a Lee-Metford barrel in about 4500 rounds. The Royal Small Arms Factory at Enfield therefore devised a new form of rifling, more resistant to cordite, and the rifles were fitted with new barrels to become Lee-Enfields.

In the 1890s, it was customary to have two basic weapons; a long rifle for the infantry and a shorter carbine for cavalry, artillery and engineers. It gradually became apparent that this practice was really redundant; the long rifle was too long, the carbine too short, and a standard rifle somewhere between the two would suffice for the entire army. In 1903 the "Rifle, Short, Magazine, Lee-Enfield Mark 3" was introduced, supplanting the long rifles and the carbines, and it remained the British service rifle for over 50 years.

To the soldier the Lee-Enfield was probably the best weapon for combat

ever devised; the Lee bolt was exceptionally smooth and fast in its operation, the notched backsight was easy to use and allowed quick pick-up of the target, the ammunition was accurate and the rifle itself felt "all of a piece" and handy to use. But the pundits despised it; South Africa had demanded long-range rifle fire as a matter of course, due to the peculiar circumstances of an elusive enemy and wide open country, as a result of which long-range rifle fire became a fetish. Theorists and target shooters demanded that the army be furnished with a weapon capable of shooting to 2000 yards with accuracy and with as flat a trajectory to that range as could be achieved. The theorists also proved that the Lee design could never be accurate since the bolt was locked in place by lugs at its rear end, so that at the moment of firing there was a compressive stress on the bolt which rendered the weapon inaccurate. What the army needed, they said, was a totally new rifle using a Mauser pattern bolt with locking lugs at the front end, accompanied by a powerful cartridge.

By about 1910, the arguments were so loud that Enfield sat down to design a new rifle. It was decided that .276in calibre would provide the ideal ballistics, and a new rifle with a Mauser bolt was developed; a limited number were put into the hands of troops as the "Pattern 1913". It was a disaster. The cartridge was designed to propel the bullet at 2785 feet per second (the Lee-Enfield .303 left the barrel at 2440 ft/sec) and to do this it had an extremely powerful charge of cordite which gave rise to excessive blast and flash, overheating of the barrel, severe erosion – few barrels managed to fire 3000 rounds before being worn out – and irregular chamber pressures. Manufacture was postponed while experiments took place to try and cure these problems, but before any cure was found the war arrived and the whole affair was quietly forgotten.

From 1910 therefore there had been

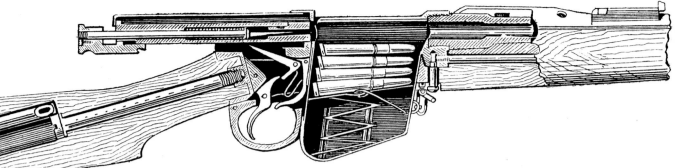

The .303 rifle British adoption of the Lee-Metford magazine rifle in 1889 (later the Lee-Enfield) paved the way for smaller calibre infantry weapons. One of the weapon's strongest points was the fast, smooth action of its bolt, which enabled the British infantry to produce a rate of rifle fire unmatched by any other army in the world.

a question hanging over the army as to what calibre the next rifle would be, and as a result of that the provision of machine guns had been halted; it would, obviously, have been stupid to continue making and issuing .303 calibre guns if the army was going to change suddenly to .276. For this reason alone the army went to war in 1914 with its basic outfit of machine guns – two per infantry battalion – but with very little in reserve stocks. Moreover the gun which was held up was the Vickers, an improvement on the Maxim, which had been formally adopted in November 1912, but which, due to the calibre question, had been almost immediately postponed. No sooner was war declared than the hesitation went out of the window, and within one month Vickers had been asked to manufacture 1792 guns, to be delivered at the rate of 50 a week. In November 1914, this had been quadrupled to 200 per week; by February 1915, a further 2000 guns had been ordered from makers in the USA who obtained licenses from Vickers.

But in the years before the war, with the supply of machine guns slowed to a trickle, the Chief Instructor of the School of Musketry for the British Army decided that if the massed infantry attacks to be expected in the future wars were to be stopped, then rifle firing had to be improved. This led to the "Mad Minute" component of the British soldier's annual shooting test. In one minute he had to put 15 aimed rounds into a target at 300 yards range, relying on the smooth and fast bolt-action of the Lee-Enfield to achieve this. By 1914 there were few men who could not put their 15 shots into a two-foot circle in the allotted time, and many could reach 25 telling shots. It mattered little where the shot landed, so long as it was on the target; a high velocity rifle bullet striking the human body at 300 yards would immobilize the victim.

The justification of this training was seen during the retreat from Mons in

Marching to war British infantry recruits equipped with Lee-Enfields on the march in 1914. At the Battle of Mons, the hail of accurate fire that British regular infantry produced convinced the German infantry that they were facing machine guns.

1914, when Von Kluck's army, applying their standard tactic of an advance in close order – a line of men almost shoulder to shoulder moving across country in the direction of the enemy – were decimated by the blast of rifle fire put up by the regular infantrymen of the British Expeditionary Force. The volume of fire was such that German commanders were convinced that the British had at least twice as many machine guns as they had been led to believe, and it was a long time before they could be convinced that rifle fire alone had done the damage. Unfortunately, the retreat from Mons and the battles of 1914 were the last time this skill was seen in its full effect; rifle shooting of this nature takes years to perfect, and wartime conscripts never had the time that was necessary to learn it.

THE TANK

The answer to the stalemate of Flanders bogs down with bad tactics

The machine gun, in the hands of both sides in the First World War, became a potent factor. It was never the major killing device, as has often been asserted; this dubious distinction belonged to the artillery, since medical records eventually showed that something like 60 percent of casualties came from artillery fire, about 30 percent from small arms fire, and the remainder from grenades, gas and other weapons. The distinctive point, though, was the timescale; while a regiment might suffer 1000 casualties in a month from artillery fire and consider this no more than average, if it suffered the same in one day from machine gun fire during an abortive assault, the sudden shock engraved itself on men's minds and the machine gun grew to have a particularly malevolent reputation. When, as in the case of the British Army, 20,000 were struck down in a day in the famous First Day of the Somme, then it had an influence for years into the future.

The machine gun's best accomplice was barbed wire; not the homely strands which surround a farmer's field, but savage ribbons of steel with barbs as thick as a man's thumb, ranked in thickets yards wide and feet high. With these obstacles to channel an attack it became a simple matter to locate machine guns where they could enfilade any attackers as they attempted to find a way through the maze, and thus an assault was cut down before it could become a threat.

Between them wire and the machine gun stifled tactical manoeuvre from the end of 1914, once the trench lines ran from the North Sea to the Swiss border. The only hope was to batter the wire flat with gunfire, use gunfire to blow the machine guns out of their nests, and then hope that infantry could advance over the shattered landscape before the enemy could mount a counterattack. The problem was that gunfire merely re-arranged the wire in a less orderly fashion and frequently failed to find a proportion of the machine guns. Or the machine gunners sat out the bombardment in some deep hole, and when it stopped, a sure sign that the infantry assault had begun, still had sufficient time to run up into the open, set up their gun and begin firing before the first waves of advancing infantry were upon them.

The Tank Solution

It was this dilemma which brought forth the tank, an armoured track-laying gun-carriage which could batter down the wire so that infantry could cross behind it, and which could straddle trenches and clamber over obstacles to get at the machine gunners. In the years which have passed since the tank's first appearance there have been several contenders for the honour of being its inventor, and several names have been shown to have produced drawings well before the outbreak of war, drawings which could well be construed as being the

"Somewhere in France"
British infantry advance into no man's land during the Battle of the Somme in 1916. From 1914 until the last year of the war, the stalemate of trench warfare on the Western Front continued unbroken, offensive after offensive being halted in its tracks with great loss. On the first day of the Somme battle alone, the British suffered 20,000 casualties. The chief obstacles to success were artillery, barbed wire and the machine gun.

Breaking through A British tank in action during the Battle of Cambrai in 1917. This was the first battle in which tanks fulfilled their intended purpose of smashing through the German defences to clear the way for the advancing infantry, though, through lack of reserves, initial success was not exploited. Previously, tanks had been the victims of the artillery barrage fired to clear the way for their attack; this so churned up the ground that their crews found it impossible to manoeuvre effectively.

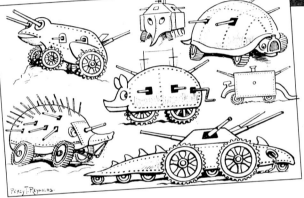

Fact and fantasy The initial breakthrough at Cambrai caught the public imagination, because it seemed that, at last, a weapon had been devised that could break the stalemate of trench warfare. Tanks had hitherto been a closely guarded secret – even the word "tank" had been chosen to conceal their true purpose.

progenitor of the tank. But drawings are not the whole story. Such claims need to be accompanied by a tactical purpose and a plan of employment, and the man who meets this specification is Major-General Sir Ernest Swinton who, while travelling back to England from the front, late in 1914, recalled seeing a tracked tractor and, building from that, postulated a suitable armed machine, a role for it, and a set of tactical instructions to suit. Swinton prepared a paper which, eventually, led to the Admiralty Landships Committee and, in the fullness of time, to the first British tank.

But as in many cases, the same idea had occurred to other people at more or less the same time; when the same problem is apparent to several minds, this often happens. Ideas for combating wire and machine guns by means of motor vehicles with rollers or armour began to flow into the French High Command early in 1915; but private enterprise was more responsive and in May 1915, the Schneider-Creusot company began experimenting with two Holt tracked tractors but their idea

was turned down flat by the Under-Secretary of State for Inventions. Finally, in December 1915, a Captain Estienne, who had gone through much the same thought processes as Swinton, wrote to General Joffre, Commander-in-Chief of the French Army, outlining plans for "armoured infantry carriers" to carry a 20-man storming party right into the enemy position. Joffre reacted rapidly, ordering Estienne to Paris to discuss his ideas with some motor manufacturers. Renault were not interested, so Estienne finished up with Schneider, who were at least glad that somebody was taking an interest. Together they worked out a more practical vehicle and, in January 1916, Schneider received contracts to build the first French tanks.

The tank had its battle debut on 15 September 1916, when 20 British tanks were put into action in a bid to revive the flagging battle of the Somme. Although they had a morale-shaking effect on some German troops, they had very little overall effect, and by the end of the day the 20 pioneers were destroyed, bogged deep in mud or scattered far from their objectives.

The recriminations over this first use of the tank have rumbled on over the years; that it was folly to commit such a small number; that it was unwise to reveal the tank's existence before the French were ready to put theirs into action; that it would have been equal folly to order vast numbers (as the French had done) without first seeing how they functioned in battle; and so on and so forth. There is something to be said for all these arguments, but they

Grim reality Early British tanks came in two varieties – "male" and "female" – depending on their armament. The fate of this "female" Mark IV, which bogged down during the 1917 Battle of Passchendaele, shows vividly what could happen when tanks were forced to operate in unfavourable conditions.

are of little contemporary relevance. In later battles the tank was to be of more value, though it was always at hazard because of the terrain in which it was forced to operate. Flanders mud, pitted with shell craters, was difficult even for tracked vehicles, and it must be remembered that these pioneer tanks were by no means mechanically reliable. When 60 tanks were used at Arras, in April 1917, their chances were spoiled by a five-day preparatory bombardment, which churned up the ground into a sea of shell-holes. Then, on the night before the attack, it began to rain heavily, and the battlefield soon turned into a swamp. All the tanks operating with the British 5th Army bogged down within 460m (500yd) of their start line, as did most of the tanks of the 3rd Army. The only benefit to the British was that the sight of all these steel monsters buried to their waists in mud simply convinced the German High Command that the tank was without a future, and they closed their minds to it.

Success at Cambrai
The tank had its chance to prove itself at the Battle of Cambrai, in November 1917. This battle came about almost by accident; Lt Col JFC Fuller, Staff Officer of the Tank Corps, wanted to mount a "tank raid" to restore morale after the disastrous battle of Third Ypres – or Passchendaele as it is more usually known. Fuller looked for a piece of undamaged ground on which tanks could operate without being stuck and settled on a stretch of country near St Quentin. He proposed his idea to Sir Hugh Elles, Commander of the Tank Corps who turned it down, since most of Fuller's proposed battlefield was inside a French sector

of the front. On the spur of the moment Fuller looked at a map, pointed to Cambrai and said "What about here?". Elles agreed, and as casually as that the plans for the first major tank battle began to take shape.

Fuller wanted a short and sharp battle against some strictly defined objectives, simply to prove the worth of the tank as a weapon. But, as it happened, the 9th Division had already suggested a battle in the same area, using smoke screens to cover a tank attack and without the usual artillery bombardment to announce the onset of the battle. Then came General Byng of the 3rd Army, a cavalry enthusiast, who wanted a role for the 40,000 or so cavalry who were awaiting their chance to exploit a break in the German lines. The three ideas were merged and superimposed so that the final plan was that of making a tank attack, supported but not preceded by artillery, so as to punch a hole through the Hindenburg Line that the cavalry could then sweep through and exploit.

At 0620 on November 20th 1917, 1009 British guns opened fire on prearranged targets – German artillery positions, machine gun posts, trench lines, headquarters – and also laid smoke screens to conceal the movement of 216 tanks. A rolling barrage of gas, shrapnel and high explosive shells moved 275m (300yd) in front of the tanks as they advanced. Behind the tanks came the infantry, running 45m (50yd) behind and relying on their individual tanks to crush the wire and protect them from machine guns. The tanks were carrying fascines – large bundles of brushwood – on their roofs, and as they came to a trench so the fascine was dropped in to fill the gap, and the tank drove across, leaving a bridge for the following infantry.

This sudden onslaught in the misty dawn completely unnerved most of the German front line troops, and the British success was overwhelming. By 10 a.m. the first objectives had been taken, and another 96 tanks had entered the battlefield, rolling forward to pass through the initial line and take over the lead. In addition, 32 special "grapnel tanks" fitted with chains and hooks had come forward to drag away whole sectors of German wire and clear the way for the cavalry.

But after this initial success, things began to falter. In the centre of the advance lay the village of Flesquières, now a German strongpoint. The 51st

Highland Division were to deal with Flesquieres, but their commander had no experience with tanks and tended to think that the drills he had been instructed in were wrong. Instead of keeping his infantry in tight groups behind each tank, as everyone else had done, he chose to spread them out in lines alongside the tanks. This meant that when the tank flattened a belt of wire, the entire line had to turn inwards and run to get through the gap, then fan out on the other side, wasting time and energy and making them a more vulnerable target. Added to this was the famous "Gunner of Flesquieres", Unter-Offizer Kruger of the 8th Field Battery who manned a 77mm field gun single-handed after its crew had been killed, and personally knocked out seven British tanks before being killed alongside his gun. With this, and the general dogged German defence, Flesquieres failed to be taken, and remained as a threat to the flanks of those troops who passed alongside it.

Due to misunderstandings a flank attack against Flesquieres failed to get under way before darkness and rain overtook it. Then, in response to a misleading message, the cavalry decided to march up to the new front via Flesquieres, and in doing so got into a tangle with 51st Highland Division which took several hours to sort out. And further advance was stopped by a canal which was securely held by the Germans and had no bridges by which to cross it.

By the evening of 21 November, the attack had run out of steam. The tanks and their crews were alike exhausted,

and there had been a failure in the resupply of petrol. The infantry were exhausted and the reserves had failed to appear at the proper time and place. So the hole was never punched in the Hindenburg Line and the 40,000 horsemen turned around and went back to their stables. After a week of stalemate the inevitable German counterattack came and drove the British back to their start line. Cambrai was over, and there was very little to show for it, largely because it had been put in motion with little or no thought given to what would be needed if it did succeed. It did succeed, exactly as Fuller and Elles expected, but there were no worthwhile reserves to go in and keep up the momentum once the initial assault began to slow down.

Nevertheless, when all the arguing was over, one fact was indisputable. The Tank Corps had done precisely what they were supposed to have done; they had delivered the infantry on to their objectives exactly as planned, protected them and defended them. Whatever the future was to bring, the existence of the tank was vindicated and assured by the Battle of Cambrai.

The French version Although the British were the first to put tanks into action, Schneider-Creusot paralleled British development independently, winning the contract to build the first French tanks in January 1916. By mid-1918, the French army could field an impressive force of both light and heavy tanks.

Missed opportunity
Germany's High Command saw little value in tanks after their initial failures in action and only a handful were built, though raw material shortages also played a part in the decision. To beat off British and French tank attacks, the Germans relied on their existing field artillery, plus the first antitank guns and antitank rifles.

TANK TACTICS

In the initial stages of the tank's development, battle tactics were relatively simple. The chief aim was to break through the massive barbed wire entanglements, with which the Germans protected their trenches, and then to cross them and provide covering fire for the supporting infantry. The main problem the tank tacticians faced was to convince their own High Command that their machines, which were cumbersome and could be mechanically unreliable, needed relatively undamaged ground over which to operate. The conventional prolonged artillery barrage was therefore the tank's worst enemy; before Cambrai, however, only a short whirlwind bombardment preceded the attack.

Tanks in action The first echelon of an attack consisted of four tank sections, numbering three tanks per section. Each section was supported by four platoons of infantry, advancing in extended order behind the main body of tanks. Behind them came a further four platoons, with half a battalion in support.

The initial crossing The leading tanks crush the wire, cross the enemy fire trench, dropping a fascine, and then advance to crush the second belt of wire.

Providing support Supporting tanks cross the "bridge" provided by the fascine, then swing to the right to flank the fire trench.

Bridging the gap The fascines each tank carried were essential bridge-builders – for the tanks themselves and for their supporting infantry. The latter had specific tasks; the first wave's role was to clear the German fire trenches of the remaining enemy, while the second wave secured the trenches and cleared more gaps in the wire ready for the supporting advance.

LESSONS OF THE GREAT WAR

*New ideas and weapons that would change
the face of conflict for ever*

The second innovative weapon by which the First World War is remembered is poison gas, and at the end of the war it was widely held to be the decisive weapon of the future. Events, however, proved that it was the tank which became the decisive weapon while poison gas stayed no more than a nebulous threat.

Realities of war

It is often assumed that the German Army had planned the First World War down to the last button and the last cartridge, but the truth is that the arrival of the war took them by surprise as much as it did the other belligerents, and their long-term planning was non-existent. Every combatant thought that they were in for a re-run of 1870, with a quick and decisive campaign, which would be over by Christmas 1914. When it wasn't, the quartermasters suddenly realized what sort of expenditure of ammunition and weapons was taking place and how minuscule were the replacement plans.

As early as October 1914, the German Army were casting about for cheap and quick methods of replenishing their artillery ammunition stocks. Shells could be manufactured fairly readily by engineering firms, but the explosive to go into those shells was rather more difficult and slower to produce. In September 1914, a suggestion was made to use an irritant powder to replace the TNT used in "Universal" shrapnel shells. By using the irritant chemical, TNT was saved and there might be a useful physiological effect. These shells, it is reported, were used against the British at Neuve Chapelle on 27 October 1914, but the idea was a complete failure. Since shrapnel bursts about 12.5m (40 ft) above the ground it is probable that the irritant drifted away on the wind.

Next they filled 15cm shells with xylyl bromide, a tear-provoking liquid, together with a small bursting charge of explosive. These were fired against the Russians at Bolimov, on the Eastern front, on 31 January 1915. Once more the idea was a failure, because the intense cold froze the liquid inside the shells and the detonation failed to disperse it as a gas.

Finally, on the advice of Professor Haber, Director of the Kaiser Wilhelm Institute for Physical Chemistry, chlorine gas in cylinders was adopted, and it was this weapon which was used against the French and Canadian lines at Ypres in April 1915. Over 5700 cylinders of gas were opened to release 168 tons of gas to roll across No Man's Land against the Allied line. This was a resounding success but, as was to happen at Cambrai and other battles, the planners had neglected to provide for success, and the Allies were able to plug the hole in their line before the Germans could take advantage of the havoc they had caused. By the end of the Second Battle of Ypres some 20,000 men had been gassed of whom an estimated 5000 died – they died in a horrifying manner.

Once gas made an appearance on the battlefield, all the combatants hurried to take advantage of it. The Germans soon found that their innovation of the cloud attack was a bad choice, because the

Clouds of death Poison gas was one of the most feared weapons of World War I. It was first used by the Germans in 1915 (right). Chlorine was the first gas used, but others swiftly followed, as both sides took up the new weapon. Methods of release and protection soon became more sophisticated as well; gas mortar bombs and shells quickly went into mass-production, while the infantry were equipped with respirators, (above).

Tactical revolution German assault troops rehearse their role before the attack on the Russian positions at Riga in September 1917. The German commander, Oskar von Hutier, relied on small groups of picked infantry to infiltrate the Russian defences, supported by a complex pattern of artillery bombardment. His success at Riga paved the way for the same tactics to be used in the German breakthrough in France in March 1918.

prevailing wind in Flanders was usually from west to east, giving the Allies a considerable advantage in this form of warfare which they were quick to exploit. The British Army became particularly adept at mounting sudden and massive cloud attacks which caused heavy casualties. Mortar bombs and artillery shells were soon brought into use as gas carriers, and the British invented the "Livens Projector", a primitive mortar which, fired by the thousand in massive volleys, literally swamped an area of German trenches with an instant concentration.

Yet in spite of the number of varieties of gas used, its actual lethal effect of gas was remarkably small; less than 6 percent of all casualties, and less than one-third of one percent of war deaths, were due to gas. A survey of 4575 cases of wounding by gas in the British Army showed that 94 percent were fit again within nine weeks.

Tactical rethinking

In the end it was not technology alone which brought the First World War to its conclusion. Leaving aside economic and political factors and looking solely at the military aspect, what brought about victory was simply a rethinking of tactics in conjunction with technology. The breakthrough came when someone thought of a different method of pushing the assault forward.

In September 1917 the German Army sought to capture Riga from the Russians; they had attempted this before and had been bloodily repulsed, but Riga was the Queen of the Baltic and would be a great morale-booster for the Germans if it could be taken, a

considerable setback to the Russians if they lost it. The Russians, of course, had no intention of parting with it and had prepared an immensely strong defensive position. The German attacking force was numerically inferior, and thus all the book solutions said that an attack must fail. The officer in charge of the attacking force, the German 8th Army, General Oskar von Hutier, had different ideas.

Von Hutier devised the technique of infiltration; instead of throwing solid lines of men against the defences, small independent groups would move stealthily across No Man's Land, probing the defences, ease their way in where the line was weakest, and then fan out behind to take troublesome redoubts from the rear. This was to be done with the assistance of artillery fire, but not the blunderbuss approach of week-long bombardments and rolling barrages. Von Hutier's artillery commander was Colonel Bruchmuller, another man who had an independent mind and was prepared to abandon the textbook approach when it appeared to be wrong. Instead of formal programmes, Bruchmuller's control of artillery stressed flexibility and an approach tailored to suit the problem in front of him. He would use rolling barrages, concentrations, smoke, gas, shrapnel in combinations and permutations, placing concentrated fire on specific targets such as communications networks, headquarters, rallying points, quite arbitrarily and in a manner which rapidly disoriented his opponents.

Bruchmuller produced 750 guns and 550 mortars to accompany von Hutier's approach to Riga, which had to begin by crossing the Dvina river. The guns were split into two groups, IKA (Infanterie Kampfzug Abteilung) and AKA (Artillerie Kampfzug Abteilung). IKA guns were for infantry support and were provided with ammunition in the proportion of four-fifths high explosive and one-fifth gas. AKA guns were for countering Russian artillery and headquarters areas, and used a proportion of one-quarter explosive and three-quarters gas.

The battle began at 0400 hours on 2 September with all the guns hammering the Russian artillery positions, three batteries of 15cm howitzers being specially detailed to bombard command posts and communications points. At 0600, the AKA continued their pounding while the IKA group turned their attention on to the Russian infantry defending the river line. This bombardment continued until 0910 hours, shifting from target to target and from explosive to gas and back again in a bewildering sequence, all the time at hurricane intensity. At 0900, the AKA group joined in, each AKA battery leaving one gun to "stoke up" the gas clouds enveloping the Russian artillery targets.

At 0910, all the guns switched to a massive rolling barrage which dwelt on the Russian infantry positions until the German assault troops had crossed the river, and then rolled forward into the defensive zone. After it came von Hutier's troops in small parties, probing, bypassing, enfilading and enveloping.

The operation was a complete success and vindicated the theories of von Hutier and Bruchmuller. German casualties were relatively light, mainly confined to engineers and pioneers operating the river crossing. The intense bombardment and the concentration of gas entirely unnerved the Russians, many of whom fled, and within 24 hours Riga was safely in German hands.

As a result both von Hutier and Bruchmuller were removed from the east and sent to the Western Front, where their tactics were repeated to give the Germans their astonishing success in the offensive of April 1918. But to ensure success, certain technological advances were required.

The machine gun
One of these, which had appeared well before von Hutier's success, was the light machine gun. The original machine guns used in the early part of the war were almost all based on the Maxim design, heavy water-cooled belt-fed weapons requiring two or three men to move and operate them. These were ideal for defensive positions, where they could sit on their tripods behind a breastwork and spew out bullets for

German equivalent One of the German answers to the British Lewis gun was the Bergmann light machine gun. Surprisingly modern in appearance, it was a standard weapon in the German Army from 1917 onwards.

The need for mobility The machine guns with which the Allied and German armies went to war in 1914 were cumbersome weapons, suited to defence and not attack. The British answer to the problem was the Lewis gun, which could be carried by one man and even fired from the hip, if necessary. The conventional belt feed was abandoned in favour of a flat drum containing 47 cartridges.

The first sub-machine gun
To increase the firepower carried by their crack storm troops, the Germans were the first to adopt the sub-machine gun. Designed by Hugo Schmeisser, the Bergmann "Maschinen Pistole" was a handy weapon, which fired standard pistol cartridges from a feed drum fitted to the side of the gun. Its rate of fire was around 400 rounds per minute.

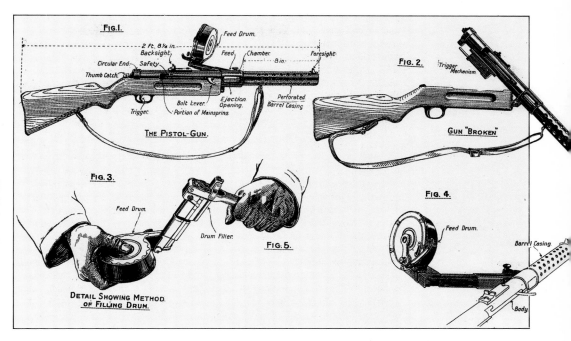

hours on end without stopping for anything but to have a new belt inserted into the breech. But this sort of weapon was a liability in the attack; the three or four men carrying the gun, tripod, water can and ammunition made an obvious group which became a prime target for snipers, their speed of advance was slow, and they took time to set up their gun and commence firing once their objective was reached. What was needed, as General Haig himself pointed out in the summer of 1915 when he was Commander, First Army, was "A lighter machine gun, with tripod and gun in one part…"

The answer was already there, in the shape of the Lewis Gun; developed in America but totally ignored there, it had been put into manufacture in Belgium and Britain and supplies began reaching the British Army in France in July 1915. This weapon could be carried by one man, was fed from a flat drum containing 47 cartridges, and could even be fired from the hip while advancing. The idea was taken up by other combatants and such designs as the Light Hotchkiss, the Bergmann, the Chauchat, the Dreyse and the Madsen appeared in large numbers throughout the remainder of the war.

The light machine gun, then, allowed the infantry to take its fire support along in the assault and it eventually came to overshadow the heavy machine gun, as we shall see. But for von Hutier's "Storm troops" something even more

portable was required; his tactical theory demanded heavy firepower from every man, more than could be easily delivered by a conventional rifle. But every man could not carry a light machine gun, from considerations of weight, bulk and ammunition supply. Something different was needed, and this led to the sub-machine gun.

The first sub-machine gun had been under development since some time in 1916; there was no military demand for it, since no military mind had visualized such a weapon, but Hugo Schmeisser, chief designer for the Theodor Bergmann Company of Berlin, was a far-seeing man who began work, sure that once he had an operating weapon the army would find a use for it. The resulting "Bergmann Maschinen Pistole 18" was an extremely simple weapon which fired standard 9mm Parabellum pistol cartridges from a 32-shot "snail" magazine inserted into the side of the gun. It fired at a rate of about 400 rounds per minute and was sighted for a maximum range of 200 m (220yd) though in practice it was to be used at much shorter distances. Weighing less than 6.4kg (14lbs) fully loaded, it was only 81cm (32in) long, a handy and easily operated weapon which gave the individual soldier immense firepower. Armed with these weapons the Storm Troopers of von Hutier's 18th Army on the Western Front made savage inroads into the Allied lines in the spring of 1918. The Allies did not adopt the

Tank developments Two British experimental tanks of the inter-war period – a Light Tank Mk1 *(left)*, an A6E Experimental Medium Tank *(centre)*. The differing views of military planners on the part that tanks would play in a future war had an inevitable impact on tank design. According to some, light tanks would operate as scouts, taking over the role of the cavalry, while fast, lightly armoured "cruise" tanks would provide the main hitting power. These theories, however, were to be exploded by the Blitzkrieg.

sub-machine gun – it was too late in the war for that – but they were well aware of the possibilities of infiltration and once they had absorbed and contained the German advance, they, in their turn, moved on to the offensive, using much the same sort of tactics. That a frontal attack now succeeded was simply due to the German advance having disrupted their tight defensive line and allowing the Allies the opportunity to move forward. Once the wedge had been inserted, assisted by tanks and concentrated artillery fire, the German line began to crumble and suddenly mobile warfare returned to the Western Front.

In the post-war years, as the armies of the world were run down from their wartime strength and lapsed into their normal peacetime obscurity, the lessons of the war were reviewed; some were learned, many were forgotten. The weapons which had appeared were also reviewed, and more notice was taken of the hardware than of the theories which had accompanied it. Although much of the wartime equipment had to stay in use for economy's sake, the soldiers and the designers saw that virtually everything in use in 1918 was obsolescent and that new weapons would be needed for the future.

In the between-wars years there were certain themes which overshadowed all the rest of military technical development: the tank, then the defence against tanks, and finally the defence against aircraft.

Re-evaluation of the tank

One of the first difficulties was to ensure the survival of the tank at all; one senior British officer, during a

lecture assessing the war's lessons, declared that "The tank proper was a freak. The circumstances which called it into existence were exceptional and are not likely to recur. If they do they can be dealt with by other means", overlooking the fact that the tank came into existence because no "other means" could be found. Tanks were scrapped as a matter of course in all countries, tank regiments were disbanded, amalgamated, dismembered and parcelled out among other corps.

And yet the only major army in which the tank corps survived as an autonomous arm was the British Army, the one which the majority of observers would have unhesitatingly called the most reactionary. The Americans and French dismembered their tank forces and gave them to the cavalry and infantry as support weapons, but the British retained their Tank Corps and allowed it to examine its possible role as an independent force on the battlefield. In fact the pendulum appeared to swing a little too far to the side of independence, and with the aid of such vociferous partisans as Major General J. F. C. Fuller and Captain (later Sir) Basil Liddell-Hart the air became thick with proposals for Tank Marines, Tank Artillery, and the entire army subservient to the all-conquering tank.

Fuller had been the author of a grandiose plan for the 1919 offensive, "Plan 1919" as it became known. This, he claimed, revolutionized warfare by striking not at the enemy's immediate front. Instead, a combined flank and frontal attack would threaten his rear areas and headquarters, lines of communication and supply and thus "destroy the nerve centres and hence

Heavy metal The British "Independent" Experimental Heavy Tank. Given the demands of battle, many tank experts differed as to the best way to proceed. Some argued that a tank that was more heavily gunned than its opponents could outshoot them from a distance and so could be lightly armoured; others argued that thicker and heavier armour was essential, even at the price of speed. What both sides overlooked was the need to standardize hull design, so that armament could be up-rated without changing the entire design.

paralyze the fighting element" by depriving it of command and control.

Liddell-Hart was a Captain of infantry who was introduced to tanks by Fuller after the war. In 1921, he expounded his "expanding torrent" theory. While he claimed to have traced the idea back to Sun Tzu he never appears to have acknowledged that this was basically what von Hutier had used at Riga and on the Western Front: probe, pierce and spread out at the rear. After Fuller had drawn his attention to the tank, he began to look at its possibilities and was soon writing glibly about "an army composed principally of tanks and aircraft, with a small force of siege artillery..." and advocating a mixture of "scout", "cruiser", "battle" and "supply" tanks.

While these and other theorists wrote and painted castles in the air, the soldiers had the job of making what they could of what they had, a ragbag of leftovers from the war and the handful of newly-designed tanks which could be afforded in the lean postwar years.

The Panzer scheme
The basic problem of between-the-wars theories lay in determining the correct method of employment of tanks. The alternatives were (a) to use them simply as they had been used during the war, to lead and protect the infantry; (b) to make them an entirely independent force with their own accompanying infantry and artillery, capable of sweeping drives through enemy lines, encircling movements, and generally "Plan 1919" at its best; or (c) to weld them as an integral part of a balanced fighting formation which would then apply tactical principles.

Only the Germans gave the matter

anything approaching rational thought; and that largely because under the terms of the Versailles treaty they were not permitted to have any tanks. When they finally made their move it was to option (c): the Panzer division.

The Panzer division was a balanced force of all arms – armour, artillery, infantry, engineers, services – capable either of independent operation or of operation in concert with other divisions. But the point was that it carried its immediate needs with it; the tanks advanced, accompanied by motorized infantry and supported by motorized artillery, with motorized engineers available for bridging and demolition, and supplied by a column of motor vehicles, the whole division being capable of moving at speed and not being tied to the pace of marching troops. When faced with action the various elements, having trained together, moved into operation smoothly, each knowing what the other would do and was capable of.

The second advantage which the Panzer division had was that it was supplied with supporting air power – the "Stuka" dive bomber was perhaps the most famous element of this but there were also conventional bombers and fighters available on call to the division. For the Germans had looked at the various possible ways of using air power and had decided that its primary use was in direct support of land forces.

Guderian, the Chief of Staff of the Panzer troops, spent his time studying everything written on the employment of armour, watched the British and French experiments, and knew precisely what he wanted to do with armour. And in 1939 he put his theories into practice.

WORLD WAR II

The inspired use of new hardware and tactics creates 'The Lightning War'

In 1914 the German plan for waging war was carefully balanced; it was obvious that they would have enemies on both flanks, the Russians on the east and the French on the west, and their famous Schlieffen Plan was devised to perform a lightning strike against the French while the ponderous Russian war machine was still mobilizing. It almost came off; indeed, had Schlieffen's original plan been left alone it might very easily have succeeded; but von Moltke's nerve failed, he tinkered with it, upsetting the balance, and it just failed, setting the scene for four years of all-out war.

The Third Reich strikes

In 1939, the problem was similar, but Hitler circumvented it in his own manner by concluding a treaty with the Russians, offering them half of Poland for their acquiescence in his attack on that country. The Soviets, mindful of their ignominious defeat by the Poles in 1920, were only too pleased to be given the opportunity to even the score, and Hitler then had one threat removed from the board. On 1 September 1939, he moved against Poland and precipitated the Second World War.

Six Panzer and four Light divisions formed the spearhead of the German attack on Poland, and they were entirely equipped with PzI and PzII tanks. In addition, there was the Panzer Lehr Battalion, an advanced training and instructional unit, equipped with the first specimens of the PzIII and PzIV models, mainly so that they could be evaluated in combat. The PzI was a light tank, the first to be developed for the Germans in 1934, armed with no more than a machine gun; PzII was larger, though still a light vehicle, and carried a 20mm gun. Both were interim designs which had been produced more or less as peacetime training vehicles, to be replaced by heavier tanks in due course. But design and funding was slow, and so only the handful of heavier tanks operated by the Panzer Lehr Battalion were ready when war began, and perforce the armoured divisions had to go to war with lightweights. PzIII was a medium tank, armed with a 37mm high velocity gun, and PzIV was also a medium but with a potent 75mm gun for close support. Altogether about 2100 tanks attacked Poland; they were well-designed, reliable, and operated by a well-trained and highly motivated army.

Facing them were 1065 machines of doubtful efficiency; the Poles had a motley collection of models, some of which were several years old and obsolescent by anybody's standard;

Panzers on parade PzKpfw I's lead a review in Berlin late in 1939. These light tanks, the first fruits of the Nazi rearmament programme in 1934, were only equipped with a machine gun and, though used in the Polish campaign, were obsolescent before the Second World War began. However, they provided a sound basis for the perfection of Panzer tactics.

"Achtung Panzer!" A Panzer commander poses in the turret of his PzKpfw IV for a photograph for the German propaganda magazine "Signal". Originally intended to provide support for the PzKpfw III, this tank became the mainstay of Germany's Panzer divisions from 1941, since it was relatively easy to upgrade both its armament and protective armour.

they also had about 50 new French tanks, bought late in 1938 and so new that few of their crews were completely familiar with them. Although the Poles fought to the best of their considerable ability, the result was a foregone conclusion to anyone who understood the armour theories of the new German Army. But at that time, of course, few people, even inside the German Army, appreciated what the Panzers were capable of doing. Most people were still thinking of war in terms of trench lines, artillery bombardments, and infantry advances, and the speed of the German advance, the surgical precision with which the Panzer divisions sliced the Polish defence into pieces, was a terrible shock. Added to the armoured thrust was the tactical air support in the shape of the Stuka dive bomber, bringing a new dimension to war, that of the "Blitzkrieg" – as Poland was swallowed up the rest of the world wondered what sort of war this was going to be.

The German armoured force was accompanied by 27 infantry divisions, four motorized infantry divisions and a cavalry brigade. It is of interest to note

The winter war Warmly protected against the onset of the Russian winter, the crew of this PzKpfw II pause at a supply station. Hitler's tanks, however, proved no match for the Soviet T34, whose impact was such that new German tank designs were hastily rushed into production.

that the German plan of attack specifically stated that its aim was "the destruction of the Polish Armed Forces"; interesting because of the predominance of pre-war theorists who had suggested that destruction of an enemy's force was no longer necessary, that striking at the "nerve centres" would paralyze an army to the point where it could no longer function effectively. It is apparent that this idea had not made much progress in the German High Command; it was still formulating its aim in the traditional manner. Destroy the army and the nation collapses.

The plan called for a vast double pincer movement. One massive thrust moved east out of Germany and, once through, the initial Polish resistance would split, one arm curving up to the west of Warsaw, the other bypassing Warsaw to the south and aiming for Brest-Litovsk. A second thrust would move down from Pomerania between Lodz and Warsaw to meet the first arm of the major attack. A third thrust moved out of East Prussia towards Brest-Litovsk to meet the second arm, so that these three axes of attack would constitute a massive encircling manoeuvre. A fourth, minor, thrust moved out of Slovakia via Krakow to sweep across the southern flank of Poland and cut off any formations retreating from the major axis.

The cutting edge of the attack was to be the Panzer divisions, supported by tactical air forces. When the armour was stopped by any opposition, a Luftwaffe observer accompanying the column would call up the Stukas while the infantry closed up behind the tanks and prepared to attack as soon as the bombing was over.

In general, the German plan worked well, with little on-the-spot modification

required. It did not, though, run as smoothly as is often thought. The troops were undergoing their first experience of war, and many peacetime attitudes had to be revised; thus advance guards would reach a river and sit down to await further instructions instead of pressing on. There was also a reluctance on the part of army commanders to rely upon the armour, a fear of committing mobile forces too far ahead in case they were cut off by a sudden counterattack. The general attitude, after the first day or two, was that the Poles had exhausted all their efforts, there was no hurry, and an orderly occupation of Poland could be conducted at walking pace. But the Poles had by no means given up and suddenly began developing dangerous counterattacks, and Guderian was suddenly let off the leash and allowed to show what he could do. In spite of dogged resistance by the Polish 18th Division – Guderian himself was cut off and very nearly captured – the German XIX Corps broke through and shot across north-eastern Poland to reach Brest-Litovsk inside 24 hours, an unparalleled rate of advance.

On the following day, to everyone's surprise, the Russian Army crossed their border to meet up with the Germans on a line running through Brest-Litovsk, and for all practical purposes the Polish campaign was over. Warsaw held out for a further week before capitulating, but in 17 days the German Army had captured 120,000 square miles of territory, 700,000 prisoners, and whatever was left serviceable of the Polish Army's equipment. German losses were 8082 killed, 27,279 wounded and 5029 missing. Tank losses were 217, and a larger number were damaged but repairable.

The drive to the east A PzKpfw III Ausf.E in action on the Russian Front in the summer of 1941. This variant, with its 37mm main armament and two machine guns, was the first mass-produced Panzer III design. Later models were equipped with a 50mm gun in both short and long versions.

After the Polish campaign was over, there was little or no action for several months. The French were satisfied to sit in the Maginot Line and wait for the Germans, the Germans satisfied to let them sit. The British Expeditionary Force formed the left flank of the French line, and were fairly certain that when things eventually began to move they would advance into Belgium, but political considerations prevented any reconnaissance of possible locations. The Belgians were happy in their neutrality, but wisely looked to their frontier fortifications. The Germans bided their time and prepared for their next move, safe in the knowledge that the Soviets would remain quiet, digesting their gift of Polish territory and seeking out any Pole misguided enough to have fought them in 1919-20.

The next move was to occupy Norway and Denmark, campaigns which were short and sharp and which the British and French could do little to counter. On 10 May 1940, the long-awaited attack in the west began, and with it the application of new technology. In broad outline it was another armoured thrust, which we need not examine too closely. But there were one or two surprises.

The first was the employment of glider-borne troops to assault a fortress considered to have been impregnably sited. The Belgian fort of Eben Emael was in an angle of the Albert Canal, so

that the canal formed a deep and wide wet ditch across its face, enough to deter any sensible enemy from attacking. But the Germans needed to take Eben Emael out to be able to use the bridges it commanded, allowing them to pour their armour into Belgium, and thus make a flanking move against France and evade the Maginot Line.

Late in 1939, the 1st Company, 1st Parachute Regiment of the Luftwaffe began intensive training with a new device: a shaped demolition charge. In the 1880s an American experimenter had discovered that if the face of a slab of high explosive was recessed, when the charge was detonated in contact with steel the shape of the recess was reproduced in the steel. Later, a German scientist found that by hollowing out the face of the explosive into a hemisphere or cone and lining this recess with a thin metal plate, the detonation could pierce steel. From this a demolition charge had been devised, a 50kg hemisphere of high explosive sitting on three legs and with its underside hollowed out into a lined hemispherical cavity. When placed on top of armour and fired, this charge would blow a hole through at least a foot of protecting plate. With these charges the 1st Company practised against old Czech and Polish fortifications in great secrecy throughout the winter of 1939. On 9 May 1940, they assembled at

airfields near Cologne and took off, in gliders towed by bombers, for Eben Emael. In the misty night the gliders swooped silently out of the sky and landed on top of the fort. Machine gun posts were soon silenced, the shaped charges placed on the gun cupolas, and within minutes all the armament of the fort was crippled. By this time the Belgians were alerted and fire from mobile artillery and other forts began to search out the attackers, and they also managed to blow up a bridge across the Maas which a German relieving force was intending to use. Eventually, assault pioneers crossed the canal in rubber boats to assist the paratroops and the fort surrendered for the loss of only six German soldiers killed and 10 wounded. The gliders were removed from the fort almost immediately, before any local inhabitants could see them, and it was not until after the war that the precise method of silencing Eben Emael was known.

If the use of gliders against Eben Emael was kept under wraps, the use of parachute troops in other parts of the Low Countries was not, and indeed the word seems to have been spread assiduously as a propaganda move; some hair-raising stories came out of Holland, of paratroopers dressed as nuns (but you could always tell them by their boots...), paratroopers dressed as postmen, policemen, tramps.... The list was endless and entirely fictitious, but it stimulated the British and other armies to investigate the use of parachute troops.

The German paratroops were part of the Luftwaffe, closely integrated and virtually "airborne marines". Their early operations were conducted with dash and efficiency, but they were decimated during the attack on Crete in 1941, after which they became merely a sort of elite light infantry.

The British paratroops were army troops from the beginning, though their parachute training was always conducted by the Royal Air Force. The birth of the British paratroops was on 21 June 1940 when the "Central Landing School" was opened, 24 hours before Churchill directed the War Office to investigate the formation of a parachute force of 5000 men. Training began in July and by 6 August 500 men were at the School. But there were no suitable aircraft, no gliders, no tactical thoughts on employment, and until 1942, when American Dakota transport aircraft became available, the British parachute force was little more than a paper promise. It was not until the arrival of the first gliders in mid-1942 that the airborne forces really had a practical system of transport to battle. Hitherto the ability to drop parachutists had been one thing; the ability to supply them with heavy weapons and transport a quite different matter. With the availability of good transports for the parachutists and gliders for vehicles and light artillery, air-landing operations became feasible for the first time.

44

ARMOUR

The steel gauntlet of tanks clashes on the Eastern Front

The development of armoured vehicles made some significant steps in 1940-41. Experience in France had shown the British – and anyone else who cared to watch – that the day of the light tank was over; it could no longer survive on the battlefield against antitank weapons designed to deal with the heavier types of armour. But the British were in a trap of their own making because their tank guns were almost impotent and their tanks incapable of being fitted with heavier weapons. In the pre-war years the axiom was that since tanks and antitank guns had the same target in mind, similar armament would save development and production time. So when the antitank gun was settled as a 40mm 2-pounder, the tanks were built around the same weapon. The German Army had begun with a similar philosophy, using 20mm and 37mm tank guns, but their experience showed that these were useless and that the 75mm gun on the PzIV tank gave them a long-ranging weapon capable of dealing with tanks and also capable of firing high explosive shells to assist the infantry or to aid the tanks in suppressing antitank guns. The British had appreciated the fact that the 2-pounder antitank gun was rapidly being outclassed by improvements in German

tank design and had designed a much more powerful 6-pounder 57mm gun in 1938; but in 1940 there was no production capacity available, and 2-pounders were being made in order to re-equip the army after its losses in France. Better the gun you know when invasion was staring Britain in the face.

Antitank solutions

Eventually the British put the 6-pounder antitank gun into the field and also began developing tanks to carry it, but by that time (late 1941) the German tanks had adopted thicker armour and their 75mm gun still gave them an advantage. No sooner was the 6-pounder in production than the British Army began designing a more powerful weapon, a 3-inch 17-pounder, which appeared late in 1942 and subsequently became one of the most formidable antitank guns in existence. But it was impossible to fit it into any existing British tank, and new designs did not appear until the end of the war.

The Germans, by late 1942, had moved on from their 75mm tank and antitank standard and had adopted

From role to role The German 88mm cannon was one of the most successful artillery designs of World War II. Its high firing velocity combined with its flat trajectory to make it a multi-purpose antitank and anti-aircraft weapon.

The Sherman The US-designed M4 Sherman medium tank was one of the mainstays of both the American and British armoured divisions in the European theatre during the latter part of the Second World War. Its major drawback was the lack of armour around its petrol supply, which made it extremely vulnerable when faced with German opponents; the Sherman's crews cynically nicknamed it the "Ronson", because it caught fire like a cigarette lighter.

88mm as their universal calibre. The 88mm anti-aircraft gun, designed in secret in the late 1920s and put into production as soon as Hitler gained power, had been tested in the Spanish Civil War, and had revealed its possibility as a defensive weapon against armour. This was reinforced when a British armoured breakthrough near Arras, in 1940, had only been stopped by the fortuitous intervention of an anti-aircraft battery who had depressed their guns to fight off the attacking armour. Provided with armour-piercing projectiles, the "Eighty-Eight" became the German wonder gun, and the scourge of Allied armour. Originally an anti-aircraft weapon it became a dual-purpose gun, and then dedicated tank and antitank guns in this calibre were perfected.

In addition to developing the weapons, the German Army also perfected the tactical handling of the antitank gun; in the early days of the war the antitank gun was thought of simply as a passive device which was sited in a position to which tanks were likely to come, and then shot at whatever came within range. But the German Afrika Korps improved on that during the campaign in North Africa. It became their practice to set out their 75mm and 88mm guns in concealed positions and then send out a small force of tanks to trail their coats across the front of the British line. This inevitably produced a response and a force of British tanks would approach in order to do battle. The Germans would gradually pull back until they had drawn the British force into the antitank guns' killing ground, whereupon the Germans would turn about and make all speed for home, leaving the British tanks to be torn to pieces by the ambush. It took

some time for this lesson to sink in, but eventually it became the normal tactic.

Tanks advance
The American Army, after years of inactivity, had begun to contemplate re-arming in 1939, and had drawn up plans for a new medium tank mounting a 37mm gun in its turret. After seeing what had happened in Poland and France the War Department reconsidered, and decided that a 75mm gun was necessary. Unfortunately, the tank's turret would not accommodate a weapon of this size so an interim solution was devised. The hull was modified to mount a turret-like "sponson" on the right front, into which a 75mm gun could be fitted. This was immediately approved and went into production as the "M3 Medium", later christened the "General Lee". By this time, mid-1941, the British Purchasing Commission was established in the USA and bidding for a proportion of American production. The General Lee, slightly modified so as to conform to British ideas and accept British radio equipment, was bought and shipped to the Middle East, where it became the "General Grant" and proved to be a revelation for its reliability, ease of maintenance and powerful 75mm gun. Meanwhile, the US Ordnance Department re-designed the hull of the tank, developed a new turret to mount the 75mm and even larger guns, and put it into production as the "M4 Medium", to become more famous as the "General Sherman".

In Soviet Russia, there had been a rash of tank designs during the 1930s, since ample heavy manufacturing facilities permitted quantities of different types to be made and evaluated. By 1939, the various

Russian supremacy In the opinion of most experts, the Soviet T34 was one of the best tank designs to see service in the Second World War. Its one major weakness was in its communication system; unlike their German opponents, the Russian tank forces still relied on manual signals given from the tank commander's turret to manoeuvre, instead of on wireless communication.

The Tiger Hitler's insistence on a new heavy tank for his battered Panzer divisions led to the design of the PzKpfw VI "Tiger", mounting an 88mm gun. The Tiger in its different versions was undoubtedly superior to any tank in the British and US armies, but its complexity of design made it unsuitable for mass-production.

designs had yielded what information they could, and the designers sat down together to bring together all the lessons they had learned. The first demand was for a reliable and powerful engine, and the Kharkov Locomotive Works perfected a 3.8 litre V12 which developed 500 horsepower. Next the designers looked at the armour; it had to be thick, well-sloped to deflect shot, and cast or welded instead of riveted. Armament was to be a high-velocity 76mm gun. Tracks were to be wide, so as to give good flotation on mud and snow, and the whole thing was to be designed so that it could be cheaply made and easily maintained in the field. Altogether, an ideal specification made by men who appreciated the vital parameters of protection, firepower and mobility and got them in the right proportions. The result was the Medium Tank T34 which was to form the backbone of Soviet tank strength until the 1950s and which, in

most experts' opinions, was the best tank of the war.

Shortly after the German Army had invaded Russia the 17th Panzer Divison reported a "low-slung and formidable" tank which appeared from the undergrowth surrounding the Dniepr River and charged into the German lines with shot bounding from its sloped armour. Crushing a 37mm antitank gun beneath its wide tracks, it then destroyed two Panzer III tanks in an offhanded manner, and went on to rampage nine miles into the German rear areas before being stopped by being shot from the rear by a 105mm field howitzer it had inadvertently overlooked. This was the German introduction to the T34.

Battle of Kursk

The greatest tank encounter of the war, in which the Soviet T34 medium and KV heavy tanks were pitted against

the German Panzers and Tiger tanks, came at Kursk in 1943. The German General Staff was hoping for a quiet year in which it could consolidate while building up German military strength. This it hoped to achieve by taking up a number of strategic defensive positions along the front, anchors for a solid line of resistance, from which they could then launch intense but localized attacks against limited objectives. These were to be mounted with the minimum effort on the German part but designed to attract the maximum Soviet defensive strength into the killing ground; in other words, a war of attrition was to be waged.

One likely target for this tactic was a salient which thrust into the German lines in the vicinity of Kursk. Von Manstein suggested a quick two-pronged attack to "pinch out" this salient and capture or destroy the troops inside before the Soviet high command had time to react. The attack was planned to take place in May, after the ground had dried out from the spring thaw. But warfare is a two-sided affair, and if the Germans could see a promising target in the Kursk Salient so could the Soviets, and they concluded that this was a temptation the Germans would not be able to resist. They therefore began strengthening the area, building a series of lines of defence with mines and antitank guns, massing artillery to cover the battlefield, and bringing up great numbers of tanks.

For reasons connected with the supply of new tanks the German attack was postponed until July, giving the Soviets even more time to prepare. On 5 July 1943, Hoth's 4th Panzer Army with 10 Panzer divisions and eight infantry divisions struck from the southern side of the Salient, while Model's 9th Army with seven Panzer divisions and 11 infantry divisions struck down from the north. Altogether the Germans put about 2400 tanks and assault guns into the battle. Facing them the Soviets had 20,000 guns and 3300 tanks.

In spite of heavy opposition the northern German advance managed to preserve its momentum until brought to a halt against a strong defensive line some 9 miles into the salient. Here the 9th Army stopped to draw breath and reorganize for a day or two before moving further. But a massive Soviet counterattack threatened the flank and supply lines, and Model's troops turned about to defend against this threat, putting an end to any idea of cutting the salient.

In the south, Hoth's army, with 700 tanks, rolled forward for about 10 miles before being stopped by a Soviet defensive line which consisted largely of several hundred tanks dug into the ground with only their turrets showing. It was the negation of armoured mobility but it was decisive, and the German attack sheered away towards the small town of Prokhorovka. This sudden change of direction took the Soviets by surprise and the Germans made some spectacular advances, capturing 24,000 prisoners, 1800 tanks and 1200 guns in a very short time. Faced with this near-disaster the Soviets threw in their reserves, the 5th Guards Army and the 5th Tank Army, and on 12 July this massive force swept into the Prokhorovka area to confront the Panzers. It has since been estimated that 1500 tanks met head-on that day, to produce what was possibly the greatest tank battle that has ever taken place. At last all the pre-war visions of fleets of tanks sweeping across open country and manoeuvering like fleets at sea had come to pass. Across the open steppe, in clouds of dust and smoke, the two armoured forces roared towards each other. At first it was a comprehensible manoeuvre as the Soviet armour sliced into the Panzer flank, but within minutes all semblance of order vanished as tanks roared back and forth, firing at whatever target presented itself, crashing into each other in the dust clouds, divorced from their companions or their commanders and simply concerned with surviving. In these conditions the better training of the

German Panzer troops balanced out the Soviet superiority in numbers, and the battle became a long-drawn-out affair; it raged from dawn until dusk, whereupon both sides fell back to lick their wounds.

The cost of this battle has never been accurately computed. Soviet historians claim 350 German tanks were destroyed but are silent about their own losses; German figures are for the entire Kursk operation and do not identify the losses at Prokhorovka. But at that stage of the war the significant point was that the Soviets could afford losses and the Germans could not.

Defensive developments
All this development of armour had, of course, to be countered by the other side. The specialist antitank guns such as the 6-pounder and the 88mm were never able to cover every line of approach, and the infantryman himself demanded some sort of weapon capable of stopping tanks. In pre-war days a number of specialized antitank rifles had been developed, usually about 12mm calibre and firing a small piercing bullet at high velocity. They sufficed against the light pre-war tanks but were soon rendered impotent by improvements in armour and tank design. But the shaped charge appeared to save the day.

The shaped charge has already been described as a demolition weapon, first used at Eben Emael. The same sort of charge placed in a projectile and fired against a tank would detonate and blast a hole through the armour, then spray the interior of the tank with flame and fragments of steel. A variety of rifle grenades were first developed, by both Britain and Germany, after which the British developed the PIAT – Projector, Infantry, Antitank. This was a peculiar weapon using a principle which its inventor, Lieutenant Colonel Blacker of the Royal Artillery, had been developing since the middle 1930s. In brief, it had a finned bomb with a shaped charge warhead and a hollow tail which contained a small propelling charge. The launcher was a tube containing a heavy steel rod and an enormous spring. The bomb was laid in a trough at the front of the launcher, the device pointed at the enemy, and the trigger pulled. This released the rod which flew forward and entered the tail of the bomb, striking the cartridge and exploding it. The explosion blew the bomb off the end of the rod and to the target, while the recoil recocked the steel rod ready for the next shot. It had

Infantry protection The British PIAT (Projector, Infantry, Antitank) and the German Panzerfaust were designed as lightweight infantry antitank weapons. Disposable, cheap and easy to mass-produce, the recoilless Panzerfaust was particularly effective.

The Bazooka The US Rocket Launcher 2.36in was fired from the shoulder. Like the Panzerfaust, it launched hollow charges, but it needed a two-man crew to fire it.

a maximum range of little more than 90m (100yd), but a good shot could stop a tank with one bomb.

The American Army then developed the 2.36-inch rocket launcher, which became better known by its nickname, the "Bazooka". This was simply an aluminium tube into the rear of which a rocket with a shaped charge warhead was loaded. The firer then pressed the trigger which electrically ignited the rocket which was then launched in the direction of the target. The bazooka appeared in 1942 and some of the first were sent to Russia; shortly afterwards one was captured and by the end of the year the German Army had copied it, calling the result the "Panzerschreck" (tank terror). They then went on to develop the "Panzerfaust" (tank fist), the first disposable weapon system.

Contrary to common belief the Panzerfaust was not a rocket launcher, but a recoilless gun. It consisted very simply of a steel tube with a trigger and a small propelling charge. Into the front end of the tube went a bomb, the shaped charge warhead of which was of considerable diameter, much greater than the tube; the only part inside the tube was the tail boom and a set of metal fins wrapped around it. When fired, the charge blew the bomb from the front and also blasted out of the rear to counterbalance the recoil. The charge, some 150mm in diameter, could defeat any tank in existence, and having fired, the soldier simply threw the tube away and either got another one or went on fighting with his rifle or other weapon.

INNOVATIONS

Special weapons for special problems – new weapons to end the war

I n 1940-41, the United States Marine Corps were perfecting the tools which they were to need in the years which followed. Their involvement in a European war was a possibility; but to their senior officers their involvement in a war with Japan in the Pacific was far more probable, and if this came along the course of the war would involve landing on defended islands. For this purpose they needed amphibious equipment, and from 1934 they had been quietly investigating likely designs. In the middle 1920s Andrew J Higgins of New Orleans had developed his "Eureka Boat" for use by fur trappers and oil drillers in the Louisiana bayous. This boat featured a shallow draft and a protected propeller. In 1934 he brought it to the attention of the US Marines and from then on he and the Marine Corps worked in close cooperation to perfect a landing craft. By 1941, a design with front-opening ramp had been perfected and was ready for production when required.

In 1933, Donald Roebling, a retired manufacturer living in Florida, had invented his "Alligator", a tracked amphibious vehicle, for rescuing downed aviators or hurricane victims from the trackless Florida Everglades country. In 1937, the Marine Corps began investigating this idea and, again by mutual cooperation between the corps and the inventor, by 1941 the 'Landing Vehicle Tracked' had been brought to the brink of production.

The next German contribution to the technology of war – the rocket – had been under development since the early 1930s, and showed itself in late 1941 during an offensive on the Russian front.

International developments

The use of rockets in warfare was not new; the British had used them in the 18th and 19th centuries with some success, but they had been overshadowed by improvements in artillery and virtually neglected since the start of the 20th century. In the early 1930s, seeking a way around the restrictions on heavy artillery contained in the Versailles Treaty, the German Army began looking at rockets as a possible long-range weapon. Their researches took them in two directions; firstly the use of solid-fuel rockets as a substitute for artillery, and secondly the use of liquid-fuelled rockets as long range strategic bombardment weapons. The first line of research developed into the "Nebelwerfer" (smokethrower – a cover name adopted to conceal the nature of the weapon), a multiple-barrelled launcher which launched a volley of simple 15cm calibre rockets to a range of about 7km (4.5mi).

The Nebelwerfer This multi-barrelled German rocket launcher fired a volley of 15cm calibre rockets. The name means "smoke thrower".

Into action German artillerymen prepare a battery of heavy rockets for launch in Warsaw during the Warsaw Rising of 1944. Although the system looks crude, it was highly effective in action.

German giant The 21cm Kanone 12 was intended to out-perform the Paris Gun of the First World War. Two of these long-range monsters were built at great expense but, except for firing a handful of 107kg shells at southeast England in 1940, they saw little combat use.

This was later improved into a 21cm model with a range of 7.8km (5 mi) and a 30cm model with a 6km (3¾mi) range. These proved to be highly effective.

As it happened the Russians had also been busy with a similar project, and shortly after the Germans unveiled the Nebelwerfer, they were surprised to be bombarded by the Russian "Stalin Organ", an equally effective weapon, which launched volleys of 130mm rockets to a range of 9km (6½mi).

The British had also ventured into the rocket field, but not as a land bombardment weapon. In 1937, their air defences were deficient of guns, and in an endeavour to find a quick and simple solution they turned to rockets. Development of suitable 2-inch and 3-inch rockets proceeded smoothly, but although the Royal Navy accepted the 2-inch model for defending ships, the Army balked at the 3-inch for various technical reasons, and it was not until 1941 that they were eventually persuaded to accept it. Installed in batteries of 128 launchers they proved very effective at breaking up German bombing formations, but they had to be sited carefully, since after 128 rockets

went into the sky, 128 rocket motors fell after the warheads had exploded.

The second line of German research, into liquid-fuelled long-range rockets, eventually gave birth to the A4 bombardment rocket, commonly known as the V2 (Vengeance Weapon 2). This was a 10-ton monster with a one-ton warhead which had a maximum range of 305km and which was eventually used to attack England and selected targets on the Continent.

In addition, however, to the Nebelwerfer and V2, German scientists developed a large number of other rocket weapons, most of which were still in the development stage when the war ended. But when Allied researchers began to examine them, they found inspiration for the long string of guided weapons which have been developed since 1945.

Artillery showed relatively little innovation during the course of the 1939-45 war, largely because artillery was a known factor and most of the invention had been completed before the turn of the century. Germany developed massive weapons, partly for effect, partly for propaganda, culminating in the monstrous 80cm

"Gustav Gerät" railway gun, which, when assembled for firing, weighed over 1300 tons and pitched a seven-ton shell to a range of 38km (23¾ mi) or a four-ton shell to 47km (30 mi). More practical, and of far greater significance, were the recoilless guns developed as accompanying artillery for their airborne forces. These allowed a major proportion of their propelling charge to exhaust through a venturi nozzle in the breechblock, so countering the rearward thrust due to recoil, enabling the gun to be made without the complex and heavy hydraulic recoil system required in a conventional gun. By using the recoilless principle they could provide a 105mm gun capable of firing a 15kg shell to a range of 8km (5 mi), yet weighing no more than 388kg. The principle was later taken up by Britain and the USA, though only the latter was able to get recoilless guns into production in time to be used towards the end of the war.

D-Day

The principal problem confronting the British and Americans in 1944 was that of landing an invasion force on the shores of Europe, held from the North Cape to the Pyrenees by German forces. Much of the coast had been strongly fortified, certainly all those parts which the Germans assessed as being possible landing areas, and thus the operation took on two component phases; firstly making a landing in the face of the defence, and secondly blasting a way through the fortifications. To assist in the latter phase the British developed a special formation, the 79th Armoured Division, and gave full rein to inventiveness. Specialized armoured vehicles were developed, including swimming tanks which could be launched from landing ships at sea and could then swim ashore to support the initial landings; tanks

carrying bridges to span antitank ditches; tanks carrying frames packed with explosive which could be laid against defensive structures and detonated by remote control after the tank had backed away; flame-throwing tanks for dealing with pillboxes containing guns; tanks mounting special heavy demolition guns for breaching reinforced concrete defences; tanks which could cross soft beaches and lay trackways behind them along which wheeled vehicles could drive; tanks with ploughs and flails which could discover or detonate mines buried in the ground; and tanks which could fire rockets dragging explosive-filled hoses across minefields to detonate the mines by blast. The Americans appear to have regarded these devices – "The Funnies'" as the British called them – with scorn, since they refused to avail themselves of any but a handful of swimming tanks, but when the invasion took place, on 6 June 1944, their value was rapidly apparent and Hitler's "Atlantic Wall" was breached in a matter of hours.

"Crocodile" in action
Among the adaptations made to existing tank designs during the closing stages of the Second World War was this flame-throwing device, called a "Crocodile". The tank towed a bowser, containing the fuel for the weapon, the bowser being linked to the tank by an armoured fuel line.

Dealing with a minefield
The flail attached to this Sherman tank was developed specifically to deal with enemy minefields. Tanks equipped with this device played a major part in dealing with Hitler's vaunted Atlantic Wall during the invasion of France in 1944.

MODERN TIMES

*The microchip and the missile arrive
on the battlefield*

Ready for battle A 1980s-style British infantryman, equipped with automatic rifle, respirator and NBC suit. The respirator and suit are designed to protect him against radiation and biological or chemical attack.

At the end of the Second World War an assessment of technical weapon development would have concluded that, with one exception, such development had been evolutionary rather than revolutionary. Artillery was much the same as it had been in 1939, the improvements being only of degree. The infantry's small arms were, in many cases, the same weapons which had been seen in 1918 or, at best, were evolved from those weapons. The tank, improved as it was, was no more than a logical progression, taking advantage of improvements in automative technology and production engineering. Even such apparent innovations as high-velocity antitank ammunition and the shaped charge were ideas which had been around at the turn of the century but which, at that time, were technically impossible.

The exception, the ultimate weapon which emerged from the Second World War was, of course, the nuclear explosive, and this was to colour military thinking for evermore, though most particularly in the immediate postwar years when it was little understood by the majority of soldiers.

Fortunately, warfare since 1945 has not brought the nuclear weapon into play. The Korean War was fought entirely with conventional arms, indeed largely with the arms standard in 1945, and it became the springboard for the development of the next generation of tanks and for generally reviewing the current state of weaponry.

Again, some of the development which has taken place in the past 30 years has been evolutionary, changing the form of weapons in order to take advantage of lessons learned in combat and of modern engineering ability. The soldier's basic tool, the rifle, is a good example of this; from a bolt-action repeating weapon, carefully machined from solid steel and supported by wooden furniture, firing a heavy bullet of about 8mm calibre to ranges of 1500 and 2000m (1370 and 1830yd), it has now become a lightweight automatic weapon of 5.56mm calibre, largely of pressed metal and plastic, with a maximum effective range of no more than 500 to 600m (460 to 550 yd). The reduction in range and calibre has come about as a result of conclusions drawn from experience, from the demonstrated facts that the average soldier cannot see targets much more than 500m (460 yd) away in even the best conditions and is unlikely to hit them at 400m (365 yd). Therefore there is no logic in having a rifle capable of projecting a bullet to four times that range.

The way of the future

What has proved to be the revolutionary aspect of weapon development is, strangely enough, the enormous strides in electronic technology which have taken place since the invention of the transistor in the 1950s. This, followed by the silicon diode, the microchip, the microcomputer and similar developments, has given weapon technology ancillaries which have allowed weapon effectiveness to be enormously increased. A rocket is simply another method of propelling a projectile towards a distant target, but when equipped with a computer to calculate its course, with radio to receive instructions during flight, with radar to detect a target or infrared sensors to allow it to find the hot engine of a tank, then it becomes a guided missile and the probability of it striking the target is considerably improved.

But strip away all the electronics and you have no more than a rocket, basically no more than the same type of weapon fired in the American War of Independence two centuries ago.

Mechanically speaking, today's tank is no more than a progression from the original tanks of 1916; it is still the same mixture of protection, mobility and firepower. What gives it a far greater power is the addition of a sighting system which uses a laser to accurately and instantly determine the range to a target and a computer which will then calculate the target's speed and course, assess such factors as wind speed, the tank's own speed, the temperature, the droop and wear of the gun barrel and much more, and then automatically shift the sight's point of aim so as to put the gun barrel in the correct position for a lethal shot. And having done so, an electronically controlled stabilizing apparatus will keep the gun barrel at the same attitude no matter how the tank bucks and rocks underneath it.

Night-time no longer stops the battle; electro-optical sighting devices permit direct fire weapons, from rifles to tank guns, to be fired at night since the sight gives the firer a picture which is as clear as he could expect in daylight. What effect this 24-hour capability is going to have on the conduct of future battles is something which has yet to be assessed: soldiers still need to sleep.

But, as always, every advance brings a counter-measure in its train. The development of anti-armour missiles was originally held to spell the end of the dominance of the tank. Wire-guided missiles such as TOW, MILAN, HOT and Swatter appeared to be a threat which could scarcely be countered,

Greater mobility The development of the helicopter means that the infantry is now more mobile than ever before, while helicopter gunships can provide instant close air support when necessary.

since they rely almost entirely on automatic electronic functioning. The firer sees a tank, sets his sight on it, and fires the missile. Rocket-propelled, it speeds to the target unreeling a fine wire behind it, down which controlling commands are passed to make the missile fly in the required direction. The first of these missiles demanded that the operator actually steer the missile by operating controls. Today, however, the sighting unit sees the missile, measures its deviation from the axis of the sight (which is pointed at the target) and a computer then calculates the necessary correction and signals it to the missile. All the firer need do is keep his sight aligned on the target.

The first response to this from the tank designers was the development of more sophisticated armour. Steel and ceramics will stop projectiles relying on kinetic energy, titanium and plastics will draw off the heat of a shaped charge, a soft plastic layer will prevent the vibration and blast of an explosive passing through the armour mass. And when the missile makers retaliated by making bigger and more powerful warheads, the next defensive move was the development of smokescreens containing substances making them impervious to infrared rays, so that

Anti-armour missiles Modern infantry anti-tank weapons, such as MILAN *(right)*, fire wire-guided missiles, which can be electronically aimed at their target.

The tank of the future The US M1 Abrahams is the most modern tank in American service. Its extremely sophisticated armour is layered to deal with antitank missile attack.

thermal sights, capable of seeing through ordinary smoke, darkness and dust, were now blinded, and the infrared flare in the tail of the missile, upon which the automatic sight relies for its information on the missile's position, is now smothered and the guidance system is inoperable.

Electronics have also been applied to artillery projectiles, giving them sensors capable of detecting laser emissions reflected from enemy targets. A forward observer points a laser at a tank; the beam is reflected into the sky and an artillery shell is fired into the area. As it detects the laser beam, a computer reacts and steers the shell to strike the target. Another electronic device, the proximity fuze, detects the target and ensures that the projectile is detonated at exactly the most lethal point on its trajectory.

For all these technical advances, though, most of the warfare since 1945 has been conducted along fairly conventional lines, albeit with the incorpration of some technical advances. Perhaps the most significant development in the conduct of combat over the past 30 years has been the use of the helicopter to move troops, carry supplies, evacuate casualties, and, currently under development, as a combat weapon carrier. Helicopters allow forces to be moved over long distances and, more particularly, over inhospitable and difficult terrain, at high speed. In the 1980s the use of the helicopter as an antitank weapon

platform has become a major concern among several armies. The next employment of the helicopter, it is being suggested, is as a pure combat machine to attack other helicopters so as to deal with the enemy's antitank force or his infantry-carrying fleet.

The principles of warfare change very little, and they can be found expounded in phrases varying from Clausewitz's "War is a continuation of State policy by other means" to Nathan Forrest's "Git thar fustest with the mostest" to Patton's "You don't want to die for your country; you want to make the other bastard die for his country." And in spite of the advances of technology the actual strategic principles and tactical operations which any army would use if called upon to fight today are little changed from the principles they would have chosen 100 years ago. Economy of force, concentration of effort, surprise, mobility; these things change only in degree. Technology allows us to take better advantage of them, to improve mobility, to produce better surprises, to concentrate more quickly, and to have a more devastating firepower effect. But the guiding principle behind all that is still a human brain, and all the computers in the world are not going to change that. As a British General said in Germany in 1980, when the first "Wavell" computerized command and control network was being tested, "After all the information is in and digested, it still comes back to me, with a map and a stub of pencil".

SEA POWER

The wooden man-of-war becomes the steel battleship – and war moves underwater

In 1850, as the old saw had it, the navies of the world were built of wooden ships and iron men. Except for a handful of steam tugs used for manoeuvering ships around dockyards and harbours, and an equally small number of experimental ships fitted with steam engines in addition to their sails, the wind provided the motive power and exercised considerable influence on a captain's course of tactics in battle. The British Navy, which had been built up over the centuries as a means of projecting British power overseas and protecting British trade throughout the world, dominated the rest of the world in terms of strength. Their warships and merchant ships had penetrated to almost every corner, had charted and recorded navigational data, and British captains and crews were familiar with the hazards of all the seas and oceans.

This situation did not sit well with other nations, particularly with the French. Under Napoleon III, France was attempting to foster its overseas trade and increase its dominion, but it was inevitably looking over its shoulder at the British Navy. What was required was some qualitative advance which would put the French Navy into a dominant technical position so that it could then exercise its various strategic ambitions without the fear of British intervention.

Shells and armoured ships

As early as 1822, a French artilleryman, Colonel Paixhans, had suggested that what the French Navy had to do was to adopt new types of gun, firing explosive shells instead of solid shot, and fit them into armour-plated ships propelled by steam, providing them with a force by which they could devastate any existing navy. These small and, therefore, more nimble ships would make difficult targets, while the explosive shells would wreck the wooden walls of their opponents. By concentrating two or three such vessels against the large men-of-war of the day, parity in gun-power would be obtained and success assured. It all sounded very attractive, since it avoided discussing such irksome matters as the stability of small ships in heavy seas, the difficulty of gunnery from small unstable platforms, and the problems of controlling a swarm of small vessels in a sea battle, but on the whole it was an attractive idea which had some sound features.

Paixhans's ideas were translated into equipment insofar as the shell gun was concerned; the French conducted a long series of trials which suggested that Paixhans was right, that an explosive projectile fitted with a delay fuze (so that it would burst after penetrating the wooden side of a ship) would do serious damage. In 1824, the muzzle-loading shell gun was adopted by the French. But practical considerations ruled; most sea-captains were apprehensive about carrying stocks of explosive projectiles aboard and, consequently, the average warship had only a few shell guns. Small vessels were equipped with more, since their store of ammunition would be smaller and the probability of their being blown up in an action proportionately less.

Paixhans's other idea, that of armouring the ships, was slower to be accepted. In the first place "armour" in

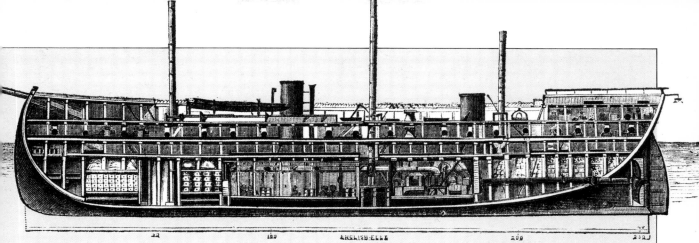

those days meant nothing more than
thick plates of iron, and no matter how
thick the plate, there was always some
keen master gunner in a proof yard who
could wheel up a bigger gun, or load
more powder, and proceed to put a
solid shot through whatever plate the
iron masters produced. Iron was not
looked upon with favour for warship
construction simply because
experiments had shown that when
penetrated by a ball it disrupted into a
shower of jagged fragments, which
caused more widespread damage and
injury than the ball alone would have
done. So wood was retained as the
prime constructional material solely on
the grounds of safety for the crew.

Crimean experiments
In 1855, in the course of the Crimean
War, the allied fleets were called upon
to bombard Fort Kinburn, a collection
of earth- and stoneworks guarding the
coastline. In the previous year the
British and French fleets had engaged a
number of forts at Sebastopol with little
effect; unwilling to hazard their ships
too close to the guns of the forts, they
had fired at ranges of 1400-1850m
(1500-2000yd) and the Russian guns
had replied, with much sound and fury
but relatively little damage on either
side. For the Kinburn bombardment
the French decided that some more
positive result was required and they
had taken the trouble to construct three
"floating batteries": the *Devastation*,
the *Tonnant* and the *Lave*. These were
shallow-draught steam-driven vessels
of wood, covered with a 10cm (4in)
layer of iron armour on top of 42.5cm
(17in) of timber and armed with 16 56-
pounder Paixhans shell guns.
Accompanied by an allied fleet the three
vessels sailed to Kinburn, at the mouth
of the Dnieper river; while the fleets
stood out of harm's way and protected
the sea approaches, the three batteries
steamed inshore to within 740m (800
yd) of the forts and opened fire.

Anchored, to give their gunners a
steady platform and the best chance of
accuracy, they presented a perfect
target to the Russians who immediately
opened fire with 18- and 32-pounder
guns firing solid shot and red-hot shot.

After four hours of fire and
counterfire the Russian forts were
devastated, while the three French
batteries had suffered only two killed
and 25 wounded, largely from splinters
which had penetrated the gunports.
Although hit by Russian shot over 200
times during the engagement, the three
ironclads were undamaged. The
Russian commander of Fort Kinburn
surrendered, and the fleet hoisted
anchor and set sail for nearby Fort
Ochakov, intending to repeat the
performance. But the Russian
commander of Fort Ochakov, having
watched while Kinburn was reduced,
surrendered forthwith without waiting
to be bombarded.

This confirmed the French in the
theories of Paixhans, that ironclad ships
with shell guns were the next
generation of warships. Once the
somewhat artificial alliance of the
Crimean War had dissolved with the
ending of that campaign, Napoleon III
began dreaming of more and greater
power. To project power overseas
demanded a strong navy; and, in 1857,
to overtake the then dominant British
Royal Navy, he appointed Dupuy de
Lome as Director of Supplies for the
French Navy.

French designs
De Lome was an outstanding designer,
who had been advocating iron ships,
steam power and similar advances for
several years. Now in the position to
realize his ideas, and with Napoleon's
encouragement, he set about the
design of a totally new type of warship
which would put France into the front
rank of naval powers. In 1858, at the
Toulon dockyard, the ironclad frigate
La Gloire was laid down.

The specification which governed the design of *La Gloire* called for a screw-propelled steamer with sufficient speed to outrun any contemporary warship; since the average speed attainable by a steamship in those days was about 11 knots, the French aimed for a minimum of 13. In addition, the ship was to be sail-rigged for cruising economically when not engaged in combat. The broadside guns were to be a clear 2m (6½ft) above the waterline, so that rough sea would not affect the aim, and they were to be protected by 12cm (5in) of wrought-iron armour which would extend below the waterline for at least 1.5m (4¾ft). This would protect the hull even when the ship was heeled over. Finally, the dimensions were to be kept compact to produce the smallest target compatible with the amount of armament demanded – 34 16-cm shell guns. The result was a somewhat beamy, barquentine-rigged, wooden ship with a skin of iron over the upperworks, a ship which was designed simply to dash out of harbour into the English Channel, devastate the Royal Navy, bombard a few dockyards, and sail home victoriously.

The territorial ambitions of Napoleon had already caused some disquiet in Britain, and when news of this new French ironclad frigate arrived, the overhaul of the Royal Navy, which was currently under discussion suddenly became a matter of urgency. The solution adopted was a naval building programme which would include both numbers of screw-propelled wooden ships for blockading, and fast ironclads

which could catch and engage any warship in existence. The British ironclad would not be a mere copy of the French, but a totally different type of ship, in accordance with the policy that being a British warship, it could be liable to operate anywhere in the world. Therefore it had to have good sea-keeping properties and be capable of making long passages under steam or sail in any sea conditions. Furthermore, instead of being a wooden ship clad with iron, the new ship would be completely built of iron; the Surveyor – the British equivalent of Dupuy de Lome – pointed out that whereas a wooden ship required complete external armouring, an iron ship would need armouring only in the vicinity of the guns and machinery, thus saving weight. The ends of the ship might be less well protected, but they would contain nothing vital to the operations, and provided they were divided off into watertight compartments a hit need not necessarily prove fatal.

British solutions

From all these considerations came HMS *Warrior*, laid down in the Blackwall yard of the Thames Iron Shipbuilding Company, in June 1859, and her sister ship HMS *Black Prince* laid down shortly afterwards.

La Gloire was launched in November 1859, and completed by the summer of 1860. On trial she reached 13 knots on a calm sea and 10 knots in squally weather, and on the strength of this France set about preparing a building

Deck gun of the 1860s As late as halfway through the 19th century, massive muzzle-loaders were still in use. This 11in smoothbore on the USS *Kearsage* had to be man-handled back after firing to be swabbed and rammed at the muzzle end, then hauled back on pulleys. Aiming was crude, over open sights.

HMS Warrior The Royal Navy's answer to *La Gloire* was an all-iron, sleek fighting ship capable of a 4-knot speed advantage over the French vessel. Until now the ability to manoeuvre had relied upon weather and sails, but now steam had been harnessed; the crudely designed screw and the sleek lines of *Warrior* gave her the ability to fight at all times, even in flat calm. In the right wind conditions both sail and steam were used to provide extra knots.

programme to transform her entire fleet into ironclads. The *Warrior* was launched in October 1860, and completed by October 1861; she reached over 14 knots on her initial trials and was the fastest warship afloat. Moreover she was far more graceful than the French ship, a lean clipper-bowed beauty with an iron skin over an iron frame. The protection came from a 10.25cm (4½in) thick layer of wrought iron laid over 45cm (18in) of teak, which was, in turn, backed by just over 1cm (½in) of sheet iron. This form of construction was designed firstly to resist the penetration of shot with the thickness of iron, then to absorb the impact and any deformation of the armour by the resilient layer of teak and, finally, in the event of a shot managing to penetrate into the mass and deform it, the layer of iron would prevent large splinters of wood being thrown into the ship to wound the crew. This armour covered the central "battery deck" and extended 1.5m (5ft) below the waterline; the ends of the battery deck were armoured fore and aft, and the remainder of the ship outside this armoured citadel was divided into watertight compartments. Her armament was a mixture of 68-

pounder muzzle-loaders and 110-pounder Armstrong breechloaders; the 68pr of 95cwt was 8.12-inch calibre and 3m (10ft) long, firing a solid ball which could pierce iron armour at fighting ranges. The Admiralty were so impressed by this new addition to the fleet that all work was henceforth stopped on wooden ships and plans were drawn up for a further 11 ironclads of various designs.

The French had, in fact, made one fundamental error in their calculation of policy; they had attempted to use technology to overtake British naval superiority. This would have been a perfectly satisfactory course to adopt had the French nation had the industrial capacity to overtake the British and maintain their lead. But at that time their industrial base was far less than that of Britain, their iron and steel output far less, their engineering works unable to compete in either design or production. Furthermore, by inciting the British to overhaul their naval technology with the backing of what was then the greatest industrial power on earth, the French were attempting to participate in a contest which they could not possibly hope to win.

CLASH OF THE IRONCLADS

The wooden man-of-war succumbs to the iron barge

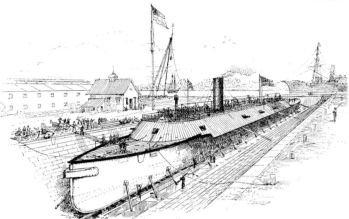

Ironclad menace After her conversion from a screw-driven frigate, the *Merrimac* (here shown halfway through the conversion process) wore a menacing look. Renamed the *Virginia* she had the fault of being confined to easy water conditions due to a low freeboard when under steam. This created problems when the ship was being manoeuvred or even simply holding a set heading in a moderate sea.

Various European nations followed the Anglo-French lead and commissioned ironclad ships which, in general, followed either *La Gloire* or the *Warrior* in their design. But while this building activity was going on, events across the Atlantic brought about the world's first combat between ironclad ships.

The American Civil War broke out in 1861, and the Confederate states, having fewer ships than the Union, decided that they would make up in quality what they lacked in quantity, and they would achieve their qualitative advantage by developing something new and unbeatable. When Norfolk, Virginia, was occupied by the Confederates, they had acquired the remains of a screw-propelled steam frigate, the *Merrimac*. The lower hull was sound and the engines capable of being repaired, so the upperworks were cut away and a new superstructure was built in the form of an armoured battery. Twenty-inch thick pine timbers were sloped at 45° from the waterline to form a pent-roof structure which occupied about two-thirds of the length of the hull. This pine foundation was covered in 10cm (4in) of oak, and on this was laid 5cm (2in) thick plates of iron, manufactured by rolling down old railway track. The battery was given ports for 10 guns, four of 7-inch rifled and six of 9-inch smoothbored, and the single funnel projected through the top. A cast-iron ram was attached to the bow.

It will be apparent that this was very much the same as the French floating batteries of the Crimean War, and certainly the *Merrimac* (now re-named the *Virginia*, was strictly a smooth-water craft. But the news of her building, doubtless magnified in transmission, reached the North and caused something of a panic. If this got loose among the wooden ships of the Union navy, it could do considerable damage; a solution had to be found. The Navy Department advertised for ideas and plans of floating batteries.

In reply came John Ericsson, ready to expound on various ideas he had been trying to promote for several years. Ericsson had been born in Sweden in 1803; in 1820, he became an engineer in the Swedish Army; and, in 1826, went to England to study the design and manufacture of steam engines. In 1836, he developed a screw propeller for ships, but he fell out with the Admiralty and went off to America in 1839, where he remained until his death in 1889. In the early 1850s, he had designed an armoured floating battery with a revolving gun turret and had offered it to Napoleon III, who turned it down. Now he appeared in Washington with more or less the same idea, and in view of the threat of the *Virginia*, Ericsson was given his head and the facilities to build his *Monitor*.

Ericsson was an engineer rather than a shipwright and, as a result, the *Monitor* differed considerably from any previous vessel. Instead of the traditional hull form, the ship was simply an armoured raft 52m (172ft) long and 12.6m (41½ft) wide, supported on a box-like hull 42.7m (140ft) long and 10.4m (34ft) wide. The overhanging raft form was supposed to give a stable platform for gunnery, and also protect the hull against ramming. The armoured sides of the raft ran 9m (3ft) below the water level, so that, as Ericsson said, any shot hitting the hull would have to go through 6m (20ft) of water to get there. The deck was of 2.5cm (1in) iron, and on it was mounted the turret, a revolving iron drum 6m (20ft) in diameter and 2.7m (9ft) high, built up from eight layers of 2.5cm (1in) iron plate and mounting two 11-inch smoothbore guns side by side. There were two ports in the turret wall for the

gun muzzles, and when withdrawn for loading the ports were closed by heavy cast-iron "port stoppers" to prevent enemy fire from coming in and injuring the crew as they loaded. The whole structure displaced 987 tons and had a draught of only 3.2m (10½ft). Two steam engines, designed by Ericsson, delivered 320 horsepower and moved the ship at 9 knots, and the recessed hull and armour skirt ensured that the propelling and steering mechanisms were well protected against gunfire.

That the designer was no shipwright became painfully apparent as the *Monitor* slogged her way down the Atlantic coast from New York, en route to do battle with the *Virginia*. The slightest sea washed over the flush deck, poured down ventilation ports and past the turret, and the sea swell rose between the armour skirt and the hull, causing the ship to vibrate and shudder.

First engagements

While the *Monitor* was making her sea passage, on 8th March 1862 the *Virginia* went into action against a Union blockading fleet outside Norfolk. The Union ships, somewhat curious about this floating apparition, sat quietly at anchor and allowed the ironclad to approach. Once it was within range the *Cumberland* and the *Congress* opened fire, only to see their shots bouncing off the sloped iron roof. The ironclad continued on her path and rammed the

Cumberland, which sank in half an hour. The *Congress*, seeing that gunnery was of little avail, slipped her anchor to make a run for it but inadvertently went aground. The *Virginia* followed, took station astern and opened fire until, ablaze, the *Congress* struck her colours.

Later that evening, as the *Virginia* had returned to her berth, the *Monitor* appeared in Hampton Roads ready for battle. News of the forthcoming battle soon spread, and next morning crowds lined various vantage points to watch. The *Virginia* steamed out, and the *Monitor* moved to intercept – and the battle began. The *Virginia*'s shot bounced off the *Monitor*'s turret, and the *Monitor*'s shot bounced off the *Virginia*'s pent-roof. The *Monitor*'s firing was more sedate, since the gunners decided against struggling with the ponderous port-stoppers and simply rotated the turret, by means of its steam engine, away from the the *Virginia* when they were ready to re-load. Unfortunately, the engine became temperamental, refusing to stop in the required place, and the gunners were reduced to firing as the guns swung past their target. Eventually the *Monitor*'s ammunition was exhausted, and the *Virginia*'s gunnery officer simply gave up; when asked why he was no longer firing he replied "I could do as much damage by snapping my fingers every three minutes." Battle was suspended and the *Virginia* retreated to the

Turret of Monitor The forerunner of the huge triple 16in turrets of the Royal Navy's twin battleships HMS *Nelson* and *Rodney* and similar major fighting ships of other nations. Inside those huge metal barrels *(above)* the concussion when the 11in gun fired must have been nearly unbearable. Rotation was achieved by an unreliable steam-engine. Note the dent to the right of the gun-port where a well-aimed round from the *Virginia* hit and bounced off.

Norfolk Navy Yard to make some repairs, while the crew of the *Monitor* turned out on deck to pick up shell splinters as mementoes.

Although the *Virginia* made a few more minor forays, she never encountered the *Monitor* again and did little practical damage. Finally, the Union Army captured Norfolk, and in the general destruction before retreating, the Confederates fired the ship, which was utterly destroyed when the fire reached the magazine. The *Monitor* was towed off to return to New York but was swamped in rough seas off Cape Hatteras, and sank with 14 of her 49-man crew on New Year's Eve 1862.

These two ships, though of somewhat aberrant form, became the prototypes of a number of similar vessels built by both sides and used in various minor naval actions, particularly up and down the Mississippi River. But there was little to be learned by other nations; the construction had been forced by circumstances and hardly represented naval engineering at its best, the ships were far from seaworthy, and the actions had all been fought in sheltered waters.

One interesting result of the American Civil War was the development of a new class of ship, which came to be called the "cruiser". Hitherto the war fleets of the world were composed of "line-of-battle ships", as powerful as possible, and frigates to act as scouts. But during the Civil War the Union forces saw the need for a fast armed ship which could defend or attack commerce; vessels were built in 1863, expressly for the purpose of catching Confederate merchant ships and sinking them. Similar light warships were used to escort Union merchants. This class of ship needed sufficient speed to catch unarmed ships and run away from heavier-armed warships, only standing to fight opponents of their own power.

The idea was soon adopted elsewhere and, by the 1870s, both Britain and France were building cruisers.

Battle of Lissa

There was not much more to be learned from the next ironclad battle, but some powerful and erroneous lessons were drawn from it which influenced naval thinking and construction for many years.

In 1866, the Italian and Austrian fleets met off the island of Lissa, in the Adriatic. Both fleets were equipped with ironclads based on *La Gloire*, and their meeting came as an "appendix" to the Austro-Prussian War. The Prussians had enlisted the Italians as somewhat half-hearted allies who hoped to benefit by acquiring Venetia and Lombardy from the Austrian empire. Unfortunately, their army was soundly defeated, while the Prussians were victorious at Sadowa. In order not to go empty-handed to the peace treaty the Italians decided to pit their navy against the Austrians. Although vast sums of money had been spent on equipping the Italian fleet, it had very little sea-going experience – and none whatever of combat, and the commander, Admiral Count Persano, was a poor leader. After vacillation and delay he was ordered to sail the fleet to Lissa and seize the fortified island.

This news duly reached the Austrians who dispatched their fleet, commanded by Admiral Tegethoff, to

Strange encounter When the *Virginia* and *Monitor* met, the first meeting in anger between armoured ships, naval warfare experts attempted to draw the lessons from this new mode of engagement. But the evidence for meaningful conclusions was lacking simply because neither side claimed victory. The only obvious certainty was that to give any warship a chance she had to be protected by armour.

intercept the Italians. On paper the Austrian fleet was technically deficient. Its ironclad ships were based on *La Gloire* and armed largely with smoothbore guns, while a good proportion of the fleet consisted of wooden ships. The Italian fleet, on the other hand, although also based on *La Gloire*'s design, had thicker armour and heavy muzzle-loading rifled guns, a preponderance of some 200 rifles against the Austrians' mixed collection of 74 rifles and smoothbores.

When the two fleets met, Tegethoff immediately seized the initiative. Arranging his fleet in three arrowheads, he turned towards the Italian line and ordered "Armoured ships will charge the enemy and sink him." While this Austrian formation steamed towards the Italian fleet, Admiral Persano suddenly decided to change his flag from the ironclad *Re d'Italia* to a turreted ship, the *Affondatore*. This necessitated stopping the ships while the Admiral was ferried across in his barge and, of course, a gap opened up in the line while this was being done. Tegethoff's advancing fleet sailed straight through the gap and out the other side, to split up and turn back to attack both elements of the Italian line, so that the whole ordered affair rapidly dissolved into a melee where every ship was looking out for itself. There were innumerable minor actions, but the principal event occurred when Tegethoff's flagship, the *Ferdinand Max*, saw the *Re d'Italia* in difficulties, a shot having damaged her steering gear. At full speed – something in the order of 10 knots – the Austrian flagship rammed the Italian ironclad square on,

tearing a huge hole in her side. As the Austrian reversed and pulled clear, so the *Re d'Italia* listed, recovered, rolled over and sank. A small Italian gunboat dashing in, possibly to rescue survivors, took a shell, which set her on fire and later blew up when the fire reached the magazine. These were the only two ship casualties of the battle, and after some more fruitless skirmishing, Persano withdrew back to his base while Tegethoff dropped anchor off Lissa.

Two lessons came out of Lissa; the first was that armour saved lives. In spite of thousands of shot and shell being fired, and excluding the losses due to the two ships sunk, the Italians had 8 killed and 40 wounded, while the Austrians had 3 killed and 30 wounded.

The second lesson was that the ram was a mighty weapon. Propelled by the force of a steam engine, independent of wind or tide, capable of being manoeuvred exactly as required, the steam vessel with its ram was obviously a most potent destroyer of ships. One only had to see how the *Re d'Italia* had gone down in minutes after a single blow! What was conveniently overlooked was that the victim was already disabled and could not dodge; that innumerable attempts to ram had been made during the battle without any other success; and that almost any competent captain could out-manoeuvre a would-be rammer. No matter; the ram was the instrument of the future, and it affected naval thought and ship design for the next 25 years, that is, until the development of long-ranging guns and torpedoes increased the battle range, thus rendering the ram totally ineffective.

Hero of Lissa Rear Admiral Wilhelm von Tegetthoff commanded the Austro-Hungarian fleet at the Battle of Lissa in 1866. This was the first major action fought between the new generation of European ironclads in which old and new tactics were combined, von Tegetthoff signalling to his fleet: "Ironclads will dash at the enemy and sink him!" The Italian commander was court-martialled after his losses were revealed for signalling that he "commanded the seas".

Salamis refought The sea action at Lissa was in part a reflection of the battle that took place in 480BC, when the numerically superior Phoenecian fleet was beaten by the Greek ships with their formidable ram-headed triremes. At Lissa, the Austrians' *Erzherzog Ferdinand Max*, commanded by Captain Sternesk, rammed and sunk the Italian *Re d'Italia*. Of the 600 crew only 168 survived, but another facet, well beyond the technology of the ancients, was that armour now could be the deciding factor when ship fought ship: decisive, that is, until armour-piercing shells countered the metallic defence.

THE TURRET

Fire from any quarter – the turret sounds the death knell for the line of battle

Turret evolution In the *Monitor* turret the gun crews' duties were not far removed from the days of Nelson, although the technology of heavy guns had moved to electrical firing and mechanical rotation. But as is obvious, the two 11in guns still had the smoothbore barrels and were cast in one piece. Even the gun carriage and trunnions are virtually identical to those of the 18th century.

The results of the gunnery at Lissa appeared to demonstrate that armour was the master of the gun; but the gunmakers were not going to let this situation last for long. Throughout the 1860s, the calibre and power of guns crept upwards; Britain began with 7-inch, went to 9-inch and then to 10-, 11-, 12-, 16- and finally 17.72-inch calibres, with the projectiles getting progressively bigger and the muzzle energy – and thus the penetrating power – increasing in vast strides. From the situation in 1860 when 11.25cm (4½in) of wrought iron was impenetrable at 275m (300yd) range, by the end of the 1870s British muzzle-loaders could defeat 60cm (24in) of iron armour plating at 920m (1000yd) with relative ease.

The penalty for this power was, of course, weight; the 7-inch gun weighed 6½ tons, while the 17-inch weighed 100 tons. The ship designers and builders therefore had to apply their minds to the problem of carrying these increasing weights, plus the weight of ever-thicker armour – for as the guns got more powerful, so the armour got thicker – in such a way as to keep the ship stable but allow the guns to fire effectively.

Shifting priorities

The first answer, since it was appropriate to the broadside technique of gunnery, was the armoured battery as used on the *Warrior*, in which all the guns were concentrated into a central armoured box with gunports. This left the remainder of the ship vulnerable, a fact of special significance since it coincided with a considerable change in the objective of naval battle. In the days of wooden walls, the objective of every captain was to batter the enemy ship into silence, close with it, and capture it. This enabled the crew to claim "prize money" and it also added to the victor's fleet, since the prizes were repaired and put into commission. In the middle of the 19th century the object of battle changed to outright sinking, and this, with the increasing power of guns, demanded some form of protection to be applied to the whole ship. The solution adopted was to place a complete belt of armour around the hull, spanning the waterline, so as to protect the integrity of the ship, and then build up the central armoured battery above it.

The success of the ram at Lissa made designers think again. If the ship was to be used in this fashion, then it followed that for much of the battle it would be pointing at the enemy; and the guns in the armoured battery were principally located so as to fire outwards in broadside fashion. Making ports in the front of the battery structure and adding more guns, or putting the forward guns on turntables so that they could fire either forward or to the beam was one solution, but not a very good one. The French came up with the idea of "sponsons", semicircular armoured bays protruding from the side of the armoured battery which allowed the guns mounted therein to fire forwards. But all these ideas were hampered by the requirement to fit ships with traditional masts and rigging so that sail power was available for cruising when not in action in order to conserve fuel and husband the engines.

THE TURRET

HMS *Temeraire* An advance in naval gunnery took place when the *Temeraire* was fitted with two 12in pivot guns. A rather cumbersome mechanism took the gun below the deck to be loaded, then raised again when needed for action. The problems inherent in sail, with their masts and the complexity of their rigging, prevented adequate firing arcs.

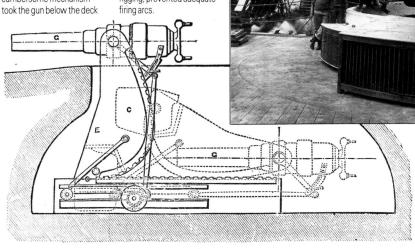

An interesting attempt to resolve the dilemma was HMS *Temeraire*, which was completed in 1877 at Chatham dockyard. This had an armoured belt and central battery mounting broadside guns, but it also mounted two pivot guns, one at each end of the ship on disappearing mountings. These were hydro-pneumatic mountings on which the gun was carried on top of an arm pivoted at its foot and supported by an hydraulic ram. The whole affair was located in a sunken well surrounded with armour and, in the normal course of events, the pressure in the ram was released and the gun allowed to retract into the well, where it was concealed from view. When combat threatened, the gun was loaded and pressure applied to the ram, forcing the gun up so that its muzzle cleared the armour and it could fire. The recoil force overcame the pressure in the ram and the gun descended into the well for reloading. Each mounting on the *Temeraire* carried a 12-in muzzle-loading gun. The design was a technical tour de force, but it was a dead end; better things had begun to appear.

The turret controversy

While the development of the central battery had been proceeding, a totally different system was being vigorously promoted by several enthusiasts – the turret. Here was a method of mounting guns which allowed them to be used in any direction, wherever the target chose to appear. It may seem obvious today, but the protagonists of the turret had a hard time convincing people.

The *Monitor*, as we have seen, used a turret, and because of this it is usually assumed that Ericsson was the father of the turret. But the idea was in use in Europe before Ericsson built the *Monitor*, and can be traced back, like many other naval innovations, to the Crimean War. Captain Cowper Coles RN was commanding HMS *Stromboli* in 1855, when he was called upon to carry out a bombardment of a Russian store depot at Taganrog. The surrounding waters were too shallow for a warship, so Coles designed a raft upon which he mounted a 32-pounder gun. This worked well, and he next suggested an improved version, in which the gun would be protected by a simple turtleback armour shield, to be used to bombard Kronstadt. His superiors thought the idea good and Coles was ordered back to London to perfect the idea; but peace arrived and the project was abandoned. Coles continued working on his idea and, in 1860, he proposed a low-freeboard ship with a number of the armoured cupolas he had suggested for his improved raft, now containing two guns each. He then went on "The horizontal motion, or training, is effected by turning the shield itself, with the gun, crew and the platform on which they stand. The whole apparatus thus becomes, as it were, the gun carriage, and being placed on a common turntable can be revolved by means of a winch."

HMS *Monarch* The pathway toward a recognizable warship took the form of HMS *Monarch*, bearing a pugnacious, jutting prow. But still the impediment of rigging and masts led to turrets placed amidships.

The Admiralty thanked Captain Coles, but had committed themselves to the *Warrior* and her sisters and were not inclined to perform any experiments at that time; in 1860, however, Coles put forward a design for a ship carrying nine turrets, seven on the centre-line and two offset in order to permit frontal fire from three turrets at once. Still the Admiralty wavered, but several smaller nations were interested and some small coastal turret ships were built, notably the *Rolf Krake* for the Danish Navy, which mounted two turrets armed with twin 68-pounder guns.

Eventually, with Coles gaining support from various influential quarters, the Admiralty agreed to build a coastal defence ship with four turrets. A wooden ship, the *Royal Sovereign*, was cut down and given an armoured belt, and four turrets installed on the deck, the forward one carrying two guns, the other three a single gun in each. A similar vessel, called the *Prince Albert*, was built of iron to the same specification. Completed in 1864, the two ships proved successful; but Coles insisted that a seagoing turret ship was feasible and pressed for this. The Admiralty gave in and laid down the *Monarch*, which was little more than a belt-and-battery ship with a turret at each end of the central battery. Since the ship's masts obstructed ahead and astern fire, smaller guns were mounted at the ends of the hull. The result was a powerful ship but one with indifferent sailing qualities; indeed, it was now obvious that turrets and rigged sailing ships did not go well together.

Coles persisted in his argument that the Admiralty had not yet got it right and, in order to settle the question once and for all time, he was given leave to have a ship built to his own design; so much to his own design that the Admiralty's ship design department distanced itself from the project as far as it possibly could, making it very clear that it did not agree with Coles's theories. In his ship, the *Captain*, Coles got around the problem of the rigging by building a "flying deck" above the turrets which carried the masts and rigging. The ship had an exceptionally low freeboard in order to make it as small a target as possible, and due to a draughtsman's error the final freeboard was even less than Coles had designed: 1.8m (6ft) from waterline to turret deck instead of 2.3m (7½ft).

The *Captain* was completed in 1870; she sailed well in her trials and steamed at 14½ knots. But in September of that year, in the Bay of Biscay, she capsized in a light squall, carrying Cowper Coles (who was on an inspection tour) and all but 18 of her 509-man crew to the bottom. The subsequent court-martial found that *Captain* had been "lost by pressure of sail assisted by the heave of the sea" and that she had been "built in deference to public opinion...in opposition to the views of the Controller and his Department."

This might have been the end of the turreted seagoing warship, but for the fact that the Constructor of the Royal Navy, Sir Edward Reed, had begun a new ship which embodied many of Coles's ideas except for the sail plan. The *Cerberus* was a coastal defence ship built to the order of the State of Victoria, Australia, and introduced a new type of ship – later called the "breastwork monitor" – which was to lead to the battleship of later years. The hull was the raft-like hull of the original *Monitor*, with an armoured citadel mounting a Coles turret at each end. Between the turrets was a small deckhouse supporting a flying deck which carried the bridge and single mast. Since the vessel was designed solely for coastal work there was no need for full rigging. There was more freeboard than on the *Captain*, and the turrets were protected by their lower section being surrounded by the armour of the citadel or breastwork.

Ships without sails
Using this as a basis, Reed then developed the *Devastation*, the first mastless seagoing turret ship. This had the same armoured breastwork of 30cm (12in) thickness, two turrets each mounting two 12-inch 35-ton muzzle-loading guns, and a small flying deck carrying the bridge and funnels. Two engines drove twin screws and she carried 1300 tons of coal, far more than any previous ship. Completed in 1873, *Devastation* proved to be an excellent seagoing ship, but was restricted to operating around the coasts of Europe and the Mediterranean due to its capacity for coal. It was this restriction which was to lead the Admiralty to set up defended coaling stations throughout the British Empire so that, in future, warships could rove the seven seas, confident in the knowledge that they could always rely upon a convenient fuel resupply.

The last of the breastwork monitors was the *Dreadnought*, laid down in 1872. She was similar to the *Devastation*, but with more freeboard, with the armoured breastwork carried out to the edge of the hull and with 35cm (14in) of wrought-iron armour. For a displacement of 10,866 tons she carried 3690 tons of armour and four 12-inch guns.

There was still some doubt about the stability of ships with turrets, and the French, in 1876, introduced something different. The *Admiral Duperre* did away with the armoured battery superstructure in favour of a complete encircling belt of 55cm (22in) armour spanning the waterline. The remainder of the hull was unprotected, and the guns were mounted in "barbettes", short armoured screens sufficient to

protect the elevating and training mechanism and the crew but over which the gun barrel projected. The gun itself was mounted either on a turntable or a central pivot, and the ammunition supply came from below deck into the protection of the barbette. This gave an element of protection to the gunners, but removed a great deal of the weight by doing away with the walls and roof of the turret. It also allowed the guns to be carried well above the waterline, giving a clear field of fire in virtually any sea conditions and, the French claimed, gave them command over vessels of lower freeboard so that they could fire downwards, behind protection and into the deck. Whether by this they hoped to overawe the Royal Navy's low freeboard designs is not clear, but certainly the Royal Navy had no high opinion of the French design; it was still a full-rigged sail plus steam ship, and the general opinion was that long before the French could gain any advantage from their high battery, accurate gunfire would have brought down the masts and rigging and piled them on top of the guns in their open barbettes.

In transition The wide beam of HMS *Inflexible* – the epitome of the 1870s transitional stage of battleship design – made her a stable platform for her four 80-ton, 16in muzzle-loading guns. Mounted in turrets amidships and set to port and starboard, they gave a clear field of fire. But the day of the rigged warship was soon to end.

NEW DIRECTIONS

The torpedo – a new method of attack means new methods of defence

Spar torpedo The misnomer given to the first mine. Suitable only for clandestine operations – the unseen approach – a delayed-action explosive charge set on the end of the spar had to be placed next to the intended target.

In the latter decades of the 19th century, the armament of warships was something of a mixture. French and German ships were using breechloading guns, but British ships were armed solely with rifled muzzle-loaders, since the Armstrong gun, which had been enthusiastically embraced by the Royal Navy in the 1860s, had proved to be incapable of firing heavy enough shot and charges to penetrate armour. The Armstrong RML gun advanced in power and weight until the Italian ship, the *Duilio*, carried four immense 17.72inch guns each weighing 100 tons; it was the threat of a ship mounting this massive ordnance which led to the British Army buying four of them and mounting two in Gibraltar and two in Malta for defence of the naval bases.

The torpedo had also arrived on the scene and was posing several problems. Torpedoes appeared in the 1860s. Admiral Porter, at New Orleans, went down in history with his cry of "Full speed ahead and damn the torpedoes!"; but the devices to which he then referred were what today would be called mines – anchored explosive charges sited so that intruding ships would cause them to detonate on impact.

This idea then advanced to the "spar torpedo", usually a waterproofed keg of powder on the end of a long spar, carried in a small boat. The object was to get close to the target without being discovered, lower the spar into the water so that the charge rested against the hull of the enemy ship, ignite a delay fuze and make off before the explosion.

In 1869, Captain Harvey of the Royal Navy invented the towed torpedo, a fish-like container full of explosive towed at the end of a line and manipulated so as to strike an enemy ship. The idea may have been sound, but putting it into practice appears to have had its problems and few of the many towed torpedoes were ever adopted for service.

Below the belt
With the arrival of ironclad ships with armour belts stretching below the waterline, the torpedo took on an even greater attraction, since it promised to be the only method of getting beneath the armour to strike at the less protected hull.

From this the idea of the self-propelled torpedo was devised by an Austrian naval officer, Commander Lupis. He worked from 1860 to 1864 on his design and then called in an English engineer, Robert Whitehead, who was designing warship engines in Fiume and, by 1866, the Whitehead Torpedo was being manufactured. Four metres (13ft) long and 35cm (14in) in diameter, it was propelled by compressed air, which drove a small engine and propeller. The warhead was loaded with 8.2kg (18lbs) of dynamite, and there was an ingenious depth-regulating mechanism which was the heart of the device. Travelling at six knots, it had a practical range of about 183m (200yd) and was fired from an underwater tube by compressed air.

The Austrian and French navies immediately purchased specimens of this new weapon but, in 1868, Whitehead sold the sole rights to the British Admiralty, who immediately set about improving it. By 1875, they had increased the speed to 12 knots and the range to 275m (300yd) or, by regulating the speed down to 9 knots it could reach a range of 1100m (1200yd). Furthermore, it had been shown that it

Torpedo boat Since the spar torpedo and its brave operators were all too vulnerable, some means of fast delivery was necessary. The torpedo-boat concept, as illustrated here by the attack and "capture" during naval manoeuvres of the *Conquest* by Lieutenant Knight of the *Sultan* in a second-class torpedo-boat, was the forerunner of the E-boats and MTBs of World War II.

was possible to fire torpedoes from the deck of a moving vessel with accuracy.

Obviously, the arrival of a new weapon set the designers the task of protecting the ships, and the general tendency was to increase the number of watertight compartments and also to fill otherwise empty spaces with cork to add to the buoyancy should the ship be holed. As an active defence the torpedo net was adopted, a massive net of steel rings about 20cm (8in) in diameter which was suspended from the side of the ship and sank into the water to below the keel, preventing torpedoes from reaching the hull. In spite of several experiments, it soon became obvious that torpedo nets were totally unsuited to protect a moving ship; but they became the regular routine when ships were anchored in waters liable to torpedo attack.

To go with the torpedo, in 1873, came the torpedo-boat, a small, narrow, very fast craft, armed with perhaps a light gun but usually only with torpedo tubes. Their role was to dash in to anchorages, loose off their torpedoes against the ships there and dash out again, relying entirely on their speed to protect them. And to counter the

torpedo-boat the warship began to adopt light fast-firing guns and machine guns. The Nordenfelt and Gardner mechanical machine guns in calibres up to 1-inch were widely fitted in the Royal Navy; many continental navies adopted the Hotchkiss 37mm revolving cannon.

The active counter to the torpedo-boat appeared in 1893, and was known as the torpedo-boat destroyer, a name which eventually dropped the descriptive part and simply became the "destroyer". These were extremely

Whitehead torpedo Looking very much like the modern torpedo, the Whitehead set a new standard in naval warfare. It led to improvements in ships' armour and to the use of protective netting when they were at anchor.

Torpedo-boat destroyer
To combat the threat of the fast and nimble torpedo-boat Thorneycroft were commissioned to design the speedy torpedo-boat destroyer, in time to be known just as a destroyer.

fast and light warships especially designed to keep guard around anchorages and to have sufficient speed to intercept torpedo-boats and sufficient light artillery on board to deal with them once intercepted. Indeed they were so effective that they could fill the roles of both poacher and gamekeeper, and with their arrival the torpedo-boat was abandoned, both attack and defence being done by the destroyer. The only navy to attempt a specialist defence was that of Britain, which developed a number of "Torpedo Gunboats" in the middle 1890s; over 30 were built but they proved to be too slow for the task and were eventually used up in patrolling, minesweeping and coastal defence roles.

The steel solution

The next major advance in the 1870s was the adoption of steel in ships, both for structural purposes and for armour. This had the twin virtues of being both stronger and lighter than the wrought iron used hitherto, and the question of weight was becoming a matter of serious concern to ship designers. Steel, though, was not entirely trusted at that time, particularly in large pieces, since flaws frequently developed, and it took some considerable efforts on the part of steelmasters to convince naval architects that their product was reliable. The first extensive use of steel was by the French, who used it for ship's frames; the first to adopt steel armour were the Italians, impressed by the resistance of 56cm (22½in) steel plate made by Le Creusot in France.

This, though, was simple mild steel, and it resisted attack by shot simply by virtue of its thickness. The problem was that pure steel plate was liable to shatter once the shot had overcome it, whereas wrought iron was more resilient and, when defeated, merely opened a hole for the shot to pass through without affecting the rest of the plate. The Sheffield steelmasters solved this problem by developing compound armour, a wrought-iron plate on to which a facing of steel was cast, so that the two were permanently welded together. With the steel face on the outside, this armour resisted attack due to its hardness. When it finally failed, the wrought-iron backing both held the steel together, preventing shattering, and also resisted the entrance of the shot, which already had been considerably slowed down by its penetration of the steel. The adoption of compound armour allowed armour thickness to be reduced by as much as one-third, with a consequent saving in weight.

Until the early 1880s, it will have been noticed that the armament of the ironclad warship was generally no more than six or eight heavy guns; this was simply because the whole objective was to penetrate armour at as great a range as possible. But there were still many critics who considered that it was wasteful to send 10,000 tons of ship to sea in order to support, in some cases, no more than four guns. But when the torpedo-boat appeared in the middle 1870s, things changed rapidly. First, as we have already noted, multiple heavy-

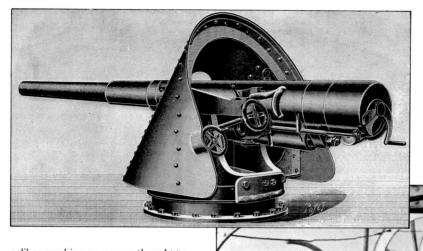

calibre machine guns were thought to be the answer. But these had limited range and the torpedo soon progressed to a point where it could be launched outside the range of these small defensive weapons. In 1881, the Royal Navy called for some fast-firing gun capable of projecting a six-pound shell to a range greater than any torpedo could reach, and within two years it had adopted two designs which had been put forward, the Hotchkiss and the Nordenfelt six-pounder "quick-firing" guns. The significant feature of these weapons was firstly that they were breechloaded through a very rapid-acting sliding blockbreech, and secondly that they were loaded with "fixed" ammunition, i.e. ammunition in which all the components were in one unit and were loaded in one movement. The cartridge case was of brass and carried a cap and a charge of black powder, and the shell was fitted tightly into the neck of the case – just like an overgrown rifle cartridge. With this round of ammunition a well-practised gun's crew could get off 20 or more aimed rounds in a minute, a storm of fire which no torpedo-boat could survive. The "quick-firing" (QF) concept having been tested and found good, the gun was enlarged; 3-inch, 4-inch, 4.7-inch, 5- and 6-inch QF guns were developed in Britain and similar calibres in other countries, though in time it came to be appreciated that the fixed rounds for the larger calibres were too difficult to handle. An alternative was to use "separate loading" ammunition, in which the shell was loaded and rammed and the cartridge case inserted afterwards; but in the larger calibres this was no quicker than a normal bag-charge gun and eventually QF guns in

calibres above 5 inches became rarities, except in German service. There Krupp's grip on the gunmaking business was such that he was able to impose his sliding blockbreech and brass cartridge system right up to the heaviest calibres.

By the middle 1880s, therefore, warships began to bristle with light armament, secondary batteries which were there, in the first place, to protect them against the ubiquitous torpedo-boat. But once the armament was aboard and the gunnery officers began to think about it, they realized that these weapons could be put to good use in bombarding the upper works of the enemy while the heavy guns were attempting to penetrate his armour.

The first British ships to appear with mixed armament were the *Trafalgar* class, laid down in 1886. These carried four 13.5-inch breechloading guns in two turrets, one at each end of the central superstructure, and between them three 4.7-inch QF guns on each side behind an armoured breastwork.

Six-pounder practice Gun crews at practice with the fast-firing 6-pounder under the watchful eye of a gunnery instructor. The arrival of rounds with the shell, case and charge all in one gave these weapons a high rate of fire.

New planning approaches

Through all these years naval building had proceeded on a somewhat haphazard basis – they have built one, we will build two, they have built 8000 tons with four guns, we will build 9000 tons with six guns. But, in 1888, the Royal Navy sat down and thought about naval strategy and the uses of naval power in a rational manner. They concluded that their potential worst case was a combination of France and Russia; that their principal task would be to keep the seas open for merchant shipping to supply Britain in time of war; and that considering such factors as resupply, maintenance and repair, which could reduce the number of ships actually available for duty, the task could only be performed if they had an actual superiority in battleships of five to three and in cruisers of two to one. With some judicious lobbying, the Naval Defence Act of 1889 was passed, making £21.5 million available for the provision of 70 new ships within five years, 10 of them to be battleships – a term coined to replace the old "ironclad" as a generic name for the big

armoured ships with the heaviest guns.

The next task was to determine what shape these battleships would take, and after long discussion it was resolved that they would mount four 13.5-inch guns in barbettes, accompanied by 10 6-inch QF guns. There would be a thick armour belt about two-thirds the length of the ship, with an internal armoured deck stretching the entire length of the hull. Above the belt the skin would be 10cm (4in) armour backed by coal bunkers, since trials had shown that such a combination was adequate to prevent most QF projectiles from penetrating (what managed to get through the plate was usually smothered by the coal within the ship itself). The result of this detailed planning was the *Royal Sovereign* class, which displaced over 14,000 tons and was capable of 15 knots continuous speed and a speed of 17 knots under battle conditions.

The reasoning which led the British to their Naval Defence Act was followed by other nations, who analyzed their own requirements and then made their decisions. Thus the

HMS *Revenge* Seen in typical stiff poses, officers and men of HMS *Revenge*, in about 1890, stand next to the barbette which houses the ship's twin 13.5in guns.

French, in 1891, voted £37 million for 10 battleships, 45 cruisers and several smaller vessels. But even when cold analysis had been done, there was still considerable apprehension whenever another nation increased its fleet, and so, in their turn, Britain again raised the ante in 1894 by ordering seven battleships, six cruisers and 35 destroyers. This led to the *Majestic* class of battleship in which the barbette was abandoned for a new type of turret, not the heavily-armoured, round, Coles design but a wedge-shaped structure with heavy armour on its front face and a lighter steel covering. The guns were 12-inch calibre, a drop from the previous 13.5-inch but justified since these guns were to use cordite smokeless powder, more powerful than black powder, and with lighter shells and mechanical ramming could put up a

higher rate of fire. The armour adopted was of a new type known as "carburized" or "Harveyized" (after the inventor), in which the carbon content of the steel was artificially enhanced by burning charcoal on the face of the white-hot plate during manufacture or by playing coal-gas across it.

Another important feature of the *Majestic* class was the introduction of an armoured "splinter deck" inside the ship which met the side armour and protected the engines, machinery and magazine beneath should a shell pierce the belt and detonate inside the ship. Secondary armament consisted of 12 6-inch guns on two decks and a number of smaller QF guns for anti–torpedo-boat defence. The *Majestic* displaced 14,000 tons, sailed at 17½ knots and had a steaming range of almost 8000 miles.

HMS *Benbow* With a quick-firer high up in her fighting top, HMS *Benbow* sits at anchor, ship's boat fussing round her. Naval authorities were beginning to feel that such large vessels should carry more than that single large gun on the *Benbow*, shown elevated a few degrees. These vessels still did not have the menacing look of the grey fighting ships soon to form the world's navies.

GUNNERY

Accurate gunnery crushes the pride of the Russian Navy

Hitting the target Guns were only as good as the gunners who fired them. The increased rate of fire of the breechloader with a quick-action sliding breechblock was ineffective without accurate targeting. Thorough training was the only means to produce this accurate gunnery.

In 1898, came a sudden political shift which had far-reaching effects. Hitherto the British had always seen the French, perhaps combined with the Russian Navy, as the main enemy at sea. But, in the mid-1890s, the Germans began to feel that they were not getting their fair share of the world's trade and real estate. It was obvious that the British, protected by their navy, were intent on colonizing everything in sight. It followed, therefore, that a strong German navy was a prerequisite to their own expansion. And so, in 1898, the Reichstag approved construction of a sea-going fleet to replace their present somewhat small and basically coastal defence fleet. Admiral von Tirpitz, in a masterly political stroke, convinced the politicians that what was needed was not simply a vote of money from time to time, but a fixed locus of strength, so that whenever the strength began to falter the Navy could obtain funds without the need to plead before the Reichstag every time. And so the Navy Law came into force, setting the German fleet strength at 19 battleships, 22 cruisers and sundry smaller vessels. Tirpitz was honest enough to point out that future events might require him to come back for "supplementary estimates", and sure enough, in 1899 when the British and Boers began to fight in South Africa, this was considered enough of an excuse for him to return and obtain a supplementary Act raising the fleet strength to 38 battleships and 32 cruisers.

There were two counters to this for the British; the first was, obviously, to increase their own naval building. But this had to wait because the South African War was taking up much of the country's energy and finance and the Navy were anxious to see just what sort of ships the Germans had in mind. The second was to improve the efficiency of the existing fleet, and this meant improving its gunnery.

The Scott revolution

Throughout the battle fleets of the world the gunnery left much to be desired. The reason was that the capabilities of the guns had outstripped the methods used to aim and control them; the sights on most naval guns of the early 1890s were no more complex than those of an infantryman's rifle – a vee backsight and a bead foresight – and this, coupled with the motion of the ship, made accurate shooting impossible. Practice was generally carried out on a calm day with the ship either stationary or moving at a slow speed, so that a skilled gunner could make a good score; but in battle, moving at high speed in rough water, with the enemy moving and both ships manoeuvering, there was little chance of a hit unless the two opponents got within 915m (1000yd) of each other. There was no method of determining the range to the enemy except by firing one gun until it got a near-miss, whereupon that range was communicated to the other gunners – since the ships were moving this figure was invalid within seconds. When optical rangefinders were eventually introduced in the late 1890s, they were only 1.4m (4½ft) long, which restricted their use to ranges no more than about 3660m (4000yd). And by that time the major naval guns had ranges in excess of 18,300m (20,000yd).

Captain Percy Scott had been a gunnery officer who could see the defects in the system; once he obtained command of his own ship he began to apply some original training methods, and in the first annual practice obtained an 80 percent hit rate. This was thought to be the result of inaccurate scoring and was generally disbelieved. When he

Well-armed but vulnerable
The Japanese battleship *Hatsuse*, 15,000 tons, typical of the new ships with which Japan was building her Navy. The *Hatsuse* struck a mine laid by the Russian minelayer *Amur*, and sank with 495 of her crew off the Tiger Peninsula, near Port Arthur, on 15 May 1905. The Japanese were the final victors, but at enormous cost. The action itself foreshadowed the battle of Tsushima, later the same month, when the Japanese put to good use all the lessons they had learned and with brilliant tactical use of their powerful navy, crushed the Russians decisively with little loss to themselves.

repeated it the following year with another ship, it suddenly seemed that accurate gunnery was within everyone's grasp.

The justification of Scott's doctrines was seen in battle for the first time in 1904, when the Japanese and Russian fleets met. In February of that year the Japanese began the Russo-Japanese war by a torpedo attack on the Russian fleet in Port Arthur. Shortly afterward, the Russian Admiral Makarov, a highly competent naval leader, died when his ship struck a mine outside Port Arthur, and he was succeeded by Admiral Vitgeft, a man with nowhere near Makarov's abilities. The upshot was that the Russian Far Eastern Fleet failed in its break-out from Port Arthur, so the Russians' only hope of relieving their Far Eastern bastion was, as a last-ditch attempt, to sail their Baltic Fleet around the world, under the Command of Admiral Rozhestvensky, to break the Japanese naval stranglehold.

Battle of Tsushima
In fact, the Russian break-out had been closer to success than the Russians

realized. The Japanese learnt many valuable lessons and, as a result, began an intensive overhaul of their gunnery technique. The Russians' epic voyage culminated as it started to steam through the straits of Toshima, 27 May 1905. Japanese intelligence had anticipated this, so Togo's fleet was waiting. Japanese cruisers, placed out as a screen, spotted their approach and signalled to Togo, who set sail with his fleet on an intercepting course.

The Russian fleet consisted of eight battleships, four of the newest design, and a collection of less battleworthy vessels. The Japanese had only four battleships, backed up by eight armoured cruisers. In gun strength, the Russians had a considerable advantage for long-range fighting, with 26 12-inch and 17 10-inch, whereas Togo had but 16 12-inch. In secondary armament, the weight was still with the Russians, a total of 121 6- and 8-inch guns available on any broadside. Togo had slightly less, 112 6- and 8-inch guns capable of firing on any broadside. The difference was to lie not in hardware, but in training.

Tsushima During the battle, speedy Japanese gunboats harried the Russians until they began to make tactical errors, and Admiral Togo took full advantage of these errors in a conclusive victory.

Just after 1 p.m. Togo's fleet met that of Rozhestvensky, the two moving in opposite directions. Togo turned about and from a range of about 6400m (7000yd), began moving in towards the Russian battle line. As he did so the Russians opened fire, their first shot falling no more than 20m (22yd) from the leading Japanese battleship. They kept up a hot fire at the turning point of the Japanese line, so that each ship came under attack in turn, but although there were a number of hits there were no instances of the armour being penetrated. Once the Japanese ships completed their turn and settled alongside the Russian line, all began firing and the battle became general.

Togo had the advantage of speed, and aimed to cross ahead of the Russian line, a manoeuvre in which he was aided by the Russians turning to cross behind the Japanese. Togo then turned, hoping to cross ahead once more; during this manoeuvre the Russian flagship *Suvoroff* was brought under intense fire.

Behind the Japanese battleships the cruisers had been attacking the second division of the Russian fleet and had damaged the battleship *Osliaba* so badly that she had begun to sink. The Russians attempted to turn away from Togo's main division of battleships, and in doing so they ran against the Japanese cruisers. By this time, the mist of the day had been thickened by funnel and gun smoke, so that the whole battle was beginning to fragment, with the two Japanese divisions virtually

fighting independently as they came into contact with the Russian fleet. The *Suvoroff*, in the confusion, became separated from the remainder of the fleet and blundered into the Japanese battleship division, drawing a storm of heavy gunfire at a range of only 915m (1000yd). In spite of being on fire, and in spite of a massive magazine explosion, she continued to fire her guns at the Japanese.

Eventually the Russian ships were clustered together, moving aimlessly, while the two Japanese divisions, still keeping perfect formation, circled around and pounded them at ranges from 2750 to 5500m (3000 to 6000yd). Taking advantage of the poor visibility a group of Russian ships broke away, heading for Vladivostok, but they were spotted and soon Togo's main division caught up with them to resume the punishment. First the *Alexander III* capsized and sank, then the *Borodino* took a shell in her main magazine and sank immediately.

The sun was setting as Togo drew away and began disengaging. The *Suvorov*, still attempting to fight even though she was burning and listed to one side, was finally sunk by three torpedoes, and during the night torpedo attacks sank a further two Russian battleships and some lesser ships. When dawn broke next morning it found only four Russian ships still making for Vladivostok, led by the battleship *Oryol*, listing and almost incapable of fighting. When Togo's force appeared, the Russians surrendered.

Tsushima was probably one of the most decisive naval battles ever fought. It was also the only decisive battle ever fought between battleships without the intervention of aviation. As a result the Russian fleet virtually ceased to exist for the next 50 years, while its effect on Japanese morale and naval thinking was to colour their actions for the next 40. The outcome of the battle was due entirely to two things; firstly that the Japanese had a four-knot advantage in speed, and secondly that the Japanese had developed their gunnery to a very high standard. Moreover in the after-battle analyses made by observers from various navies who had been present with one side or the other, it was apparent that the secondary armament had contributed enormously to the victory by smashing the unprotected parts of the Russian ships, setting fires and damaging equipment. Relatively little damage had been done to the armour belts, and the sinkings were due either to magazine explosion, which rent the ships apart, or to torpedo attacks which reached beneath the belt; and even then the *Suvorov* needed four torpedoes before she finally sank.

Post-Tsushima insights

The battle of Tsushima vindicated the gunnery experts' concern with improved shooting, and it also vindicated the theories of those who had advocated secondary armament for its power of damaging the less well protected areas of warships. In addition, it showed up some areas in which technique was deficient, particularly in the matter of controlling

the fire of the multitude of guns which a modern fleet carried. Although the Japanese ships carried a gunnery controller aloft in a small command position up the mast, he could do very little once the battle had begun. The fall of shot into the water, throwing up a screen of splash and spray, the rolling smoke from the guns, and the impossibility of deciding which shot had been fired by which gun – or even which ship – rendered him powerless once he had determined the initial range to open fire. After that the individual gun captains and captains of turrets took the matter into their own hands, seeking their own targets and firing as and when they felt they had a chance of hitting. The only overall command was simply to vary the rate of fire, stop firing or recommence firing as the commander or the ship's captain considered the tactical movements.

Much of this had already been appreciated in naval circles and steps were being taken to bring the gunnery of every ship under centralized control. Every fleet was faced with the same problem and devised similar solutions;

Vice Admiral Petrovich Rozhestvensky *(left)* Commander of the Russian Fleet *(below)* at Tsushima. His ships' guns had the advantage of using armour-piercing shells, but managed only one percent of hits in over 3000 rounds. The Japanese fired 5000 rounds, scoring nearly six percent hits.

for the sake of convenience we can trace the steps taken in the British fleet during this period. In the 1890s, the practice of salvo firing by electrical means had been developed; the guns were fired by electrically-initiated primers, the current for which was derived from a circuit controlled from the gunnery controller in his "control top" on the mast. All guns were loaded and laid, the crews stepped back and lay on the deck clear of the recoil, and all guns on the broadside fired simultaneously. This meant that all the shells landed together and it became possible for the gunnery controller to derive some information from seeing where the shells fell; hitherto, with shells falling erratically around the target it was impossible to make a correction since the controller could not know who had fired which shell. Now he could assess the error, make a correction, have it applied to all guns, and again fire a salvo for observation. Once he had the "straddle" – one salvo over the target, one short – he could "split the bracket" and order independent fire, the guns loading and firing on the final data as fast as they could. Meanwhile the observer watched, and if the enemy sheered away and the range changed, he could return to salvo firing to get another straddle.

From this came various mechanical devices to simplify his task. Optical rangefinders began to lengthen their baseline, from 1.4m (4½ft) to 3.7m (12), 5.5m (18) and even 11m (36ft). Since optical rangefinding, as practised by the British, relied upon triangulation, it followed that the greater the width of the optical base, the greater the range which could be measured with acceptable accuracy. It might be noted that the German fleet, when it adopted optical rangefinding, took to an entirely different system, that of stereoscopy, which allowed a comparable degree of accuracy with a shorter base, or better accuracy with a longer one, but also demanded some very specialized operators with unusual optical skills.

Having established the target's range, it was next necessary to determine its speed and course, and for this other instruments were devised, measuring the angular travel and comparing it with elapsed time and range. Then came the problem of compensating for the time taken for the shell to get to its target; at a range of 9150m (10,000yd), a shell would take some 18-20 seconds to reach the enemy, and if the target was moving at 15 knots he could have moved about 155m (170yd) in that time. Forecasting what might be the case with faster ships and longer ranges made it apparent that a 25-knot target at 18,300m (20,000yd) could move over 460m (500yd) during the shell's time of flight, and unless some compensation was made, gunnery would be useless. First came the "Dumaresq", named after its inventor, a graphical plotter which drew out the course of the ship and of the target on a moving sheet of paper, so that their comparative positions could be seen. Then came the "Dreyer Table", also named after its inventor, a mechanical plotter which permitted data extracted from the Dumaresq, the rangefinder and the other instruments to be collated and produce a forward plot of where the shell would land were it to be fired at any given moment. By use of the Dumaresq and the Dreyer Table together, it was now possible to bring the point of impact and the forecast position of the enemy into the same point in space and fire the guns at the appropriate moment to bring the salvo and the target together at the same point in time. All that remained was to bring the control of the guns into one "director centre" so that they could be fired electrically at the correct moment. All the gunners had to do was apply the range and bearing information sent from the controller, load the guns and wait for them to fire.

Once this revolution in fire control had been accepted, and the necessary instruments developed and installed, there was a good argument for changing the tactics. The observation of fire and its correction was a mathematically precise affair on one condition; that all the guns were of identical performance. Where the ship was armed with a collection of various calibres, each one developed a different trajectory, had a different muzzle velocity and a different time of flight to a given range, so that it became extremely difficult, if not impossible, to control a mixed armament against a single target. The second element of the argument was that if the major armament could be accurately controlled at long range, then there was little point in having secondary armament since the enemy would be sunk before he got within its range.

THE DREADNOUGHT

As guns get larger, so do the ships that carry them

In October 1904, Admiral Sir John Fisher became First Sea Lord, and immediately set about shaking up the Royal Navy. Admiral Sir Percy Scott was appointed Inspector of Target Practice, and Captain John Jellicoe became Director of Naval Ordnance; all three were technical men and between them they were to revitalize the British naval strength. One of Fisher's first acts was to set in motion the building of a totally new type of capital ship, the *Dreadnought*. This was to be based firstly on the premise that one major calibre was all that was required in a battleship and, secondly, on the premise that speed was the answer to the growing threat of the submarine. As a result the *Dreadnought* carried 10 12-inch guns, with 24 3-inch guns for repelling torpedo-boats, and had a speed of 21 knots. At 17,900 tons, she was larger, faster and more expensive than any previous British warship and was the first of any nationality larger than a light cruiser to use turbine engines. The 10 heavy guns were in five turrets, three on the centre-line and two abreast on the beams so that eight guns could be brought to bear on any broadside.

It might be thought that the arrival of the *Dreadnought* would have pleased the Royal Navy; in fact, many naval authorities were aghast, arguing that it made everything else obsolete and

HMS *Dreadnought* At last, in February 1906 the launch took place of the Royal Navy's first large-calibre gun, turbine-driven battleship. Her speed of over 21 knots and her formidable broadside capability of eight 12in guns made her one of the most powerful warships ever built.

After _Dreadnought_ A new class, the battle cruiser, followed the _Dreadnought_. The new ships were of hybrid design, the first being the Tyne-built HMS _Invincible (left)_, having equivalent firepower but noticeably thinner armour, her defence lying in speed. Next in capital ship design was the _Queen Elizabeth_ class _(above)_. They had oil-fired turbines, and the _Queen Elizabeth_ herself bore a burnished shovel on the quarter-deck as a reminder of the filth generated when coaling was the order of the day.

threw away the years spent in building up the British battleship fleet. This was true, but it also made every foreign ship obsolete, put every nation on an equal starting footing, and relied upon Britain's manufacturing superiority to maintain the quantitative lead.

The _Dreadnought_ was followed immediately by three of a totally new class, the "battle cruiser". These, beginning with HMS _Invincible_, were smaller than the _Dreadnought_ but adhered to the same all-big-gun policy, mounting eight 12-inch guns in four turrets. They were capable of 25 knots, but in order to save weight they had a maximum of 15cm (6in) of armour, whereas the _Dreadnought_ class had 27.5cm (11in).

The German response was to stop building, spend two years planning, and then to lay down four _Dreadnought_-type ships of their own, the _Nassau_ class. These mounted 12 11-inch guns, had armour of 30cm (12in) thickness, but, due to production difficulties, were fitted with piston engines and could therefore not reach 20 knots. They also displaced more than previous designs which meant that German tactical dispositions were set at naught until the Kiel Canal, between the North Sea and the Baltic, was widened and deepened.

Von Tirpitz went back to the Reichstag and obtained another supplementary Naval Law, allowing the laying-down of four new battleships every year until 1911, two per year thereafter. This, coupled with indications that Germany was stockpiling materials for guns and armour and that Krupp was laying in machine tools for the manufacture of large numbers of naval guns and mountings, caused the British to speed up their building rate to keep step with the Germans, and the naval armaments race was on.

Britain came out of it the leader by producing what many experts consider to have been the finest battleship design of the time, the _Queen Elizabeth_ class. These were the first British ships to carry 15-inch guns, the first to use oil as fuel for the turbine engines, they displaced 27,500 tons and had a speed of 25 knots. The armour belt was 37cm (13½in) thick and the armour deck 5cm (2½in) thick. There was a reversion to secondary armament; in addition to eight 15-inch guns in four turrets (the inner turrets being superelevated above the outer) she carried 12 6-inch and four 3-inch guns, principally for anti–torpedo-boat firing. She also carried five submerged torpedo tubes.

WAR UNDERWATER

The submarine adds another dimension to war at sea

Admiral Fisher had made one other far-reaching decision; in 1901, he had persuaded the Admiralty to order five submarines from Vickers. The idea of a submersible boat can be traced back to the 17th century, but in spite of attempts by Ericsson, the first really successful design came from Nordenfelt, a Swedish company which, in the 1880s, managed to sell one or two submarines, notably to Greece and Turkey. The defect of the Nordenfelt boat was that it would only remain submerged so long as it was moving forward; once it stopped, it floated to the surface. This was corrected in the design developed in the USA by J.D. Holland, who set about designing a submarine in order that he and his Fenian friends would be able to strike a blow for Ireland by sinking British warships in harbour. He used electricity to propel the boat, a fact which interested Isaac Rice, who had become a millionaire from manufacturing storage batteries. Holland completed his first boat in 1898, and in the following year Rice drew it to the attention of the US Navy. They were slow to see any point in the invention, and Rice therefore went to Europe where he managed to conclude an agreement with Vickers, a skilled shipbuilding yard, whereby Rice's Electric Boat Company would provide the designs and "know-how" while Vickers provided the manufacturing capacity, Electric Boat to receive a proportion of Vickers' profit for the next 25 years. In the long run, Vickers were smarter than Rice, and within five years, by buying up minority shareholders, Vickers had virtual control of the American company.

Early submarines

It was to Vickers that Fisher turned in 1901, and they were to hold a monopoly of submarine building until shortly before the First World War. After the first five experimental craft had been assessed by the Royal Navy, and suggestions for improvement made, Vickers began the "A" class, then the "B" and "C" classes, a total of 56 of

these being built by 1910. These boats had petrol engines for propulsion on the surface at a speed of 12 knots, and electric motors for submerged movement at considerably slower speeds. Then came the "D" class, 49m (160ft) long and capable of 14 knots, and finally the broader-beamed "E" class. These proved to be excellent boats for their time; two sailed to Australia, and another completed over 48,280km (30,000 miles) before requiring a refit, something of a record for such complex and delicate vessels.

After 1909, Vickers were also permitted to sell submarines – though not of Admiralty design – to foreign powers and, by 1912, had sold 18 to America, seven each to Russia and Japan, two to Austria and one to Holland, in addition to 61 to the British Royal Navy.

Underwater war During the Fleet Review of 1907, Admiral Sir John Fisher told King Edward VIII: "The submarine will be the battleship of the future." Had he known of today's huge and powerful nuclear submarines with their awesome and hugely destructive weapons he would have seen the realization of his prophecy. But the beginning of submarine warfare lay in the tiny *Holland*, designed by Irishman John Philip Holland and launched in 1901.

Nordenfelt The whale-like appearance of the Nordenfelt submarine *(above)* was not echoed in its maximum safe depth of 15m (50ft). The print illustrates a Turkish Nordenfelt approaching Constantinople in 1888.

The Nordenfelt design was taken up in Germany by the Hansa Deutsche Werft shipyard in 1890; they built two boats which were not particularly successful and which failed to interest the Imperial Navy. But the general interest in submarines at the turn of the century led the Krupp company to begin their own development; by 1903 they had produced a practical design, the "Forelle", which was then improved into the "Karp" class, three of which were sold to the Imperial Russian Navy. The principal drawback to this boat was that it used the Korting engine, a crude oil machine which used kerosene as fuel and thus advertised its presence by a large cloud of white smoke. The "Karp" became the prototype for the first German U-boat, U-1, which was launched in 1906, still using the Korting engine. It was not until 1912 that the Krupp company adopted the diesel engine, some years after it had entered service with Britain and other countries.

The general naval view of submarines was that they would be legitimately employed in attacking warships or troop supply and transport

ships, but that merchantmen and passenger liners were not a proper target. Many and varied were the tactical theories put forward, most of which revolved around the concept of escorting a fleet with a screen of submarines or decoying an enemy fleet into a waiting submarine ambush. Unfortunately, the performance of the early submarines was not such that a submerged boat could keep station with a surface fleet, so that most of these theories withered and the submarine came to be acknowledged as a lone patrol vessel.

The other naval weapon to show improvement in the early 1900s was the submarine mine, the original torpedo. It received its initial impetus as a coastal defence weapon, an auxiliary to the artillery which began to proliferate in the 1870s, mines being laid in areas in which hostile ships would have to pass – such as narrow straits – or to protect areas which could not conveniently be covered by gunfire. These mines were simply metal canisters of explosive anchored in fixed spots and connected by electric wire to an observation post. Some countries

Vickers & Maxim The Royal Navy's submarine arm came into being when the first Vickers-built *Holland* went down the slipway at Barrow *(above)*, starting her sea trials in 1902. Five were built, costing £35,000 each.

placed the responsibility for coastal defence upon their navy, as a result of which navies began to explore the possibilities of using mines as offensive weapons to deny stretches of sea to hostile fleets. The typical design of the pre-1914 period was a cylinder or sphere of metal containing a heavy charge – 230kg (500lb) or so – of guncotton, and provided with horns which protruded from the surface of the mine. These were of copper or some other malleable metal and concealed a glass tube filled with acid. The mine was anchored to the sea bottom and had sufficient buoyancy to float at a predetermined depth below the surface. On being struck by a passing ship the horn would bend, breaking the glass tube and releasing the acid; this would establish an electrical circuit and discharge a current into an electric detonator to fire the mine. The tamping effect of the surrounding sea would ensure the maximum pressure against the relatively fragile ship's hull, sufficient to sink or seriously damage the ship.

When war broke out, in 1914, it was generally assumed that a major sea battle between the two great fleets of Britain and Germany would take place, in much the same way that everyone expected overwhelming air raids to follow the declaration of war in 1939. In neither case did the expected happen. Both fleets adopted a defensive posture; the British fleet sat down to operate a blockade of the North Sea,

preventing anything getting in to Germany and also preventing any German ship from getting out into the world at large to influence British commercial shipping. A number of German warships were already at large, and managed to do some damage, but they were all hunted down. Meanwhile the German High Seas Fleet sat in its bases at Wilhelmshaven and Kiel and waited for the British Grand Fleet to show itself in the North Sea.

Devastation by U-boat

It was unlikely that the Royal Navy, with its tradition of carrying the fight to the enemy, would sit down under this regime for long and, late in August 1914, the Admiralty decided to make an offensive sweep into the Heligoland Bight. Fortunately, Admiral Jellicoe heard of the plan, thought it somewhat foolhardy, and sent his battle-cruiser squadron under Beatty to support the sweep. Two light cruisers and 33 destroyers swept into the Bight early in the morning of 28 August. After sinking one German destroyer and suffering some casualties the British force began to get the worst of it as the Germans realized they were unsupported and began to bring up heavier ships. In mid-morning, just as things were getting critical, Beatty's battle cruisers arrived, roared in and sank three light cruisers, rescued the light forces and shepherded them away. This singeing of the Kaiser's beard was bad for the

Underwater menace At the outbreak of World War I, the naval authorities did not see any real need to look much beyond the threat of the surface fleet when planning battle strategy. However, a devastatingly effective attack by only one German U-boat on three armoured cruisers, which it sank, shocked the admiralty and the nation into recognizing the true potential of the submarine as the decisive weapon at sea.

morale of the German Navy and led to an instruction from the Kaiser that the High Seas Fleet was not to venture outside the Bight.

If the High Seas fleet could not stir, then some other method of carrying the war to the British had to be sought, and this allowed the submarine to show what it could do. On 22 September, the Royal Navy were shocked when a solitary U-boat, *U-9* under the command of Leutnant Weddingen, sank three armoured cruisers within the space of an hour. The *Hogue*, the *Aboukir* and the *Cressy* were part of the Harwich Flotilla, a force whose task was to keep the North Sea clear of German minelayers and torpedo-boats, and the three cruisers were assigned to supporting the destroyers of the flotilla. Because of severe weather the destroyers had been withdrawn, leaving the cruisers operating alone; when the weather improved the destroyers were sent back to resume their duty of screening the cruiser force from possible submarine attack. At much the same time the *U-9* had left Kiel, intending to patrol the coast off Belgium, but due to a compass fault found herself well out in the North Sea. On surfacing to recharge the batteries, Weddingen spotted the masts of the cruiser force to his south. He submerged again and fired a single torpedo at the leading ship, the *Aboukir*, obtained a hit and the cruiser immediately began to sink. Captain Drummond of the *Aboukir* thought he had struck a mine and signalled the *Hogue* and the *Cressy* to close up, which they did, their captains then stopping them in order to pick up survivors. The *U-9* had dived deep to reload her forward torpedo tube and now came back to periscope depth and fired two torpedoes at the *Hogue* from a range of 275m (300yd). The *Hogue* sank within minutes. The *U-9*'s batteries were almost expired by this time and Weddingen surfaced and turned stern-on to fire at the *Cressy* with his stern torpedo tubes. The *Cressy* saw the U-boat and the captain ordered full speed in an attempt to out-manoeuvre the submarine, but one of the two torpedoes struck and stopped her. The *U-9* then turned and fired a bow torpedo, obtaining another hit and sinking the cruiser. The U-boat made off, leaving some 2000 men swimming for their lives.

The news struck England like a bombshell; it was first thought that the sinkings were the work of a "pack" of submarines, but when it became known that it was the work of a single U-boat, the shock was even greater. Sixty-two officers and 1397 men had been drowned and scapegoats were sought; but the simple fact was that the submarine, hitherto an unknown quantity and untried in war, had suddenly arrived on the naval scene and effectively demonstrated its offensive capabilities.

At the outbreak of war the German Navy had little faith in the submarine's ability; it was not until the exploit of *U-9* and effective patrols by other submarines convinced the High Command that these craft were seaworthy that their possibilities began to be further explored. In February 1915, with the High Seas Fleet bottled up and their surface raiders being whittled away by British warships, the submarine began to look like their one effective weapon. Since the British blockade was beginning to make itself felt in Germany, the obvious course was to apply the same treatment to Britain by using submarines to sink merchant shipping, both belligerent and neutral, which traded with Britain. On 2 February 1915, the Germans declared "all the waters surrounding Great Britain and Ireland, including the English Channel, an area of war" and that they would "therein act against the shipping of the enemy". They also pointed out to neutrals that they would be wise to avoid this area because "in view of the misuse of neutral flags ordered by the British Government... their becoming victims of attack directed against enemy ships cannot always be avoided."

On 18 February, when unrestricted submarine warfare was to commence, Germany had 20 U-boats available, though only four were ready for immediate action. But within days two boats already at sea sank seven merchant ships and, joined by the other two sailing from Kiel, increased the score to 13 within a week. The most prominent sinking to occur as a result of this first U-boat campaign was, of course, the Cunard liner the *Lusitania*, sunk by torpedo on 7th May 1915 with the loss of 1198 lives. Although Germany rejected American protests – there were 128 American citizens among the dead – they did, in practice, order submarine commanders to be more restrained in their attacks on passenger liners.

THE FLEETS COLLIDE

A test of strength in the North Sea ends in acrimony

The next major fleet action was the Battle of the Dogger Bank in January 1915. The Kaiser had rescinded his previous order and given his Admirals a degree of freedom, and Admiral Hipper led a reconnaissance into the North Sea, hoping to meet some destroyers or other light forces he could punish. The German radio messages having been intercepted, the British battle cruisers under Beatty were sent out to intercept Hipper, though due to a signal failure Jellicoe and the Grand Fleet were not informed in time to take part.

The two forces began firing at about 18,290m (20,000yd) range, and as this dropped to 14,630m (16,000yd) the shooting began to tell. Hipper had four ships and all concentrated their fire on the *Lion*, Beatty's flagship leading the attack. For her part the *Lion* gave as

good as she got and dropped a shell into the *Seydlitz*, Hipper's flagship, which struck a gun turret and ignited a column of cartridges, the fire from which killed two turret crews and put both turrets out of action. The *Seydlitz* got in two hits on the *Lion* which stove in her side so that seawater got into the boiler feed system and stopped one engine. The *Lion* began to slow, and Beatty sent up a flurry of flag signals instructing the remainder of his force – four ships – to close with the enemy. This instruction was mis-coded and misunderstood, so that the British ships now clustered around the German heavy cruiser, the *Blücher*, which had suffered damage to her steering gear, and sank her with a storm of fire. The rest of Hipper's fleet took their opportunity and made off.

In February 1916, Admiral Scheer took command of the German fleet and

Dogger Bank When intercepted enemy signals gave the Royal Navy, here shown sailing out, the chance to hit the German fleet hard in 1915, the resulting action was a severe disappointment to the Admiralty. The oldest German ship of the group of four, the *Blücher*, was sunk, the others getting away. The action might be described as an example of how not to fight a naval battle.

Admiral Sir John Jellicoe, described by Winston Churchill at the time as "the only man on either side who could lose the war in an afternoon".

began plotting an involved ambush which would lure Jellicoe from his base at Scapa Flow to where the German fleet would be waiting. This led to the famous Battle of Jutland, the activity of which was completed in an afternoon, but the arguments over which have continued to this day. To be brief: the first part of the action, which began close to 4 p.m. on 31 May 1916, was between Beatty's six battle cruisers and Hipper's five, a running duel fought at about 14,630m (16,000yd) range. Hipper was some 160km (100mi) ahead of the High Seas Fleet, and he turned back to draw Beatty towards the heavier force. Visibility and wind – which blew funnel smoke – favoured the Germans and their gunnery was extremely good, finding the range with their first salvoes. The *Indefatigable* and *Queen Mary* both took shells into turrets, raising fires which communicated to the magazines and the two ships were instantly destroyed. Then the British Fifth Battle Squadron of Queen Elizabeth class battleships arrived and the fight began to go in the British favour.

Now Hipper had made contact with the High Seas Fleet, and upon seeing this Beatty turned his force about to lead the Germans back to Jellicoe and the Grand Fleet which had steamed down from Scapa Flow, curving his course ahead of the Germans so as to prevent them seeing the Grand Fleet approaching. Jellicoe, upon seeing the approaching mass, turned his wing column away from the German line so as to pass around them out of torpedo range and thus cut off their escape route back to Germany; this move has been at the heart of the criticism of his handling of the battle, it being suggested that he should have turned inward to the torpedo threat and closed with the enemy. This was, however, the accepted manoeuvre when faced with the possibility of a torpedo attack and, in fact, some 23 torpedoes were launched by the Germans at this time, none of which managed to find a target due to Jellicoe's turn. Be that as it may, the result was that Scheer was now surrounded on three sides by battleships. He made two attempts to turn away, and eventually extricated the majority of his fleet by having Hipper make a suicidal charge towards the British guns. By this time mist and darkness supervened and the Germans were able to slip away.

Assessment of Jutland

The gunnery of the Grand Fleet had been superb, and at extreme ranges, in failing light, considerable damage was done to the German ships. More would have been done, but for the fact that the British shells were failing to penetrate the German armour. At the end of the affair both sides claimed victory: the Germans because they lost 11 ships out of 110 and suffered 2586 killed and 490 wounded, against the British losses of 14 out of 149 ships, 6447 killed and 564 wounded; the British because, as Admiral Sir Percy Scott later put it, "The Germans came out for the Battle of Jutland and they went home and never came out again except to surrender." That wasn't quite true, but it was true enough, and certainly the British fleet was left in possession of the field of battle, while the German fleet never again attempted to try a major action. Jellicoe became the victim of a whispering campaign – he had failed to press home the attack, turned away at a crucial moment, had striven too hard to preserve his ships instead of risking them – and in November was appointed to the Admiralty, ostensibly to deal with the German submarine campaign. Beatty became Commander-in-Chief in his place, and, according to some critics, immediately orchestrated

a campaign to prove that his battle cruisers were the only effective force at Jutland. It was all very pitiful.

The failure of the High Seas Fleet to force a conclusion led the Germans to increase the scale of submarine warfare. The unrestricted warfare begun in February 1915 had been terminated in the waters around Great Britain, in September 1915, in the face of protests from neutrals in general and the United States in particular. Even so, the sinking of British merchant ships continued and, by late 1915, had reached the point where the tonnage was being sunk faster than replacements could be launched. The problem facing the Royal Navy was twofold: firstly their anti-submarine weapons were relatively ineffective, and secondly their tactical system was based on guarding sea routes rather than on guarding ships. In February 1917, therefore, the U-boats were given permission to attack anything they found which was not German. This, it was hoped, would once again deter neutrals from trading with Britain and, by sinking upwards of half a million tons of shipping a month, would break Britain's ability to sustain the war within six months. Germany at that time had 111 submarines, of which 50 were operational, and within a month they

had sunk 250 ships. In the next month they increased their score to 430 ships and, in accordance with their prophecy, the flow of neutral shipping to Britain was reduced by three-quarters. After the tally of sinkings had exceeded the 800,000 ton mark, the Admiralty adopted the convoy system, basing the decision on the relative probabilities of a submarine finding a convoy and finding one of the same number of ships scattered around the ocean. Convoys, supported by the surface fleet, gradually gained the upper hand and the submarine threat receded. At the same time the threat led to increased activity in developing devices and weapons for detecting and sinking the submarine.

The war ended in 1918, and part of the price of armistice was the surrender of the entire German fleet and its internment in Scapa Flow. Its end was not glorious; in October 1918, the German Admiralty ordered the fleet to sea in the hope of one final and conclusive battle with the Royal Navy, but the sailors declined the honour, setting in train much of the unrest which helped to bring about the final collapse. And on 22 June 1919, the crews quietly opened the seacocks, took to the boats, and scuttled the fleet rather than see it fall into other hands.

Jutland One of the great sea battles of modern times, Jutland had all the ingredients of the epic. It was a fast and furious action, with no fewer than 148 Royal Navy ships and 99 German at each other's throats in the confines of the North Sea. By the end of the afternoon of 31 May 1916, 6097 British sailors had died compared with 2551 Germans. The Royal Navy had lost three battle cruisers, three cruisers and eight destroyers. Joining them at the seabed were a German battleship, battle cruiser, four cruisers and five destroyers. It was a sad end to the last great deliberately planned set-piece naval battle.

BETWEEN THE WARS

The machinations of governments breed a new kind of warship

In the immediate postwar world the British Royal Navy was the predominant naval force, but there were others about to dispute their position. The United States had begun building the "Great White Fleet" under Theodore Roosevelt in the early 1900s, and having abandoned the policy of non-involvement in European affairs with its entry into World War I, now intended to place itself on a level commensurate with the other world powers. The Japanese, strengthened by the long-standing Anglo-Japanese Alliance, had guarded the Pacific Ocean area during the war years, and as their reward had acquired most of the German colonies in that ocean. In the absence of British and American mercantile shipping in the quieter parts of the world during the war years, the Japanese merchant fleet had trebled and the Japanese, reasonably in their eyes, were determined upon a navy capable of protecting all their new-found interests. Moreover, the United States did not appear to take kindly to the Japanese influence spreading across the Pacific. When they discovered that the Japanese were not only building two enormous battleships mounting 16-inch guns, with a view to increasing their strength to 16 such warships by 1927, but planning even bigger ships with 18-inch guns, the alarm bells rang in Washington and London. The Royal Navy began planning four 48,000 ton battle cruisers with nine 16-inch guns to be followed by another four with 18-inch guns, while the US Navy began

developing an 18-inch gun of unprecedented power.

The thought of all this building, with its effects on the shaky postwar economy, was daunting. Congress and Parliament both rebelled at the prospective costs and, after much discussion, an Arms Limitation Conference was proposed; the "Washington Conference" took place in November 1921.

The result of this momentous conference, after much wrangling, was an agreement between Britain, the United States, France, Italy and Japan to limit the size of their fleets. Britain would have 22 battleships, the USA 18, Japan, France and Italy 10 each. These could be replaced, in 20 years' time, with new construction not exceeding 35,000 tons and armed with no larger than 16-inch guns. There were also agreements preventing Britain and the USA from making any additions to their fortified bases in the Pacific, and forbidding either country, and Japan, from building any new bases in the area.

Newly emerging needs

This was a considerable achievement, though it can be seen, from hindsight, to have concerned itself only with a weapon which was already becoming obsolescent. There was no mention in the treaties of submarines or aviation. But these were, at that time, the fancies of enthusiasts and given little credence by the naval pundits of the day. The battleship was the outward and visible sign of naval power, and

Husho The carrier *Husho* was built in 1934, as part of Japan's plan to build a formidable navy – a strong weapon to aid her expansionist plans. When Japan entered World War II the carrier was so old that she was relegated to training duties; but at the Battle of Midway she joined seven other main fleet carriers in a show of massive naval air power.

thus he who had the battleships made the rules.

But there were forward-thinking naval officers who could see some prospect in these two new weapons. Some power was added to their arguments with a series of trials carried out by the US Army and Navy in 1921, in which several old German warships, which had escaped the Scapa Flow indignity, were subjected to various forms of attack from the air. The lighter craft were sunk quite quickly, but it took rather more to sink the *Dreadnought*-type battleship *Ostfriesland*. Both the aviators and the surface sailor found points to strengthen their arguments. Then came some tests by Britain against another old German warship in which bombing failed to produce much damage. Finally, the Americans, having scrapped a new battleship under the terms of the Washington Treaty, attempted to sink her by bombing, but without success. The aviators retired from the arena in some disarray.

The idea of an aircraft carrier, a ship totally designed as a floating airfield, had begun in the closing months of the war and was followed in the postwar years, for even if aircraft appeared to hold little danger as a weapon, the navies of the world were agreed that they made excellent reconnaissance devices and also had their virtues as submarine-hunters. So naval aviation was by no means ignored; it was simply

discounted as an offensive weapon, or at least discounted until some type of armament could be devised which would cope with the armoured target. The only prospect appeared to lie in torpedo-carrying aircraft which could fly low above the water and drop torpedoes which would then continue in their usual manner through the water to deliver an underwater attack. But this was not seen as a method of destroying an enemy fleet, merely as a method of disabling a fugitive so that he could then be caught by conventional surface warships and bombarded in the conventional manner.

The two nations who contributed most to the future of naval air power, in the 1920s, were the United States and Japan. The US Navy, ignoring much of the uproar which surrounded Colonel Billy Mitchell and the US Army's attempts to sink ships from the air, moved quietly ahead. By the end of the 1920s, they had two modern aircraft carriers and their aviators were experimenting with dive-bombing and with the basic tactics of seeking out and destroying other aircraft carriers. The Japanese had laid down their first carrier in 1919, and began flying trials from her in 1923. Even though the aviators did not have an entirely trouble-free time, largely because the overall control of their navies remained in the hands of battleship-era admirals, they derived strength from the fact that in both Japan and the USA the naval air

USS *Saratoga* In 1941, the carrier *Saratoga* shared with the *Lexington* the doubtful honour of being the oldest carrier in the US Navy. Both were converted 33,000-ton battle cruisers in 1927 and at that time were the world's largest aircraft carriers. The *Saratoga* was at sea on 7 December 1941, and so missed the destruction when the Japanese hit Pearl Harbor. This 90-plane carrier had a long and eventful war and was still operating in 1944 when she and her aircraft supported the Allied assault on Sumatra.

forces remained independent, part of the Navy, responsible to no-one else. In Britain the Fleet Air Arm became subordinated to the Royal Air Force and many of the roles it would have preferred to have in Naval hands were arrogated to the RAF. The design of aircraft was controlled by the Air Ministry and it was not inclined to listen to sailors when it came to developing naval aircraft. Moreover, the shortage of money in the 1930s meant that whatever was available had to be parcelled out between the various competing ideas, and battleships came higher on the scale of priorities than did submarines or aircraft carriers. The long-term result was that the Royal Navy entered the war in 1939 with insufficient carriers and aircraft which were either badly designed or obsolete by world standards.

Similar thinking obtained with the other European powers. The Germans had laid down one carrier, but since the air arm was the Luftwaffe no attention was paid to naval aviation except for the provision of a few float-planes which could be catapulted from warships for reconnaissance flights. The Italian Air Force was another third service, under Mussolini's special care, and the Italian Navy therefore had little attention paid to its air needs. In the case of Italy, though, there was some excuse; since the Mediterranean was the *Mare Nostrum* of the Italian Navy, as they fondly believed, it was provided with Italian air bases on both sides, there was really no need for carrier aircraft. The French had one carrier and a few aircraft, but no clear idea of what they intended to do with either. In spite of the fact that the Royal Navy had such

lead as there might be in naval aviation in Europe, their equipment was not good enough for them to derive much benefit from it, nor was there much incentive from the higher command.

Although there had been a series of treaties in the years after the First World War in an attempt to limit the size and number of battleships, by the middle 1930s they were effectively dead. The German Navy, severely limited by the Versailles Treaty, had decided to build a "limited offensive" fleet and developed the "Panzerschiffe" (armoured ship), which became popularly known as the "pocket battleship" because of its combination of small size and powerful armament. This, the *Deutschland* class, had a speed of 27 knots so as to be able to elude battleships, armour protection which would suffice against 203-mm shells, and six 28-cm guns in two triple turrets so that it could outgun heavy cruisers. Once the construction of these ships was announced, the French immediately began work on a design which would neutralize them and, in 1931, announced the *Dunkerque* battle cruiser class.

On hearing of the French decision the Italian Navy began the rebuilding of four battleships to bring them up to a more modern standard, and, in effect, the naval armament race of the years prior to 1914 was beginning to be repeated. Within a few years new battleships were being planned or built in every major nation, for irrespective of the claims of the submarine or aviation branches, the gun was still the major armament and the battleship was the most effective way of taking the gun into action.

WORLD WAR II

*Sovereignty of the seas is the key to survival
and final victory*

Admiral Graf Spee This fine pocket-battleship, well armed, fast and powerful, was lost to the German navy by the orders of Hitler. The warship was harried by the royal Navy's *Belfast*, *Exeter*, *Achilles* and *Ajax* and she entered Montevideo harbour for repairs to holes in her bows. But after a few hours, during which time there was hectic diplomatic activity, her captain, Hans Langsdorff, acting on the direct orders of the Führer, took her out to the mouth of the River Plate. After getting the crew away he set timed high-explosive charges in the hull and magazines, then left the ship to her fate. After she exploded, Langsdorff returned to Montevideo, where he shot himself.

The Second World War was barely a few hours old when the first blow was struck at sea by the German submarine *U-30*, sinking the liner *Athenia* off the northwest coast of Ireland. The U-boat captain believed the *Athenia* to be an armed auxiliary cruiser, but it was, in fact, unarmed and 112 people were drowned. Britain assumed this to be the start of unrestricted submarine warfare once more, but the German Navy actually imposed even stricter controls on their U-boat captains to prevent a recurrence, though these controls were soon to be relaxed.

A more serious blow was received by the Royal Navy on 17 September, when the aircraft carrier *Courageous*, employed on an anti-submarine patrol off southern Ireland, was sunk by the *U-29*. This misemployment of aircraft carriers to perform tasks better suited to other types of warship was rapidly discontinued, since the *Ark Royal*, Britain's newest carrier, had had a near miss from a U-boat torpedo only a few days before.

The most devastating blow to Royal Naval pride, however, came on 14 October, when U-boat *U-47*, commanded by Kapitanleutnant Gunther Prien, passed through the defences of Scapa Flow, the principal British naval base, to torpedo the battleship *Royal Oak* as she lay at

anchor; what was even worse was that the *U-47* then sailed back through the defences unscathed and returned to Germany. As well as being a severe blow to naval prestige, it also indicated some serious weaknesses in the defensive arrangements.

Lessons of the *Graf Spee*

The first significant naval action was the battle of the River Plate, in which three British cruisers drove the German "pocket battleship" *Graf Spee* into Montivideo harbour where her captain scuttled her rather than risk another battle. This result came about because of the fortuitous combination of ships; the *Graf Spee* was of the *Deutschland* class and armoured to withstand shells up to 203mm calibre; the British cruiser *Exeter*, one of the opposing force, had 203-mm guns and had sufficient armour to withstand the 28-cm shells of the *Graf Spee*. This victory caused great public jubilation, but behind the scenes the *Graf Spee*, when examined by British naval observers, produced two surprises. The first was that she was provided with radar for controlling her guns. Radar was, by this time, under development in Britain, the USA and Germany, but each nation had placed a different emphasis on the route which the development took. In Britain, the primary requirement was for radar as a method of detecting aircraft and warning the defences in good time; gun direction, whether for air defence artillery or naval gunnery, came a poor second to this and therefore naval radar was by no means well advanced in 1939. The USA were experimenting with radar for early warning and also for gun direction, but at a relatively slow rate. German development had been instigated by the Naval Radio Research Establishment with both early warning and naval gunfire direction in mind, and by the outbreak of war most German warships had radar fitted. The discovery of this set on the *Graf Spee* gave an impetus to British naval radar development.

The second discovery was that too high a proportion of the British shells had either failed to penetrate armour which, theoretically, they should have done or, if they penetrated, had often failed to detonate. It seemed that British naval shell design had progressed little since the same complaint had been made after Jutland.

The importance of the air came into sharp focus in the Mediterranean. In July 1940, a British force under Admiral Cunningham protecting two convoys met an Italian squadron on similar duty and the two squared away at each other. Within a few moments the *Warspite* scored a direct hit on the Italian battleship *Guilio Cesare* at a range of 23,770m (26,000yd), the Italians turned away under cover of smoke and the British pursued them back to their base. But as they approached the Italian mainland strong forces of bombers appeared and began attacking the British force to such effect that its commander turned about and sailed back out of their range. The hit on the Italian battleship was enough to deter the Italian fleet from trying a head-on battle for some time, but the ability of the Italian bombers to turn back a battle squadron was not overlooked either. From then on convoys through the Mediterranean were constantly harassed by Italian, and later German, aircraft attacks, and not even when the Royal Navy had been reinforced with a new aircraft carrier and with special anti-aircraft cruisers, with radar and heavy air defence armament, were the attacks contained. It soon became apparent that naval forces could no longer operate inside bombing range of enemy bases without the strong fighter cover provided by carriers.

The other side of the coin was seen when Admiral Cunningham mounted an air attack against the Italian naval base at Taranto. Twenty-one old Swordfish biplanes carrying torpedoes flew off the aircraft carrier *Illustrious* and made a low-level attack in two waves. Three torpedoes struck the new Italian battleship *Littorio*, and the battleships *Caio Dulio* and *Conte di Cavour* each took one hit. Two other ships were damaged and only two Swordfish aircraft were lost in the attack.

The *Bismarck* threat
In early 1941, the new German battleship *Bismarck*, accompanied by the heavy cruiser *Prinz Eugen*, made a foray into the North Atlantic. The *Bismarck* was a fast and powerful ship; she, and her sister ship, the *Tirpitz*,

were commissioned in August 1940, and were the largest battleships ever built for the German Navy and the heaviest ships ever completed by any European naval power.

With a displacement of almost 50,000 tons fully laden, armed with eight 38-cm, 12 15-cm and 16 105-mm guns and with 320mm (12⅔in) of armour on the main side belt, they could reach a maximum speed of just over 30 knots and could sail almost 10,000 nautical miles at reduced speed without refuelling. Their potential for mischief meant that the British had to permanently station their best battleships at Scapa Flow in order to be ready to make a countermove if and when these two threats decided to make a move, which meant that other theatres of war had to be neglected. The thought of the *Bismarck* loose across the supply line caused the Royal Navy to react rapidly and despatch the *Hood*, a First World War battle cruiser with 15-inch guns, and the *Prince of*

Wales, a new design fresh from the
dockyard, to deal with the threat.

A patrolling British cruiser in the
Denmark Strait picked up the two
German ships on radar and began
shadowing them, reporting their
position back to the *Hood*. After losing
and then refinding the quarry, the
British force finally met them early in
the morning. Fire was opened at a
range of 23,770m (26,000yd) and the
Prinz Eugen immediately had the range
and within one minute scored a hit on
the *Hood* with a shell from her 8-inch
guns. The *Hood* turned so as to bring
her full broadside to bear, but a few
moments later was struck by a salvo
from the *Bismarck*; the magazines blew
up almost instantaneously and within
four minutes, the *Hood* was gone.

The *Prince of Wales*, closely
following the *Hood*, had to manoeuvre
sharply to avoid the wreckage, and
came under fire from the *Bismarck* at
14,460m (18,000yd) range. Struck by
three 38-cm and four 203-mm shells,

she was forced to turn away under
cover of smoke. But she had managed
to get three 14-inch shell hits on the
Bismarck, two of which made holes
which allowed water to flood into the
ship and also isolated about 1000 tons of
fuel oil and for this reason the Germans
also turned away and the engagement
came to an indecisive end. Since the
cut-off fuel curtailed her cruising range,
and since water was being shipped
through the holes in her hull, the
Bismarck turned to make for St.
Nazaire to seek shelter and repair the
damage. Because of the shell damage
her speed was reduced, she was
shadowed by British cruisers and two
carriers, the *Ark Royal* and the
Victorious, stood across her path. A
force of Swordfish torpedo bombers
from the *Ark Royal* found the *Bismarck*
and two torpedoes struck home; one
jammed the rudder and the other
caused some flooding at the stern; this
slowed her so that two more British
battleships, the *King George V* and the

Okinawa sacrifice Admiral Yamamoto's flagship, the *Yamato* was another case of refusing to believe that the age of battleships was over. At just under 73,000 tons and mounting nine 18in guns, she was the largest battleship ever built and firmly believed by her builders to be unsinkable. What no one had taken into consideration was the possibility of long-range aircraft, which were carrier-based. After seeing no major action all through the war, the *Yamato* was sent as part of a relief force in April 1945 and was attacked in the Van Diemen Strait by US aircraft. As the result of an enormous sustained bombardment, the giant battleship took 20 torpedoes and 17 bombs, sinking in just nine minutes.

Rodney were able to catch her and silence her in a furious gunnery duel. They were, however, unable to sink the *Bismarck*; this was left to cruisers to accomplish with torpedoes once the *Bismarck*'s guns had been silenced. In fact the final coup de grace was done by the crew of the *Bismarck* setting scuttling charges in the engine room.

This battle seemed to confirm what the conservative naval elements had been saying all the time: that air could be useful as an ancillary, but when it came to destruction the battleship was the only sure method. Before long there came a series of events which turned this theory on its head. In December 1941, the Japanese using carrier-based aircraft, attacked the American naval base at Pearl Harbor and decimated the US fleet.

The Pacific theatre

Japan entered the general conflict with a view to gaining possessions, and more particularly a source of much-needed oil, by an expansion southward, to form the so-called "Greater East Asian Co-Prosperity Sphere". If it could manage this without going to war, so much the better, but if war was necessary, then war it would be. The most dangerous enemy appeared to be America; Britain had a relatively small presence in the Pacific and, after the setbacks to British military prowess of 1940 and 1941, the Japanese felt they had little to fear from her. The Japanese Navy began planning their opening strike against Pearl Harbor over a year before it took place, long before the Japanese politicians and soldiers began looking seriously at such a war, and their planning was in large part influenced by the British success against the Italian fleet at Taranto.

December 1941 would be the critical point; the oil stocks would not last much longer, and if a move was going to be

made it had to be made then, and not later. In the summer of 1941, the Army and the political establishment began talking about war and the Navy produced their plan. After much argument, on November 3rd it was approved and the Navy began putting it into effect.

It has long been a joke in military (and naval) circles that the best way to attack a western force is to attack on Sunday morning, when the officers are relaxing with their families and the men are sleeping off the previous night's debauch. The Japanese attacked on a Sunday morning, but for more prosaic reasons; it had to be early in December since the best weather conditions were likely, and Sunday the 7th was selected as being the day when moon conditions were at their best for the final approach to Pearl Harbor.

The attack group consisted of six aircraft carriers carrying 423 aircraft, escorted by two battleships, two heavy cruisers, 16 destroyers and three submarines. Piecemeal, to avoid arousing interest, these ships assembled in remote Tankan Bay in the Kurile Islands. There they took on extra fuel, shallow-water torpedoes and special armour-piercing bombs. Then, preceded by a screen of 27 submarines, on 26th November the force set sail, initially to rendezvous with tankers, then onward to Pearl Harbor, by a route which kept them clear of the most commonly used shipping lanes.

Enroute, by listening to American naval and military radio traffic, the Japanese established that all was normal in Hawaii, and from a Japanese agent-in-place they ascertained that eight American battleships were in harbour. Unfortunately, they discovered, the two American aircraft carriers which they had expected to be there, the *Lexington* and the

Enterprise, were absent; nevertheless, the destruction of the battleships was worth the endeavour, and there was always the possibility that the carriers would, as usual, return to Pearl for the weekend and be there when they struck.

The attack was to be launched in two waves. The first would consist of 140 bombers, accompanied by 50 fighters, and would be launched at 0600 local time from a point 460km (275mi) north of the target. This wave would attack the five known airfields, the seaplane base, the battleships and, if possible, the carriers. The second wave, of 134 bombers accompanied by 36 fighters was to take off at 0700 and make for the same targets in order to take care of anything missed or overlooked by the first wave. All aircraft would return to their carriers, which were being guarded by a patrol of 30 fighters, and the force would then turn for home, pausing only to rendezvous once more with their tankers.

In Pearl Harbor, the US Naval authorities were not in any state of readiness; although code-breakers were hard at work trying to produce some forecast of Japanese intentions, by the time they had anything resembling a clue it was too late. A radar station, one of the few which the Americans had in operation at that time, was operating in a fitful manner; due to a shortage of skilled operators it would be switched on for a time and then switched off. On the morning of 7th December, it had begun operating during the night and was due to close down at 0700. But the truck to take the operators back to barracks was delayed, and the set was kept running, the operator being keen to get all the practice he could. Shortly after 0700 he detected a flight of aircraft approaching; he informed his headquarters who told him that it was nothing to worry about, doubtless a flight of "Flying Fortress" bombers which were being flown in from the USA and which were expected that morning.

The attack, therefore, was a complete surprise. The Japanese pilots had been repeatedly practised on models and plans of Pearl Harbor and needed to waste no time on reconnoitering their targets; they went straight for their assigned objectives,

Pearl Harbor Smoke and flames shroud the sunken USS *West Virginia* as navy launches seek survivors during the raid on Pearl Harbor. Roosevelt's "Day of Infamy" left six battleships and three destroyers sunk and many others badly damaged. It brought the US into the war and led eventually to the defeat of the Axis Powers.

and a few minutes after 0800 dive bombers and torpedo-bombers swooped down on the fleet, while high-level bombers devastated the airfields and destroyed practically every aircraft on them. In "Battleship Row", the mooring in the harbour, five battleships – the *West Virginia*, the *Arizona*, the *Nevada*, the *Oklahoma* and the *California* – were ripped open by torpedoes within minutes. Only the *Maryland* and the *Tennessee*, which were moored to inside berths, and the flagship *Pennsylvania*, in dry dock, escaped the torpedo attack. The American crews responded to the best of their ability, manning anti-aircraft guns and shooting down some of the attackers, while damage control parties attempted to minimize the effects of the bombing. Next came the dive bombers and high-level bombers dropping armour-piercing bombs which sliced through the decks and did immense damage; one tore through several layers of deck to detonate in the magazine of the *Arizona*, totally destroying the ship which sank with 1000 men trapped aboard.

The first wave, having completed its attack, flew off, leaving the American sailors to deal with the wounded and attempt to bring the fires under control. They also managed to man more air-defence guns and restock with ammunition, so that when the second wave appeared shortly after 0900 they met with a much hotter reception. Nevertheless, they managed to

damage the *Pennsylvania* and two destroyers sharing the dry dock and also caused the battleship *Nevada*, which had, amazingly, managed to get under way and was making for the open sea, to beach itself.

Pearl Harbor aftermath

By 1000 it was all over and the Japanese planes were on their way back to their carriers. Their success was so overwhelming that the commander of the air group, Commander Mitsui Fuchida, urged Admiral Nagumo, commanding the attack force, to mount a third raid. Nagumo, however, was a cautious man and considered that they had been fortunate in achieving as much success as they already had, and that a third attack might be taking the pitcher to the well once too often. This was fortunate for the Americans, since had a third attack been mounted it might well have caught the aircraft carrier *Enterprise*, returning from her exercises, and might well have caused immense damage to the fleet repair facilities and oil storage tanks in Pearl Harbor, neither of which had been damaged in the first two attacks. As it was, for the loss of 29 aircraft, the Japanese had effectively neutralized the entire battleship force of the US Pacific Fleet.

Immediately after this the Japanese launched an attack against Singapore, the British naval base at the tip of the Malayan Peninsula. The battleship *Prince of Wales* and the battle cruiser

Yorktown Another American carrier that probably paid the penalty of its open-hangar construction, thereby creating difficulties in fire control. On 4 June 1942, during the battle of Midway, the carrier came under bomb attack from the air and torpedo attack from Japanese submarines. Two of the torpedoes struck the American ship and she was soon blazing fiercely. Two days later she sank.

Repulse were there, and Admiral Phillips, the British Commander-in-Chief called for shore-based fighter cover and set forth to attack the Japanese ships supporting the invasion. The next day Phillips was bluntly told that no fighters were available and that the Japanese were believed to have strong bomber forces in the area. Already committed, he carried on but upon being spotted by a Japanese reconnaissance aircraft Phillips thought it wiser to turn back rather than risk his ships against bombers when he had no adequate means of defence. En route to Singapore he received information – which was later found to be incorrect – that the Japanese were making fresh landings close to Singapore. He therefore turned aside to investigate, was again spotted by reconnaissance aircraft, and at 1107 on the morning of December 10th came under attack from Japanese bombers and torpedo-carrying aircraft sent from land bases in French Indo-China. The first attack struck the *Repulse* with a 500lb bomb, then the torpedo-bombers swept in at low level. The *Prince of Wales* was hit twice, damaging her rudder and propellers. A second torpedo strike hit the *Prince of Wales* four times and the *Repulse* five. The *Repulse* eventually sank, about one and a half hours after the attacks had begun. the *Prince of Wales* began listing badly, and the destroyer *Express* came alongside, at considerable risk, to take off 1500 of the battleship's crew. Then, at 1320, the

Prince of Wales rolled over on her port side and sank, Admiral Phillips and Captain Leach, the battleship's captain, standing on the bridge as she went under. The entire affair was over inside two and a half hours.

In a matter of a few days the pre-eminence of naval air power had been underscored and the battleship had been made obsolete. From that time onwards the significant naval engagements were done with air power rather than gun power. The first of these came in May 1942, when two American task forces each with an aircraft carrier were sent to intercept a Japanese force intent upon putting troops ashore in New Guinea. For the first time a naval battle was fought in which neither side sighted the other; it was entirely fought by carrier-based aircraft. Each force lost one carrier, but the Japanese expedition was severely damaged and the landing was prevented.

Midway turning point
A few weeks later came one of the most important battles of the Second World War, when a strong Japanese force of seven battleships, four carriers and 270 aircraft sailed east to support a Japanese invasion of the island of Midway. By this time the Americans had broken the Japanese naval code and were fully aware of what was in train; they positioned three carriers, and by superlative tactical timing struck against the Japanese while most of their aircraft were on the carriers refuelling. Three Japanese carriers were put out of action and the fourth succumbed to another attack on the following day. Bereft of his air support, the Japanese admiral turned his battleships about and the Battle of Midway was over.

This had a considerable effect on the Japanese. They were in the process of building, in the closest secrecy, three monster battleships of the *Yamato* class, displacing over 70,000 tons, mounting nine 18-inch guns and protected by 41cm of armour and yet capable of 27 knots. Now the building of the third of these, the *Shinano*, was stopped and the design changed to convert it into a massive aircraft carrier, and two battleships were withdrawn from the fleet to be similarly converted. The three superships eventually saw brief action; the battleship *Musashi* was sunk in the Battle of Leyte Gulf, having taken 20 torpedoes and 17 bombs; the battleship

Yamato was part of a suicidal attack on Okinawa in the closing days of the war and was sunk after three hours of air attack; and the supercarrier *Shinano* was caught on the second day of her maiden voyage and sunk by four torpedoes from the US submarine *Archerfish*.

Wolf pack

While aviation was showing its superiority in the Pacific, the Atlantic almost became the preserve of the German submarine. Germany had been forbidden submarines under the terms of the Versailles Treaty, but managed to keep its designers occupied until Hitler, in 1934, ordered construction of U-boats to begin once more. By the outbreak of war, 65 U-boats had been built and production facilities were ready for an immediate increase. But all U-boats had to run the gauntlet of British patrols in the North Sea, and thus their effectiveness was greatly reduced. Once France fell, and the French naval bases on the Atlantic coast were available to the U-boat force, the picture changed dramatically and from August 1940, British mercantile losses in the Atlantic increased sharply. Seeing this opportunity, Germany stepped up its submarine building programme; 54 were launched in 1940, 202 in 1941 and 238 in 1942, so that building was faster than Allied sinkings.

In 1941, Admiral Doenitz introduced the concept of the "wolf pack", largely because the expansion of U-boat commissioning had outstripped the training of crews and there was a shortage of U-boat commanders capable of operating effectively on lone patrols. By grouping the boats into packs and concentrating attacks on convoys at night, the rate of exchange – Allied ships sunk for U-boats sunk – was extremely favourable to the Germans. Any U-boat which spotted a convoy would signal its location to base, shadow the convoy, and wait until more U-boats had been guided to the spot before launching the mass attack. Night attacks could be made on the surface, and many terrible battles were fought with scores of ships sunk and very few U-boats damaged.

When the United States entered the war, Britain hoped that this would reduce the U-boats' toll, but, in fact, things got worse. The Americans were sceptical about the danger, and it was not until U-boats began sinking ships within sight of the American east coast that the lesson was driven home. From then on anti-submarine warfare took on a major importance: new types of ship – the corvette – designed primarily for finding and destroying submarines; new types of improved sonic detector, now almost universally known by the American term Sonar rather than the original British term Asdic; new types of depth charge and anti-submarine bomb were developed; and, most important of all, the use of centimetric radar was introduced into the search. This radar was sensitive enough to pick up the periscope of a submerged U-boat; moreover, it could detect a U-boat cruising on the surface through cloud, so that the first intimation the submariners had was when the attacking bomber swooped out of the clouds almost directly overhead and began bombing or firing rockets which could penetrate the submarine hull. By the middle of 1943, the U-boat, while still dangerous, was no longer the menace it had been in 1941-42.

By way of counterattack, the German submarine engineers produced a number of new and ingenious devices. They first produced a homing torpedo, which relied upon the sound of a ship's engines to attract it; this was followed by the "Snorkel", a tube which, protruding above the surface, allowed the submerged U-boat to run on its diesel engines, obviating the need to cruise on the surface while recharging its electric batteries. Two new designs of U-boat were also prepared: the "Type 21 Elektro", which used an enlarged battery system to allow bursts of high underwater speed; and the Walther which used a hydrogen peroxide propulsion system. But the usual German administrative inefficiency wasted time and effort on experiments with the Walther motor instead of putting the simpler and equally effective Type 21 into production. As a result the war ended with only three Type 21 and no Walther boats in service.

Less well-known but probably as important to the Allies as the Atlantic U-boat battle was to the Germans, was the performance of American submarines in the Pacific. They were outstanding as reconnaissance units, giving much important and timely information about movements of the Japanese fleet, but as destructive devices they were of immense value in virtually strangling the Japanese

economy. Their first priority was
Japanese aircraft carriers; their second
priority was oil tankers, and after that
they could sink anything they found.
Operating usually in "packs" of three,
they took a heavy toll of Japanese
merchant shipping, even penetrating
into the Inland Sea, and reduced the
Japanese to using sailing ships and small
coasters, hugging the shallow coastal
waters in the hope of escaping torpedo
attack.

The Japanese were unimaginative in
their use of submarines; their martial

ardour led the submarine captains to
ignore merchant ships in the hope of
finding warships to attack. They were
equipped with one of the best
torpedoes of the war, combining long
range and high speed, but apart from
that their equipment was
unremarkable. They managed to sink
several American ships, notably the
carriers *Yorktown* and *Wasp*, but their
failure to deploy their weight against
supply lines meant that their efforts did
not really discommode the American
forces in the Pacific to any extent.

The U-boat war The tanker
Fern burns garishly after
being torpedoed by the
German U-boat *U99*. This U-
boat met her match on 17
March 1941, when HMS
Walker smothered her with
depth-charges. As the hull
split the vessel began to sink,
but a few crew, including her
captain, managed to get out
of the conning tower.

THE WOLF PACK

As more and more submarines emerged from Germany's shipyards from 1940 onwards, Grand Admiral Doenitz devised new tactics to suit the needs of his expanding U-boat fleet. He believed that by deploying submarines in massed groups – he christened these groups "wolf packs" – he could beat the convoy system and bring Britain to its knees.

To locate his targets, Doenitz developed a surface scouting system, augmented by long-range air reconnaissance. Once an individual U-boat had made contact with a convoy, Doenitz's strict instructions were that it was not to attack. Instead, it shadowed the convoy, signalling course and speed to German naval headquarters, who then directed other submarines in the area in for the kill. To maximize effectiveness, the "wolf packs" attacked on the surface at close range – night after night, if necessary, until the convoy had been decimated.

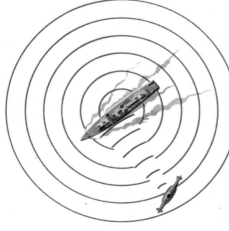

Hunter and hunted
One of Britain's most closely guarded secrets at the start of the Second World War was the submarine detection system known as Asdic. Sound waves were transmitted in pulses by a transmitter located beneath the keel. When these literally "hit" a submerged submarine, the waves bounced back, changing the signal. A destroyer equipped with this device could therefore plot a submarine's depth and course after initial detection and, so it was believed, be almost certain of making a kill. However, the system, as initially introduced, was imperfect. It could not detect a submarine on the surface, because the echoes the system relied on merged with those created by the waves; in rough weather, the transmitter beneath the destroyer's keel was inevitably exposed intermittently, with confused and distorted echoes as the result; and the echoes could not penetrate cold thermal layers, which wily U-boat commanders soon learned to use to conceal their presence.

Convoy The concept of a group of merchant ships accompanied by warships goes back at least to Napoleon and was seen as the answer to protection of lone merchantmen in the Atlantic from the marauding submarines to which they were so vulnerable. The convoys were coded and each was co-ordinated by a senior naval officer who dictated strategy in case of threat or attack. Germany's answer to this method of defence was the Wolf Pack, which attacked the convoys under the cover of night.

Depth charge This was a cannister of HE cordite with a detonator that could be set to explode the main charge at various depths. The pressure waves created, if close enough, would split a U-boat's hull open. It was hurled from the vessel by a Thorneycroft "Thrower" by means of a 2lb charge. Later improvement was the Hedgehog, which threw clusters of 24 contact-fuzed depth charges up to 230m (250yd).

Type VIIB There were over 600 of these U-boats built during World War II. They could carry 14 torpedoes and had a surface speed of 17 knots and an underwater speed of 7.5 knots. Maximum depth, sometimes exceeded in extreme emergency, was 200m (660yd). In addition, an 88mm gun could be fitted to the foredeck for anti-shipping or, alternatively twin and quadruple 20mm guns, for anti-aircraft fire.

CHANGING CONVENTIONS

*The missile strikes and the carrier
reigns supreme*

By the end of World War II, the aircraft carrier was firmly established as the capital ship, with the battleship relegated to the role of protector to the carrier. The battleships were retained for some years but, eventually, as they reached the point of requiring overhaul, most were scrapped. The utility of the big gun was also called into question with the arrival of guided missiles which could be fired from a ship and which could strike with unprecedented accuracy at targets several scores or even hundreds of miles away. This was brought into sharp focus in 1967, when an Egyptian patrol boat, blockaded in harbour at Port Said by an Israeli force, fired a Soviet Styx missile which struck and sank the Israeli destroyer *Eilat* out at sea. This incident, which resulted in a heavily armed and armoured conventional warship being sent to the bottom by a lightweight patrol boat which had not even bothered to cast off from the dockside, set the world's navies on their heels and led to a great deal of tactical and strategic re-thinking.

The other major strategic upheaval came with the development of nuclear-powered submarines which were, for the first time, true submarines, capable of staying underwater for weeks or months on end. Two basic types have evolved, firstly the missile-carrier, armed with guided missiles which can be launched from underwater. This technique had been pioneered by the Germans in experiments carried out in the Baltic during 1944, though they never brought the idea to perfection. It was followed up by the Soviets and the Americans, who both brought missile-launching boats into service in the early 1960s. The missiles carried vary. Some are cruise missiles with ranges of about 300 nautical miles, or 555km, and are intended for use as fleet bombardment weapons; others are strategic missiles with ranges of several thousand miles, and these are invariably nuclear weapons which are deployed for their deterrent effect.

Fast attack craft Most modern navies have numbers of these nimble, high-speed patrol/attack vessels. This one, a German *Pelican*, was built in 1974. It can do 30 knots, is armed with an 80mm Bofors and a 76mm gun, but its main hitting power comes from the four Exocet SSM missiles which are capable of destroying major warships.

Nuclear submarines A Royal Navy submarine of the *Swiftsure* class. These hunter/killer vessels are powered by a pressurized water-cooled nuclear reactor which drives 15,000 shaft horsepower steam turbines. Today's battleships are these manacing craft, the nuclear-weapon carrying versions being able to conduct global warfare and destroy major urban centres and distant military installations from thousands of miles away.

The second nuclear submarine is the "attack" or "hunter-killer" submarine, intended to hunt and destroy other naval vessels, both surface and submarine. The immense power and extremely complex hull shape of these boats gives them a speed and manoeuvrability denied to earlier boats and makes them extremely difficult to catch by surface vessels, so that a distinct new school of naval warfare, that of submarine against submarine in the depths of the ocean, has developed.

The nuclear submarine, with higher speeds and almost silent movement, led to enormous efforts being made in methods of detection and destruction. Sonar has been greatly improved since the Second World War and other forms of detection – using the submarine's magnetic field to alert a patrolling aircraft, laying acoustic detectors on the seabed and several other systems - have been perfected and deployed.

The most significant feature of the postwar years has been the resurgence of the Soviet fleet. In 1945, it was virtually non-existent, but since that time it has been expanded until it now outnumbers every other fleet in the world. Its principal strength lies in aircraft carriers and missile-carrying submarines, but it has not neglected conventional cruisers and destroyers, minelayers and submarine hunters.

Close encounters

From time to time, there have been calls made on naval forces which have sometimes upset the currently-accepted theories. When the United States intervened in Vietnam, for example, it was felt that naval forces employing shore bombardment could be a useful method of interdicting the North Vietnamese supply lines. Unfortunately, the US Navy no longer had any ships capable of carrying out such a bombardment, having placed all their reliance upon guided missiles. It was necessary to remove obsolescent cruisers from preservation, recommission them and send them out to exercise their guns, a process which took some time. This led to much research being done on new and compact designs of automatic-loading guns which provide the gun-power of the old-time battleship but which demand much less space in which to install them. Nevertheless, within the past few years the US Navy has recommissioned mothballed battleships and routinely uses them, notably in their Sixth Fleet, which patrols the Mediterranean.

In 1982, in the British campaign to re-take the Falkland Islands from the Argentine occupying force, the power of aviation to influence events was made obvious once more. Only the fact that the Argentine aircraft were shore-based and operating virtually at the extreme edge of their endurance and could thus only make short attacks, saved the Royal Navy from disaster. Moreover, the power of the sea-skimming missile was amply demonstrated when Argentine forces used French Exocet missiles to sink HMS *Sheffield* and also the supply ship *Atlantic Conveyor*.

As ever, sea power in the 1980s revolves around two requirements: the protection of trade and the projection of power. In the past 10 years there have been innumerable examples of both these aspects of sea power being employed, albeit on a small scale. From the sending of a warship three times to

Belize in order to deter the Guatemalan government from a rash escapade, to the Icelandic use of gunboats to achieve their claimed fishing rights, and to the Chinese taking of the Paracel Islands, there have been enough examples to prove that in many cases minimal power, in the form of naval power, is all that is required to show a nation's interest and promise more severe measures if the warning goes unheeded. It is now fairly obvious that the British withdrawal of their patrol vessel from the Antarctic area was enough of a disclaimer to encourage the Argentines in their abortive invasion of the Falklands.

The purposes of sea power have therefore not changed fundamentally since the 19th century. The emphasis may have changed, trade having become even more widespread and important and the projection of power a secondary requirement. The present tendency is for polarization into superpowers; it is perhaps for discussion whether naval alliances between the smaller nations might not, in the long run, provide a useful balance to these potent weapons.

HMS *Sheffield* ablaze After having been hit by an Exocet missile, the *Sheffield* lies mortally wounded. The fierceness of the fire was in some measure due to the aluminium used in the ship's structure, a material selected as a weight-saving measure. The sinking of this Type-42 guided-missile-armed warship and others revealed the vulnerability of warships of this kind to missile attack.

US giants America has put much faith in her huge fleet of aircraft carriers. Propulsion is achieved from power supplied by two reactors driving sets of steam turbines. The strike availability of the 90-plus aircraft, including helicopters, is formidable. However, doubt has been expressed about the vulnerability of such a hugë bulk in the face of determined and massed missile attack.

Russian sea power The *Kirov*, a 25,000-ton nuclear-powered battle cruiser, is a very sophisticated warship. She and her sister ships would constitute very powerful task forces in the event of any major conflict. They can hit hard with long-range missiles and conventional armament, which consists of two 100mm and eight 30mm guns.

AIR POWER

The sky emerges as a battlefield and a new service comes into action

Air warfare might be said to have its beginnings in Napoleon's balloon corps at the end of the late 18th century and its infancy in the various schemes for using balloons and airships for reconnaissance which were put forward in the 19th century. The actual use of aircraft for military purposes began in a tentative fashion in 1911 and was accelerated during the First World War.

Since then, military minds have been occupied in adapting the third dimension to warfare, and with hindsight, it is apparent that for much of the time they have failed to do so adequately or efficiently. This is not to deny the heroism, the loyalty, the sense of duty of the millions of airmen who have attempted to follow their orders and project their country's power by means of aerial warfare, nor to denigrate the sacrifice of the hundreds of thousands who have died in the process. What it does deny is the cogency and the accuracy of the policies and theories which drove them. For much of its existence air power has fallen short of its promise and failed to reach its full potential.

War from above

The Italian Army were the first to embrace the field of military aviation. An Army Aeronautical Service was formed in 1884, and balloons were used for reconnaissance purposes during the Eritrean War of 1887/88. In 1911, five aircraft and two small airships were employed in the army manoeuvres in Libya with moderate success, and when war broke out between Turkey and Italy later that year aircraft were used for reconnaissance. Aircraft, balloons and airships were sent to Tripoli and air operations began late in

October. One of the first problems to arise was simply the question of the aviators knowing where they were; the maps were poor, and the desert devoid of prominent landmarks, with the result that the Italian Army began experimenting with aerial photography in order to improve their knowledge of the ground and their maps. The next problem was that of communication; the aviators were asked to observe artillery fire, which they managed to do, but when it came to instructing the gunners to make corrections they were incapable of communicating to any great effect. From observation, the air arm moved to offensive action, throwing hand grenades and home-made bombs over the side of the aircraft at likely targets. Almost immediately came a complaint from the Turks that a hospital had been a target.

The Turks, without any air arm, were forced on to the defensive and retaliated by rifle and machine gun fire. Since the Italian aviators could not fly very high, these weapons had some effect; one Italian aircraft outside Tripoli was hit seven times by rifle fire while flying at 2500 feet, though neither the aircraft nor the pilot was disabled. One luckless flyer had an engine failure behind enemy lines and was captured, though there appears to be no record of his subsequent fate; with the reputation the Turks had in those days it was probably grim.

The Italians continued their campaign with success, until in October 1912, with the outbreak of the Balkan War, the Turks sued for peace, fearful that they would have problems in the Balkans and anxious to cut their losses. It cannot be said that air power had a decisive effect in the Italo-Turkish War, but there was certainly advantage to be

Aerial observation Balloons began to be used for military reconnaissance early in the 19th century, a use that continued into World War I. Here we see Russians in a captive balloon telephoning details of the fall of shells as the Japanese Fleet closes in on Port Arthur, in 1904. It is a curious fact that aircraft continued to be viewed in this somewhat subsidiary role and that its true military potential – and that of the sky as a new theatre of action – did not begin to be appreciated until well into World War I.

had from the employment of aircraft and most of the major powers had watched their progress with some interest.

In 1912, the North African desert was the arena for further military aviation, when the French Army brought aircraft into their sporadic war against the Moroccan tribes. They were entirely for reconnaissance and observation, but nevertheless two aviators were wounded when they flew too low over a hilltop occupied by armed tribesmen.

The Balkan War, which had caused Turkey to break off its conflict with Italy, broke out in October 1912. Briefly, Bulgaria, Serbia, Greece and Montenegro formed an alliance (the "Balkan League") with the object of liberating Macedonia from Turkish rule. Its importance here is simply that the Bulgarians used a number of aircraft, flown by private owners anxious to assist the army; they were usually rewarded by the grant of a commission in either the Greek or Bulgarian armies, though some appear to have retained civilian status. Their role was entirely that of reconnaissance and observation. One pilot, named Constantin, was making an aerial study of the Turkish lines at Chataja was struck by a rifle bullet from the ground and killed. He was found dead beside his crashed aircraft, which had more bullet holes in its wings and fuselage. The unfortunate Constantin thus has the melancholy distinction of being the first aviator to be killed by anti-aircraft fire.

By now other countries had begun to examine the idea of military aviation. On 1 August 1907, the US Signal Corps established its "Aeronautical Division", responsible for "balloons, air machines and kindred subjects", and it received

its first aeroplane in 1909. In France there were many army officers enthusiastic about the new technology, but the authorities remained unimpressed, General Foch observing that "Aviation is good for sport, but for the army it is useless". Germany set up military and naval aviation corps, but seemed to be uncertain as to what they were to be used for; the army corps was under the control of the Inspector General of Military Transport, while the naval service concentrated its attention on the airship.

Airships

The most famous name in airships is, of course, that of Count Ferdinand von Zeppelin. He served with the Union army in the American Civil War, and it may be that he saw balloons in use there. He returned to Germany and fought in the wars of 1866 and 1870 and, after retiring from military service, devoted the remainder of his life to the development of airships. He formed a company in 1899 and began experiments until in 1906 he made a successful flight of 60 miles in two hours. This attracted the attention of the German government which gave the company financial assistance, and both the army and navy then began to show an interest in the Zeppelin airship.

In Britain the year 1911 saw the formation of the Air Battalion of the Royal Engineers, with a company of airships, one of man-lifting kites, one of balloons and one of aircraft. In the following year the Royal Flying Corps was formed as a joint service, with Naval and Military wings, and a Central Flying School was set up on Salisbury Plain. The commander of this school was a naval captain, and his Chief instructor was a Major H. M. Trenchard of the Royal Scots Fusiliers. But this apparently sensible organization did not last for long, since there was a basic difference of opinion between the army and the navy; so far as the army were concerned the task of aviation was reconnaissance, but the view of the navy was that "The real key to the situation will be found to lie in a vigorous and offensive attack on the enemy's airsheds and on his aircraft before they reach these shores...." Since the army felt that this was hardly their business, in July 1914 the Air Wing became the Royal Naval Air Service, and the RFC reverted to being simply another corps of the army.

WORLD WAR I

Aeroplanes carry the war into the clouds

By 1914 there were two basic types of aeroplane, the "tractor" and the "pusher"; the tractor had an elongated fuselage with the engine in the front and the pilot seated behind it, and the propellor pulled it through the air. The pusher had a short, bathtub-like fuselage with the pilot in front and the engine behind him, its tail being supported on a framework that allowed the propellor to function and thus push the machine along. The tractor type had a better aerodynamic shape and thus gave a better performance, but the pusher was also popular because of the excellent view to the front. Both types of machine were built as monoplanes and biplanes (the former having the advantage of speed and agility, but the latter being stronger and more resistant to sudden manoeuvres and hard landings. Indeed, monoplanes acquired a reputation for fragility, to such an extent that, in 1912, the RFC ruled that monoplanes were unacceptable as military machines.

There was as much divergence of opinion on the matter of engines; the petrol engine of the period was a cumbersome device by our standards, and therefore the provision of a powerful engine which was light enough to be used in these early aircraft was something of a technical problem. The Germans, because of their relatively advanced automobile industry, had some sound watercooled engines available, made by Daimler, Benz and Opel. The French, being the first European nation to take to the air, had

evolved some flimsy aircraft that demanded light engines to go with them, and most of their faith was pinned on the Gnôme-Rhône rotary engine. This long-forgotten device worked totally differently to any other engine in that it had a central, fixed crankshaft around which the remainder of the engine – the crankcase and the radially-arranged cylinders – revolved, taking the propeller with it. Though delicate and temperamental, this engine developed 80 horsepower for a very light weight.

Several of the first military aircraft were no more than civil machines co-opted into service. Thus the German Taube had been developed in 1910 as a sporting monoplane but was immediately taken into use by the

BE-2 One the first military aircraft flown by the new Royal Flying Corps, the BE-2 soon became obsolete. In spite of its four-bladed propeller, which gave more "bite", the BE-2 could manage only about 70mph and was shot down in numbers high enough to discourage its continued use. Ten of Baron von Richthofen's 80 victories were against BE-2s. Amazingly, at that time, parachutes were forbidden because it was felt that such an avenue of escape could lead to cowardice.

Popular Tabloid A 1914 Sopwith Tabloid. Controls were basic and instruments minimal. The skids in front of the wheels prevented the propeller hitting the ground on take-off and landing. The aircraft weighed only 490kg (1080lb) and carried two 20lb bombs, which would be lobbed manually over the side of the cockpit. Forward-firing guns were mounted once the problem of avoiding shooting off the propeller was solved in 1915.

Germans on the outbreak of war. This was a graceful machine with swept-back wingtips, a design popular at that time, since it gave considerable stability in flight. Several of these aircraft were used successfully for reconnaissance on the Eastern Front, giving vital warning of Russian movements, and one flew from the Marne front to Paris and dropped several hand grenades, the first bombing attack on a major city. Similarly the French commandeered a number of Bleriot monoplanes for use as scouting machines.

The British at least had some "purpose-designed" machines at the outbreak of war; the first purely military aircraft was the BE2 (for Bleriot Experimental, though the design owed nothing to Bleriot), a tractor biplane designed by Geoffrey de Havilland and F.M. Green at the Royal Aircraft Factory at Farnborough in 1911. These were adopted as reconnaissance and bombing machines but carried no offensive armament. In 1912, the Admiralty had advertised for an aircraft capable of carrying a machine gun, the result of which was the Vickers FB-5, popularly called the "Gunbus". A biplane pusher, it carried an observer in the nose armed with a Lewis gun.

First steps
As soon as war broke out in 1914, an RNAS squadron was flown to Dunkirk and began planning offensive operations. An advanced base was set up close to Antwerp, and on 8 October Lieutenant Marix of the Royal Navy flew a single-seat Sopwith Tabloid biplane to attack the German airship base near Düsseldorf. He achieved two hits with 20lb bombs on the main airship shed, destroying it and Zeppelin Z-9, which was inside the hangar. Unfortunately, the same day saw Antwerp evacuated in the face of the advancing German Army, which meant that the advanced base was no longer available (the base at Dunkirk was too far from Düsseldorf for the range of the available aircraft). However, managing to persuade the French of their need, the Royal Naval Air Service were given permission to use a French airfield near Belfort, from which they flew across the Black Forest to strike the Zeppelin factory at Friedrichshafen on Lake Constance. Using three Avro 504 biplanes, the raid destroyed one Zeppelin and also the gas-generating plant.

The Royal Flying Corps had about 55 aircraft in service when war broke out, mostly of the BE2 type, and the four squadrons were immediately flown tto Belgium and France to support the operations of the army. RFC observers first showed their importance in the battle of Mons, where they were able to give accurate and timely reports of the

The "Gunbus" The Vickers FB-5 *(top)* placed the observer in front of the pilot, thus giving him a good field of view that was unobstructed by the wires and struts that held these aircraft together. The observer was also the gunner, and he operated the air-cooled Lewis machine gun while standing. Based on the Avro 500 "racing" biplane of 1913, the 504 *(above)* saw action in the first year of World War I. But it soon became obsolete as an operational aircraft and developed into a valuable training machine, due to its good behaviour in the air while suffering the usual maltreatment offered by trainee pilots. At least 8000 were built between 1914-18 and the trainer version remained in RAF service until 1933.

Voisine bomber Gabriel and Charles Voisine were French aircraft designers who established the classic "pusher" biplane. From early models such as the "Bird of Passage" of 1909, they developed a number of similar but more airworthy machines such as this bomber which carried out raids in 1918.

movement of the German Army towards the British positions, and also to report on the development of a flanking movement by the Germans at Tournai. French aviators were also instrumental in discovering von Kluck's movements against their own army and it was their reports which enabled Gallieni to make his countermove, leading to the battle of the Marne and the saving of Paris.

The Germans pioneered the use of aircraft to spot for artillery, using a primitive signalling system which, mostly, relied on flying over the battery and dropping a written message. This primitive system was effective enough for the Germans to place their shrapnel fire over the heads of Allied troops, and it was this stimulus which led two RFC pilots, Lieutenant Strange and Lieutenant Penn-Gaskell, to take to the air on 22 August with a Lewis gun and take a few shots at a German observation aircraft at a height of 5000 feet. They drove the observer off, without doing him any damage, landed and reported their feat, but they were given scant encouragement to repeat it; the general opinion was that they might well be starting something they would later regret.

As early as June 1912 a test had been carried out in the USA of using a machine gun on an aircraft to attack the ground. A Type B Wright pusher machine had been armed with a Lewis machine gun and with a two-man crew, Lieutenant Milling flying the aircraft and Captain Chandler balancing the machine gun on his foot-rest, a cloth target 1.8 by 2.1m (6 by 7ft) was attacked from a height of 250 feet. The gun's magazine held only 47 rounds, and on examination the cloth was found to have five bullet-holes in it, while the ground around it was scarred by other bullets. In

December of the same year a further demonstration of the Lewis gun took place in Belgium. But in spite of this the authorities felt that the passive role was the proper one for military aircraft.

Nevertheless, pilots began arming themselves with whatever was available; rifles, shotguns, even pistols were taken into the air and discharged, though with little effect. The basic problem was that the aircraft of both sides were slow, with top speeds of about 60 mph, and neither had sufficient advantage of speed or manoeuvrability over the other to make a decision possible. One turned away as soon as an enemy was sighted, and it was practically impossible for the enemy to catch up. Discharging firearms at long range was little more than a gesture.

French tactical shift
The French transferred their aggressive spirit from the ground to the air and set about bombing "strategic" targets behind the German lines. Using Voisin and Farman pushers and Caudron tractor two-seaters they mounted raids from a base near Dunkirk against factories and railway junctions, using 75mm and 155mm artillery shells fitted with fins and simple impact fuzes. The Germans were also examining the possibilities of bombing; as early as November 1914 the *Brieftauben Abteilung Ostende Nr 1* (Ostend Carrier Pigeon Detachment No. 1) was formed. This title disguised a squadron of bombing aircraft that was to be based near Calais and from there make attacks on England, but the battle of the Marne ruined that idea. The German advance failed to reach Calais, and the Carrier Pigeon Squadron was moved to Metz in the spring of 1915 to become a normal army supporting squadron.

As a result of these bombing attacks, thoughts began to turn to the use of scouting aircraft armed with machine guns to deter the bombers, and two-seater aircraft with "free" machine guns became the standard. (A "free" machine gun is one which can be manipulated freely in any direction by a gunner; a "fixed" machine gun is one which is built into the aircraft structure and can only be aimed by aiming the entire aircraft.) These two-seaters could be pushers, with the gunner in the front of the fuselage, commanding a wide arc forward; or tractors, with the gunner behind the pilot, commanding the rear. There were arguments on

Boy's Own **version** This is how a magazine of the day saw air combat. What appears to be half a pilot is flying a Morane-Saulnier monoplane fighter with a standing gunner firing at a German Taube, designed by Doktor Igo Etrich. The gunsmoke would be effectively blinding the pilot of the British machine who would not be able to manoeuvre into a killing attitude.

both sides, but eventually the tractor became the standard, since it could protect the vulnerable rear of the aircraft. In due course, fixed machine guns were adopted to cover the forward aspect.

The difficulty with forward-firing machine guns was the spinning propeller, so the first solution was to place the gun on the upper wing of a biplane, so that it fired outside the propeller arc. Since these early guns were generally magazine-fed, this meant that there was only a limited amount of firing possible before the pilot had to stand up and change magazines, a somewhat fraught proceeding in the middle of an aerial battle. The early Lewis used a 47-round magazine, but representations from the airmen led to the development of a 96-round version. Even so, changes were too frequent for comfort, and they could be extremely hazardous; there is one legendary exploit of a flyer who lost control of his aircraft in the middle of the operation and found himself hanging from the strap of the Lewis magazine as the aircraft rolled above him. Fortunately, it continued its roll and he was able to regain the cockpit.

Mounting a gun or guns above the engine, in front of the pilot where he could reach them to correct stoppages, was the ideal. The first attempt to fire through the propeller arc was made by

the French who simply plated the wooden propeller with steel at the area where bullets would strike; firing through the propeller arc now meant that a proportion of the bullets would pass through, while a small number would strike the steel plates and be deflected without damaging the propeller blade. Shortly after this the Dutch designer Fokker developed a cam-actuated device for the German air service, which, by means of a cable to the gun trigger, fired the gun only when the propeller blade was clear of the line of fire. Finally the Allies developed the "Constantinesco synchroniser", a hydraulic pump which did the same thing rather more reliably; once these devices were perfected the use of twin forward-firing machine guns became standard.

By the middle of 1915, air warfare was beginning to take shape. On both sides, the armies were demanding observation and reconnaissance, while their opponents were sending up fighter aircraft to attack them and so deny them the information. The solution was to protect the reconnaissance machines with fighters, so that the basic tactic which emerged was for fighters to attack fighters in order to engage their attention, while more fighters attacked the reconnaissance machines. This began as a free-for-all but, by mid 1916, it had become more formal, with the opposing forces developing combat formations designed to offer all-round protection by means of the free guns and attacking ability from the fixed synchronized guns.

Sopwith Camel This squat, pugnacious airplane was acknowledged as the "supreme fighter" at the end of World War I, having shot down 1294 enemy aircraft. It went into action for the first time as the Battle of Ypres opened in July 1917. The first squadrons to receive the Camel were units of the Royal Naval Air Service, but it soon appeared in RFC markings.

THE BEGINNING OF AIR BOMBING

The air war comes to the factories and cities

By 1917 the organization of air services had been compartmentalized; instead of any aircraft being put to any task, by this time specific types had been developed fighters, bombers, reconnaissance machines – and they were organixed in squadrons according to their role. The German Air Force (formed as a separate force in October 1916) developed "circuses" of fighter aircraft which could be moved around the front to wherever their services were required.

This represented what might be now called the "tactical" side of aviation; actions in direct support of the field armies. The other side, now known as the "strategic" side – actions against the enemy's bases and manufacturing capability – was also being pursued away from the line of combat in Flanders. The German Army's intention was to use Zeppelins to bomb England, since these had the duration and weight-carrying capacity to make worthwhile bombing expeditions possible. But technical problems delayed the preparation of this offensive, and it was an aeroplane which made the first strategic attack.

First bomb use
On 21 December 1914, a German aircraft appeared off Dover harbour and dropped two bombs into the sea just off the Admiralty Pier, turned around and flew back to Belgium, having done no damage. Three days later another aircraft appeared and dropped a single bomb into an empty field near Dover Castle. Finally, on Christmas Day 1914, a single Albatross aircraft of the German Army flew up the River Thames. It was fired on by a gun in Sheerness Dockyard, but continued upriver undamaged. Three aircraft of the RFC took off from Eastchurch aerodrome, and three RNAS machines from the Isle of Grain, and these caught up with the intruder close to Erith, whereupon the Albatross turned about and began to fly back downriver. Pursued by the British machines, he was fired at by a gun in Cliffe Fort. By this time the German pilot obviously felt he had done enough, and he played his final card by dropping two bombs which landed close to Cliffe railway station. Having thus relieved himself of weight he was able to pull away from his pursuers and escaped back to Belgium unscathed.

The German Navy also operated Zeppelins, and it was these which made the first airship attack on England, on 19 January 1915. Of the three which set out, one, L6, developed engine trouble over the North Sea and turned back, but the other two, L3 and L4, managed to reach the coast. L3 flew south and dropped nine bombs on Great Yarmouth, while L4 went north, dropped a few bombs at random on or near villages, and finally arrived over King's Lynn. Seeing lights, and thinking

Albatross The German Air Force's reply to the Allied superiority in the air during World War I, the Albatross, had one very bad habit: in a high speed dive it tended to lose its wings. It had a 180 or 200hp Mercedes DIIIa engine. The first DVa variant was based on an earlier DIII model and by 1918 over 1000 Albatrosses were flying with operational units, armed with twin machine guns firing through the propeller arc, but synchronized to miss the blades.

End of a Zeppelin
A contemporary version of the night action in which Flight Sub-Lieutenant Alexander Warneford *(inset)* destroyed LZ39. His Morane-Saulnier Parasol carried a rack holding six 20lb bombs, released by the pilot pulling a cable through a hole in the floor of the cockpit.

he was over the Humber estuary, the commander dropped the remaining bombs, seven 50kg high explosive and a number of incendiaries. Two people were killed and 13 injured, and both Zeppelins escaped unhurt.

The first German attack to reach London took place on 31 May 1915, when L38 dropped 30 high explosive and 90 incendiary bombs in the eastern area of London. The airship flew high and was unseen, so that the few gun defences of London never opened fire.

Seven people were killed and 35 injured, and the airship once again escaped free. The defences of London were given additional guns and fighter aircraft as a result of this.

From this time onward airship raids on London became more and more frequent, with both German Navy Zeppelins and German Army Schutte-Lanz machines being used, though the Army soon found they had better things to do and left the task to the Navy. And on 8th September, the Navy made their

Bomber's moon A British fighter in pursuit of a Gotha bomber. The illustration shows clearly how low these World War I bombers had to fly in order to hit targets with any degree of accuracy.

most successful raid so far, flying Zeppelin L13 across London, bombing as it went, causing 22 deaths, 87 injured, and property damage estimated at over half a million pounds. All 26 guns of the London defences opened fire without success, though they drove L13 up to 11,000 feet in order to evade the shellfire.

This led to a total reorganization of the London defences, Admiral Sir Percy Scott, a renowned naval gunnery expert, being called in to take control. His plan of defence was to put the guns and aircraft well forward so as to attack the raiders before they reached the city, reserving only sufficient guns around the capital to deal with any which got through the first line. Admirable as this plan was, it was slow to develop due to shortages of both guns and fighter aircraft.

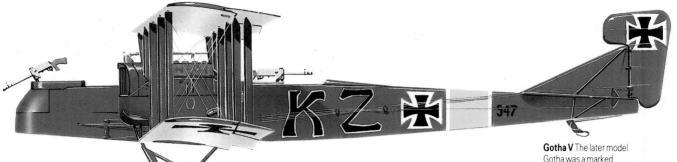

Gotha V The later model Gotha was a marked improvement on the original GII version. It could fly for six hours at 87.5mph and carry up to 1100lb of bombs. At the time it was suggested that the Germans copied the Handley Page 0/100 for their only large bomber but this was actually not the case.

Defenders strike back

The first defensive success against the air attack had come in July 1915, when Flight Sub-Lieutenant Warneford, flying a Moraine aircraft over Ostend, had managed to get above Zeppelin L37 and drop a bomb on to it. A violent explosion took place and the airship crashed into the sea in flames. Warneford was awarded the Victoria Cross, but ten days later, while collecting a new Farman biplane from a rear airfield, he crashed and was killed. In the defence of London the first aircraft success came on 3 September 1916 when Lieutenant Leefe Robinson, using the newly-developed "Buckingham" incendiary machine gun bullet, shot down the Schutte-Lanz airship SL11 near Cuffley in Hertfordshire. A few days later 2/Lieutenant Brandon of the RFC perforated the gas-bags of Zeppelin L33, which force-landed, and on the same night 2/Lieutenant Sowrey caught L32 and brought it down in flames. It began to look as if the defences had caught up with the raiders.

The Germans were of the same opinion and the last Zeppelin raid to reach England took place in October 1917. But this was simply because the airship was no longer a viable method of attack in the face of the improved defences, and a better weapon was ready. On 25 May 1917, a flight of 16 Gotha bombers, large twin-engined biplanes capable of carrying 400kg of bombs, attacked Folkestone and Shorncliffe with heavy loss of life. While this was still being talked about, on 13th June a flight of 14 Gothas flew up the Thames in daylight and delivered a severe bombing raid on various parts of the capital, killing 162 people and injuring 432. Ninety-two aircraft took off in defence, but none of them as much as saw the raiders, which escaped unhurt. The Gothas returned on 7th July, killing 54 and wounding 190; one Gotha was lost, and that was almost an accident; the machine was suffering from engine trouble and limping along the East coast on its way home when it was caught by a Home Defence Squadron aircraft and shot down.

This raid was to have far-reaching effects. The apparent ease with which these flights of monster aircraft had penetrated to the heart of London, and the appalling damage they had done, led to an uproar over the state of the defences. After much argument the War Cabinet set up a committee to look into the matter, and in looking for an impartial president they settled on Lieutenant General J. C. Smuts. In the end the Committee turned into a one-man affair conducted entirely by Smuts. His brief went beyond the simple question of air defence; for some time a political argument had been brewing over the allocation of scarce manufacturing resources between the Royal Flying Corps and the Naval Air Service. Smuts' recommendations on air defence were well-reasoned and led to a total reorganization along lines which, in effect, were to be revived for the Second World War. During the course of his conversations with various representatives of the RFC and RNAS, Smuts came to the conclusion that there would, by the middle of 1918, be a surplus of aircraft beyond what the Army required for its tactical support in France, and that this would best be employed by aggressive attacks against the German war industry. He went further than that:

"An air service can be used as an independent means of war operations. …there is absolutely no limit to the scale of its future independent war use…the day may not be far off when aerial operations with their devastation

Caproni CA-3 Gianni Caproni
was the first man to design
large multi-engined aircraft.
His CA-3 was a two-wing
variant of the triplane CA41.
The CA-3 made high-level
raids across the Alps in World
War I, where the aircrew
must have suffered from
exposure to cold and thin air.

of enemy lands and destruction of
industrial and populous centres on a
vast scale may become the principal
operations of war...."

At any other time the defence
recommendations of the Smuts Report
would have been accepted, and the
remainder of it consigned into oblivion
via the nearest waste-paper basket as
not having any bearing upon the
question in hand. But in late 1917,
under the premiership of Lloyd
George, the Army and Navy were
having a hard time. He had an
unreasoning hatred of Haig, the
Commander-in-Chief of the BEF, and
Robertson, Chief of the Imperial
General Staff, and he had no very high
opinion of the Admiralty either. And
here, gratuitously presented to him by
Smuts, was a magnificent opportunity
to score off both the Admiralty and the
War Office. With no further ado, Lloyd
George ordered the formation of an
"Independent Air Force" –
independent, that is, of tactical
direction by GHQ France – and also
ordered the RFC and RNAS to be
amalgamated into a separate service,
the Royal Air Force, on 1 April 1918.
The commander of the RFC, Sir Hugh
Trenchard, one-time Chief Instructor
of the Central Flying School, was
ordered back from France to take
command of the new service.

Trenchard, during his tenure with
the RFC, had always resisted
suggestions for an independent force,
but now that he had command, his
opinion changed overnight and he
became the most passionate advocate
of independence. However, he
quarrelled with the Air Minster Lord
Rothermere, gave up the post of Chief
of Air Staff, and went back to France to
command the Independent Air Force –
which was a separate entity from
everything else.

The Independent Force had actually
come into being some time earlier,
though not under that name. The effect
of German air raids on London and Paris
had led both the British and French to
discuss the setting up a bomber force
for raids against German cities, but a
shortage of aircraft prevented much
being done until late in 1917. In late
October, a wing was formed and began
to undertake raids and, by April 1918,
this had been developed into four
squadrons, and these now become the
Independent Force, RAF. The aircraft
varied from lightweight FE 2b day
bombers to the immense (for those
days) Handley-Page O/100. This was a
twin-engined biplane capable of
carrying 16 112lb bombs at about 75
mph for 450 miles. This British element
was then reinforced by three Italian
Caproni squadrons and a French
Groupe de Bombardement, but the
promised American element was never
provided. The Force made a number of
raids into Germany, and dropped 665
tons of bombs; their effect appears to
have been minimal, but they certainly
gave Trenchard visions of what might
be done with bigger and better aircraft.

When contemplating the air war in
1914-18 one tends to look solely at the
Western Front; in fact much important
work in the direction of strategic
bombing was done by the Italians
against the Austrians. In February
1916, three-motored Caproni bombers
raided Ljubljana; later they attacked
various targets behind the Austrian
lines and made several severe attacks
on the Austrian naval base of Pola and
the Fiume torpedo factory, once flying
over 200 bombers in one assault. These
operations were to add to Trenchard's
opinions in post-war years.

At the end of the war, in 1918, the
air forces, like the ground and naval
forces, were cut back severely. (Air
defence forces were obliterated).
Finance dwindled everywhere; in
Britain Lloyd George was keen to axe
the Royal Air Force completely as
being a luxury too expensive for
peacetime, but Trenchard had a
brainwave – "Air Control".

THE POST-WAR YEARS

The air force becomes an autonomous, potent fighting force

Pioneer Sir Hugh Trenchard, first commander of Britain's Royal Air Force, developed a philosophy of air power that was to shape the story of the force he created well into World War II. He believed in common with his Italian counterpart Douhet, that the strategic bomber was the wonder weapon of the future and that a modern air force could win wars on its own by bombing the enemy population into submission.

One of the difficulties in the post-war years of restricted finance and manpower was the perennial problem of keeping dissident tribesmen under control in the farther-flung areas of the Empire. This demanded large forces of troops, with vehicles, animals and artillery, which could operate as flying columns to march out to some dusty village and remonstrate with the headman after any act of unrest or law-breaking. Trenchard suggested that a far cheaper solution would be to keep a few aircraft at strategic spots and, when punishment was required, fly one or two over the offending village and drop a few bombs. The financial aspect appealed, and Air Control became a feature of the 1920s and 1930s in India and the Middle East. Much of its punitive effect was lost because of government insistence that warning had to be given, so that the villagers merely decamped with their belongings and livestock for a few furlongs and watched while their huts were pounded, after which they moved back, rebuilt the huts, and carried on as before. Political officers were generally scornful, maintaining that Air Control was ineffective and that the tribesmen only respected troops on the ground who could actually do them some damage, but the government approved, and with this and a well-organized public relations staff the Royal Air Force weathered the lean years.

The prime memory of the First World War in every military man's mind in the early 1920s was the bloody stalemate of the Western Front, and the prime concern was to find some tactic or philosophy of war that would avoid such a fracas in the future. Soldiers talked of tanks, but airmen were most taken with the idea of leaping over the battle line and carrying the war into the heart of the enemy nation, striking at his economy, his communications and his command structure. Trenchard, with his experience of the Independent Force, was Britain's advocate:

"In my view...it is almost always necessary as a preliminary step (to defeating an enemy nation) to defeat the enemy's army...It is not, however, necessary for an air force, in order to defeat the enemy nation, to defeat its armed forces first. Air power can... pass over enemy navies and armies and penetrate the air defences and attack direct the centres of production, transportation and communication from which the enemy war effort is maintained".

History tells us that the only key to conquering a nation is to beat its armed forces decisively preliminary to occupying it. A country is not defeated when a bomb falls on the factory down the street; but it knows it is defeated when it sees an enemy soldier with a rifle standing on the street corner.

Gloster Gladiator The Gladiator had a first and a last: it was the first RAF fighter to have a hooded cockpit, and it was the last of the Service's long line of biplane fighters. It entered service in 1937, and took part in the Battle of France in 1940 and the defence of Malta in June 1941.

Several soldiers and sailors tried to drive this home to Trenchard, but he was totally oblivious to criticism or argument. He was reinforced from Italy by the writings of General Guilio Douhet, whose book *The Command of the Air* was published in 1921. Douhet argued the use of strategic air forces, basing much of his theories on the Italian successes against the Austrians. In the United States, Colonel Billy Mitchell was another passionate advocate of strategic aerial bombing; Mitchell is famous for his bombing attacks on captured German warships in a series of tests carried out in 1921. Several old ships were sent to the bottom by bombs, though the one serious target, the ex-German battleship *Ostfriesland*, managed to survive 16 direct hits before being sunk by two one-ton bombs which landed in the water alongside and stove in her side by blast. The protagonists of air power were jubilant; their opponents pointed out that the ships were moored, were not shooting back at the aircraft, that the weather was perfect and the sea calm, yet it still took 16 hits and two near-misses to sink an obsolete warship. Mitchell over-reached himself in his proselytizing, offended his superiors more than once, and was court-martialled and dismissed from the service. But there were, in fact, few opponents of the theory of strategic air power in the USA and, as a consequence, the development of a powerful bomber force was always kept in mind.

Italy and Japan both developed long-range bomber forces during the inter-war years, since such forces complemented their expansionist aims and also made sense in the context of where their likely enemies lay. The Caproni Ca 133 of 1932, a three-motored high-wing monoplane, could carry 1000 kg of bombs for 1350km (822mi), the Japanese Kawasaki Type 88 of 1928 was designed by a German engineer and fitted with BMW engines.

Circumventing Versailles

Germany, which might most justifiably have been expected to develop the strategic bomber theory to its maximum, turned its face against it entirely and refused to countenance the theories of Douhet and Trenchard. During the 1920s, the German Air Force did not exist, having been disbanded by the terms of the Versailles Treaty; it existed insofar as pilots were trained to fly by Lufthansa, the civil airline, and once-qualified, pilots went to secret training bases in Soviet Russia where they shared the facilities with the Russians, but there was no Luftwaffe in being until 1 April 1935. When it did appear its roles were entirely tactical, since it was subordinated by the General Staff to a primary role of directly supporting the army and acting as one of the fundamental factors of the Blitzkrieg system.

Blitzkrieg ("Lightning war") is usually construed as being the application of armoured troops in highly mobile action, but what is often overlooked is that tactical air support was an integral part of the theory. The fundamental concept around which Blitzkrieg was developed was of a balanced force of all arms, and that included the air arm. Hitler's panzer troops were closely supported by dive bombers and ground attack fighter/bombers as a form of flying artillery, and the operations of the longer-ranging twin-engined bombers were closely tied to the tactical plans of the ground armies.

Medium-range bombers would attack a town which lay on the axis of advance, to disrupt communications, damage military installations and to demoralize the civil population and encourage it to flee. The close-support aircraft would then assist the advancing armour and infantry by delivering attacks on strong points and points of resistance which were encountered during the attack or on known enemy positions ahead of the advance. The object of Hitler's armed forces was to

Geodetic strength A new method of airframe construction, designed by Barnes Wallis, enabled the tough Vickers Wellington to absorb enough punishment from flak and bullets to down most other bombers. Even direct hits merely shattered sections of the structure without causing the surrounding areas to collapse.

make fast, well-defined advances and obtain local gains at high speed before setting off once more. The prospect of bombing a factory 480km (300mi) behind the line in order to disrupt the manufacture of, say, mortar bombs or tanks was of no use to this sort of tactical appreciation; the effects would not be felt in the front line for months, if ever, and only immediate results were of any use in the Blitzkrieg concept. Although there were members of the Luftwaffe who were cognizant of the theories of Douhet and Trenchard and were attracted by the prospect of strategic bombing, most of the available finance was being put into tactical aircraft. One or two manufacturers and designers put forward ideas for long-range bombers, but none were ever accepted. (Indeed, the only long-range aircraft operated by the Luftwaffe during the Second World War, the Focke-Wulf Condor four-engined maritime reconnaissance aircraft came about by accident; it originated as an airliner but the Japanese asked for a maritime version in 1938, and having seen the result the Luftwaffe were persuaded to order some.)

The monoplane enters the scene
As the 1920s moved into the 1930s, so the design of aircraft began to move forward. The First World War ended with the biplane supreme in military service, a few triplanes in existence, and a very few monoplanes, since the latter were generally considered to be marginally stable and prone to shedding their wings during violent combat manoeuvres. Air Ministries tended to the conservative, asking for more or less what they had had before but with a little more power, or lifting capacity, or ceiling, but nothing so extreme as to upset the accepted notions of what an aeroplane ought to look like. As a result, biplanes were the general rule throughout the 1920s and into the early

1930s; the last British biplane fighter, the Gloster Gladiator first flew in 1934, entered squadron service in 1936 and remained in first-line service until 1941. The American equivalent, the Curtis Hawk, had first flown in 1923 and subsequent modification kept it in service until the middle 1930s and later with some countries. Confusingly, it was followed, if not actually replaced, by another Curtis Hawk, this time a monoplane. Fokker, the Dutchman who had built most of the German fighters in 1914-18, was still building biplane fighters as late as 1938 for air forces who wanted them.

But in the 1930s designers began looking more and more at monoplanes, and particularly monoplanes made from metal; instead of the traditional ash frame covered in fabric, the new design school advocated aluminium frames covered in a riveted aluminium skin. This was accepted only slowly by airmen, largely because it meant completely retraining all their maintenance staff, who were skilled at repairing wood and cloth but totally inept as metalworkers. In the face of unarguable aerodynamic facts, the authorities began to accept monoplanes, but of traditional construction and in roles where they could be made in substantial form and not asked to do any violent manoeuvring. But if the Air Ministries

Bristol Blenheim The military version of the "Britain First", the Blenheim was a three-crew light bomber. Its main claim to fame is that it was the first RAF aircraft to cross the German frontier in 1939. It was slow for its day, but made sorties over Occupied France until faster light bombers came into service.

Junkers 88 A really outstanding aircraft the quality of which is shown by the fact that 15,000 were built during World War II, and many variants were developed. It made a formidable night-fighter, armed with three 7.9mm machine guns and three 20mm cannon.

The Schneider Trophy The competition for the Schneider Trophy, a series of air races held before World War II, led to enormous advances in aircraft design. Designed by R J Mitchell, the father of the Spitfire, the Supermarine S4, S5 and S6 streamlined float monoplanes achieved air speeds hitherto unattainable. In 1929, the S6 averaged 328.63mph; then, during 1931, in an uncontested race the Supermarine S6B flew seven laps to give Britain the three successive wins needed to retain the trophy permanently. The S6B then created a new World Air Speed Record of 407.5mph.

were unwilling to gamble, the manufacturers were, and private venture designs began to be seen at air displays and in the pages of aeronautical magazines. In 1931, Vickers were asked to design a new bomber to the usual biplane formula; they did so, but felt that the result left a lot to be desired, and so on their own initiative they developed a revolutionary single-engined monoplane which was built around the geodetic metal basketwork system of construction devised by their designer Barnes Wallis. The performance was so superior to existing bombers that the Air Ministry suddenly overcame its abhorrence of monoplanes and bought over 170; they called their plane the Wellesley. In 1934 Lord Rothermere, the press magnate, decided to push the Air Ministry into action and commissioned the Bristol Aircraft Company to built him a fast executive aircraft, which would be able to carry a pilot and six passengers at 240 mph, which was a good deal faster than any RAF fighter then in existence. Bristol built their Type 142, the first modern stressed-skin monoplane with retractable undercarriage to be built in Britain. On test its performance amazed everyone, including its designer, when it achieved 307 mph. It was then christened "Britain First" and

displayed at the Hendon Air Display to let people see just what British designers were capable of producing when asked, leaving the public to ask why the Air Ministry had not thought of it first. Inevitably the Ministry had to move, and "Britain First" became the Blenheim bomber.

The emergence of Germany
The stimulus to military aircraft design came in 1933 with the rise of Hitler and the Nazi party in Germany. No sooner was Hitler in power than the German armed forces began to be strengthened, first surreptitiously, then openly, and this led to the rest of Europe looking to its defences. Since Germany had been permitted no military aircraft under the Versailles Treaty she was in the fortunate position of having no stocks of obsolescent machines to be used up, and designers could have free rein. They had been working secretly throughout the 1920s, keeping their hands in by making paper projects, working more openly on civil machines which, with little modification, could easily be transformed into military equipment. By 1936, the Luftwaffe had begun equipping with the Junkers 86 and 88, Heinkel 111 and Dornier 17 bombers (all originally civil airliner designs), the

120

Hawker Hurricane The prototype of the hump-backed Hurricane flew for the first time in November 1935. When the Battle of Britain was at its height, 23 RAF squadrons were equipped with it. During the battle, the Hurricane, with its eight .303in machine guns, four on each wing, shot down more enemy aircraft than any other form of defence. It was a fine, strong aircraft, but it had the misfortune to be overshadowed by the glamorous Supermarine Spitfire. Behind it is seen the prototype of the Hawker Henley, an aircraft that sank into obscurity in the shadow of the Hurricane.

Junkers Ju87 dive bomber and the Messerschmitt Bf109 fighter. All were metal monoplanes, all were as advanced as the state of the art permitted, and all were to play significant parts in the coming war.

In response to this Britain and France began sending specifications to manufacturers in increasing numbers; often a fresh specification would arrive while the earlier design was still on the drawing board. All were for modern monoplane designs of single-engined fighters and twin-engined bombers, and by 1935 the results were beginning to appear. In that year the prototype Hawker Hurricane made its first flight; the Hurricane had begun as a monoplane version of an existing biplane fighter but was changed while still on the drawing board to take a more powerful engine and, most important of all, to carry no less than eight machine guns mounted in the wings outside the propeller arc. This was a result of an Air Ministry demand, since it was becoming obvious that with the increased speed and manoeuvrability of the coming generation of aircraft, the time during a dogfight which the pilot would have for shooting would be brief, and the more guns which could be brought to bear in the time, the more chance there was of damaging the enemy.

In the following year the first Supermarine Spitfire, the second eight-gun fighter for the Royal Air Force, made its maiden flight. The Spitfire could trace its ancestry back to the racing float-planes which the Supermarine Company had made in the late 1920s and early 1930s to capture the Schneider Trophy for the world's air speed record, and together with the Hurricane was to make history. The

same year saw the first flights of the Hampden, Wellington and Whitley twin-engined bombers and of the Fairey Battle, a single-engined light bomber of which great things were expected. Abroad the Dewoitine D500 fighter was going into production for the French Air Force, the Americans had flown their first DC3 monoplane airliner and the prototype four-engined Flying Fortress bomber. But perhaps the most important event of 1936 was the Royal Air Force's Specification 13/36 which asked for a long-range twin-engined bomber. Three companies responded, but all realized that the specification was unworkable and all went on to develop their ideas into four-engined machines which were to become the backbone of the British bombing offensive.

By the middle 1930s, the bomber had assumed a threatening aspect. Not knowing how the new Germany would develop, and with half an eye to France, the British government were at their wits' end trying to think of a suitable form of defence. At that time air defence was still based on the principles used in 1918; guns on the ground and patrols of fighters in the air across likely approach routes, and the odds were very much in favour of the attacker. The most telling remark, and the one most frequently quoted thereafter, was that made by Britain's Prime Minister Stanley Baldwin, in November 1932, when, during a debate in the House of Commons, he said:

"I think it is well for the man in the street to realize that there is no power on earth that can prevent him from being bombed. Whatever people may tell him, the bomber will always get through...."

This belief in the invincibility of the bomber was at the heart of the strategic bombing school of thought; it seemed entirely feasible to fly a fleet of bombers across enemy territory and blast his industries, railways, command centres and supply depots without incurring very much loss, since the bomber would always get through. With this object firmly in view the Royal Air Force tended to concentrate on building up a bomber force, relegating fighters to home defence more as a gesture than as a positive and reliable method of stopping an attack. In 1934, the RAF had twice as many bomber squadrons than fighter squadrons, and the fighters depended heavily on reservists and auxiliaries to man them in time of need.

Trials in Spain

In 1936, the Spanish Civil War broke out, and the two opposing sides were reinforced by weapons and soldiers from the great dictatorships of Germany and Italy (on the Nationalist side) and Soviet Russia (for the Republicans). Treating the war as a species of realistic testing grounds for equipment and theories, these nations sent tanks and aircraft, together with advisers and directors. One of the more publicized reinforcements was the "Kondor Legion" of the Luftwaffe, an air division equipped with a mixture of the standard German combat aircraft and transports.

On 26 April 1937, an event occurred which had repercussions throughout Europe far in excess of its intrinsic combat value; the town of Guernica was bombed by the Condor Legion. At 4.40pm a lone Heinkel 111 flew across the town and dropped a few bombs, then flew off and returned leading three more Heinkels. These were followed by three flights of Junkers Ju52 bombers, some Messerschmitt BF109 and Heinkel 51 fighters. Together this force pounded the town with about 50 tons of bombs and then machine-gunned the streets. A subsequent commission of enquiry established that some 70 percent of the houses were destroyed, 20 percent seriously damaged and the remaining houses in the town damaged to some extent. How many died has never been established, though the best authorities place it at something in the region of 200 to 250.

Guernica was – and this has never been seriously disputed – a legitimate target insofar as it was an important communications junction, with strategic bridges, and had a large arms factory on its outskirts. But neither the bridges nor the arms factory were damaged in any way, and the town was completely without defences. But the prime significance of Guernica's martyrdom was the ammunition it

supplied to the various political groups and to the argument about strategic bombing. Indeed, it was not until 1970 that the Nationalists even admitted that Guernica had been bombed; since 1937 they had argued strenuously that the damage was due to mines and Basque explosive caches set off by one or two bombs accidentally dropped over the town. But the Republicans extracted every ounce of propaganda for the horrors of war, and this was assiduously picked up and spread throughout Britain and France. This, piled on top of the general atmosphere of doubt about future warfare, was enough to turn the scales, and Europe as a whole began to voice fears of the unrestricted terror of the next war. It was generally assumed that the outbreak of war would be immediately followed by fleets of aircraft appearing over the major cities of Europe, showering them with explosives and, in particular, poison gas bombs. As might be imagined, the strategic bombing theorists were by no means upset by this; it gave them an excellent lever – if they are going to do it to us, how much better if we prepare to do it to them? Or "Do unto others as they would do unto you – but sooner."

Early radio detection

What the man in the street did not know in 1937, and what only a small number of servicemen knew, was that the seeds of the bomber's destruction had already been sown and were sprouting vigorously. During the late 1920s, the infant science of radio had been applied to various problems, one of them being the study of the stratospheric layers

Ju52 The first Ju52 was a single-engined transport plane, but following trials with three Pratt and Whitney Hornet engines it was obvious that the added power made it a much better aircraft. Here it is seen bearing the markings of the Condor Legion, which fought in the Spanish Civil War where it was used as a bomber. It was the standard transport for the Luftwaffe throughout the war, its slow speed making fighter cover necessary.

Messerschmidt Bf109E The prototype of this famous German fighter first flew in 1935 and its descendants fought right through the war. Early models received their battle experience in the Spanish Civil War on the side of General Franco. The aircraft shown here made an unplanned and accidental landing at RAF Manston in November 1940, giving the RAF's investigation Branch an unique opportunity to evaluate its performance against their Hurricanes and Spitfires.

which surrounded the earth, and it had been discovered that radio waves would reflect from the Heavyside Layer. Arising from this, scientists in different parts of the world, entirely independently, began to wonder whether radio waves would reflect from more solid objects such as ships and aircraft; some of this thought was directed to peaceful ends – the French, for example, were considering a device for detecting icebergs in time to avoid repetitions of the "Titanic" disaster – but in Britain, Germany and the USA the thoughts ran in the direction of detecting aircraft, and enemy aircraft in particular.

In 1935, Dr. Robert Watson-Watt conducted his now-legendary experiment in Oxfordshire, demonstrating that a bomber would reflect the radio waves given off by a BBC transmitter. This was enough to convince the Committee for the Scientific Study of Air Defence that there was a distinct possibility that radio-location would work, and money was made available. Within four months a radar set had been built which could detect aircraft at 17 miles range. Late in 1935, a Dr. Kuhnhold of the German Naval Radio Research Establishment made an experiment similar to that of Watson-Watt, obtained similar results and, in the middle of 1936, a German manufacturer was given a contract to build what eventually became the Freya early-warning radar. By 1936, too, both the US Army and US Navy had experimental sets for the detection of aircraft.

What distinguished the British research was its practical slant; Watson-Watt, in his first report on the possibilities of the radio system, had not only dealt with the simple scientific matter of detection, but had outlined a system of use, had forecast the accurate measurement of range, azimuth and elevation, the identification of friendly aircraft, and had even touched on the subject of counter-measures. This led to the setting up of a chain of radar stations around Britain, and a carefully organized reporting system which ensured that the information was passed rapidly to places where the defence could be organized accordingly. The British radar defences went into action during the Munich crisis in September 1938, and they have remained in operation ever since; this early start gave Britain a considerable advantage in air defence

over the rest of the world, insofar as it had an integrated system while other nations merely had radar sets.

The other element of air defence was the application of guns and fighter aircraft to the attacking bomber; guns were an army responsibility and, in general, once they had money available, guns were forthcoming. Fighters, being an RAF responsibility, were a different matter. As we have already noted, the RAF preferred to see the available finance weighted towards providing a bomber force, but at the same time it was necessary to at least make an effort to conform to the various defensive plans which were produced by the Government from time to time. These had been devised at intervals since the middle 1920s, and the final plan, which was the plan with which the air defences went to war, was the "Re-orientation Plan" of 1935, so-called because for the first time it was admitted that Germany would probably be the source of attacks, and the defences were oriented accordingly. At the same time, a series of plans were drawn up to govern the organization of the RAF for war; the final one of these, co-ordinated with the air defence plans, called for a strength of 1352 bombers and 608 first-line fighters to be in service by April 1940. That this "Plan L" was put into operation at all was due to Lord Swinton, the Air Minister; the RAF had demanded 1442 bombers and 532 fighters by April 1941, but the Minister, feeling that insufficient weight was being given to defence, held out for the revised figures and eventually got them. In the event the RAF went to war on 3 September 1939 with 536 bombers and 608 fighters.

Radar The development of this form of detection began with trials in 1931. In its most effective form it gave an accurate reading of an enemy's position in terms of range and direction. In the photograph a WAAF radar operator watches the screen and assesses the information the system has produced in visual form. Considerable experience was needed to translate this into usable data. Radar is based on pulsed electromagnetic waves striking objects and being reflected back to a receiver, the time taken to return and the direction supplying the target's position.

WORLD WAR II

*Battles in the sky – air superiority is the
key to victory*

The German Luftwaffe went into
their war on the 1 September,
with 2130 bombers and 1215
fighters. But their concern was not with
defence or strategic bombing; it was
with supporting the operations of the
army, and its technique was unveiled in
Poland. As the army advanced it was
preceded by Junkers Ju87 "Stuka" dive
bombers attacking strongpoints,
bridges, defended areas and villages on
the line of march. Ahead ranged
medium bombers taking out airfields,
railway junctions, road junctions,
factories, small towns and seaports on
the Baltic coast. And both forces were
attacking every Polish troop
concentration they could see, whether
or not it presented an immediate threat
to the advancing German army. On the
evening of 1 September Warsaw was
raided, in spite of courageous
opposition by the Polish Air Force in
their obsolete fighters. By 17
September, however, the Polish Air
Force had virtually ceased to exist, its
machines either shot down, destroyed
on the ground, or unable to fly for lack
of fuel and spare parts. After that the
German aircraft roved freely over
Poland, bombing and shooting
whatever they saw; Warsaw was left in
ruins, and on 27 September Poland
capitulated.

The tactical application of air power
by the Germans can be seen in two
forms, if we take the Polish campaign as
a "typical" example. Firstly the direct
application, blasting away obstacles in
the immediate front of the army, and
secondly the indirect application,
bombing targets well removed from the
line of army contact but which could
have a rapid effect on the fighting ability
of the defenders. Thus bombing a town
perhaps 32km (20mi) behind the line
can have a rapid effect on the immediate
of battle by blocking the advance of
reinforcements; it can also have an
effect on the ground action by spurring
the civil inhabitants to move out en
masse, thus blocking roads and
interfering with the movement of
supplies and reinforcements. It can also
have an effect on the defenders'
morale; when everything around them

is being bombed and blasted, the
tendency is to think that the enemy is
invincible and that resistance is
pointless.

The bombing of factories and
seaports well behind the lines during
the German attack on Poland could
have no effect on the progress of the
battle; the German forces were so
strong and so overmatched the Poles
that there was no likelihood of the war
lasting so long that the cessation of
operation by a factory making trucks,
for instance, would have had any effect
on the course of the campaign. For this
to happen a period of several weeks or
even months would have to ensue
before the supply line at the front
showed deficiencies. In the Polish
campaign this rear-area bombing was

Ju87 The Stuka, full title
Sturzkampfflugzeug, was a
dive-bomber that earned a
fearsome reputation for
accuracy. This was so against
undefended targets, such as
those it met in Poland and the
Low Countries in 1939-40.
But when pitted against
Britain's military targets,
defended by Hurricanes and
Spitfires, it was seen to be
slow and vulnerable. The
Luftwaffe then withdrew
it from Britain's skies and
armed it with two 37mm
cannon for antitank duties.
Germany found no
replacement for the Stuka
even though it had passed its
best by 1942 by which time
about 5000 had been built. It
is remembered for the sirens
fitted beneath the gull wings,
which howled as the aircraft
dived, creating terror among
civilians.

done entirely in order to overawe the population and promote a stream of refugees which would disrupt communications. It should be borne in mind that to the Nazis the Poles were *Untermensch* – sub-humans incapable of rational thought or behaviour – to whom bombing would be a terrible experience capable of breaking their morale. Moreover, there was no experience of such a form of attack which could be used as a reference point, and thus civil morale could, and did in some cases, crumble. On the whole, though, it was the immediate application of air power at the point of contact between the armies which proved decisive, breaking the Polish formations, destroying their equipment and defensive works, killing their soldiers. The rest of the world saw and wondered.

The phoney war

In Britain the RAF began their war handcuffed by political restrictions; they were to attack only well-defined military targets in locations where there was no risk to the civil population. As a result, and with the traditional British concentration on naval strength and strategy, the first role for the bombing force was the attack on ships of the German Navy and close support for the British Army in France, two tasks for which there was no precedent and for which there had been no training. The only flights into Germany by bombers were made with the sole task of distributing propaganda leaflets. At one stage it was even suggested that the pre-war Air Control policy of first warning the targets and then, after an interval to permit the civil population to move out, attacking them should be

adopted; fortunately, wiser counsels prevailed. One enthusiast who suggested bombing the Krupp works in the Ruhr, probably the only German name associated with armaments widely known in England, was abruptly brought to heel by the observation that since Krupp's was private property it was inadmissible as a target.

Nevertheless, the tools for a bombing campaign were being forged, if slowly. As we have seen, in 1936 the RAF had called for a large twin-engined bomber capable of overflying Germany with a reasonable bomb-load; they further specified the engines, which were to be the new Rolls-Royce "Vulture" of 24 cylinders arranged in an X-form. The Vulture turned out to be one of Rolls-Royce's less successful designs, and the three twin-engined bombers which were under development eventually appeared as four-engined machines powered by different engines. The Handley-Page Halifax flew in October 1939, the Short Stirling in May 1939, and the Avro Lancaster in January 1941; but it was not until late 1940 that first deliveries to service squadrons began and not until 1941 that there were sufficient of them to begin making bombing attacks in any number.

Until that time the backbone of the British air offensive was the Vickers Wellington twin-engined bomber, capable of carrying 4500lbs of bombs and of flying some 3200km (2000mi) (though with a reduced load). The Wellington had been designed by Barnes Wallis of Vickers, and was built with the geodetic construction which had been pioneered in the Wellesley light bomber. This form of construction allied lightness with immense strength

Boulton Paul Defiant The only two-seater fighter with no forward-firing guns, the Defiant's uniqueness lay in its power-operated turret armed with four .303 Browning machine guns. Against bombers it was reasonably effective, shooting down over 60, but the German fighter cover found the heavy Defiant easy pickings. As a night-fighter it found fresh success during 1940-41.

Supermarine Spitfire A remarkably versatile fighter, which replaced the ageing Gloster Gauntlet; by September 1939 nine RAF squadrons were equipped with it. The 1440hp Rolls Royce Merlin engine, fine workhorse though it was, was replaced by the 2050hp Griffon, the extra power giving the Spitfire Mk XII an edge on the Luftwaffe's FW190 in 1943. A clipped-wing Seafire and an unarmed photo reconnaissance version were developed as the war progressed. The Spitfire sports a squadron leader's pennant near its cockpit.

and structural integrity, and during the war Wellington bombers survived incredible damage and managed to return safely with their crews. The Wellington was augmented by Whitley and Hampden bombers, capable of lesser loads and ranges but still able to raid the North Sea coastal ports in search of German ships. Early attempts at daylight raids were severely punished by German fighters, and so the RAF went over to night raiding, using darkness as their protection.

In May 1940, the German Army struck again, first at Norway and Denmark, then into the Low Countries to overrun Holland, Belgium and, eventually, France. As the Allied armies crumbled before the onslaught of audaciously-handled armour backed up by tactical air support, their air forces fought valiantly to cover their activities, and many peacetime theories went to the wall. The RAF had placed a great deal of faith in two designs, the Boulton-Paul Defiant and the Fairey Battle; the former was a two-seat fighter, the rear seat holding a power-driven turret mounting four .303 Browning machine guns, while the latter was a light bomber with a single wing machine gun and a flexible gun manned by the observer behind the pilot. Both proved to be useless; the Battle was simply shot from the sky, while the Defiant, starting with some good results, was soon found to have a blind spot beneath, where the turret guns could not reach, after which it, too, became a sitting target for the German fighters.

Swooping from the skies

Germany used two machines which stuck in the minds of the soldiers beneath; firstly the Junkers Ju87 dive bomber, known far and wide as the Stuka. Fitted with a screaming siren

and a single 500kg bomb, the Stuka would hover in the sky and then fall vertically with an increasingly loud scream, releasing its bomb at the last moment before climbing away. The combination of the daredevil dive, the screaming siren, and the final blast of the bomb was bad for anyone's morale and it carved a way through defences for the ground troops in fine style. The second threat was the Messerschmitt Bf109 fighter, the German equivalent of the British Hurricane. Armed with cannon and machine guns this was a ground attack machine *par excellence* which could swoop down on a marching column of soldiers and decimate them in seconds.

The ground attacks, particularly when directed against columns of refugees, took precedence in the newspapers of the period, and little was heard of dogfighting or anything resembling the air combat of the First World War until the late summer of 1940 when the German Army were in occupation of northern France and the British were all back on their island. Hitler then planned Operation Sealion, the invasion of England; a prerequisite for this was command of the air over the English Channel in order to protect the anticipated fleet of troop-carrying barges which was being mustered in the ports of the Low Countries.

The Battle of Britain

Before the evacuation from France had been completed, German aircraft had begun probing raids on England; but on 30th June, Goering, commanding the Luftwaffe, gave directives for the forthcoming battle. His aim was the destruction of the RAF and its airfields and aircraft factories. The German Navy, however, were insistent that the Royal Navy should also figure in the target lists, since they were

Hawker Hurricane IIc Here a pair of Hurricane IIc types are flying in formation. The lower Hurricane is from a squadron with Polish pilots, identified by the chequerboard motif. The cloth strips covering the four .303in machine guns on each wing are untorn, showing that the guns have not been fired.

apprehensive of what could happen to an invasion force if the Royal Navy swept through the Channel. Goering agreed to take on both targets at the same time, but, fortunately, he was overruled by the Luftwaffe General Staff; the RAF was the prime target, and only after it was defeated would the Luftwaffe turn to the Royal Navy.

The battle began by bombing attacks on shipping in the Channel; this was partly to damage the ships, but principally to lure the RAF fighters out so that they could be destroyed. The first of these attacks took place on 10th July, when a mixed force of bombers and fighters formed up over northern France to attack a convoy then passing Dover. Their formation was detected by radar, and Fighter Command was alerted. It was the beginning of what has since gone down in history as the Battle of Britain.

The course of this battle has been well documented and needs little explanation in these pages; the significant feature is the tactical and strategic theory behind it. The German plan, as we have said, was to draw the RAF up into the sky and gradually whittle it away, but this was frustrated by the excellent warning and control system the defenders possessed. Instead of flying constant patrols, so wearing out machines, using fuel and tiring pilots, the RAF were able to detect German attacks as they formed up over France, forecast their probable course, and then deploy the necessary strength of fighters in the right place and at the right altitude so that they could operate to the best effect. As a result the aircraft were conserved and, perhaps more important, the pilots were given as much opportunity to rest between missions as possible; indeed, towards the end of the battle the principal concern was not so much the supply of aircraft but the supply of skilled pilots.

The next German mistake was in

Messerschmidt bF109 The traditional enemy of the Hurricane and the Spitfire, the 109 had a similar number of variants to that of the Spitfire, even to naval and high-level photo reconnaissance models. It could also be modified to take rockets and act as a ground-attack aircraft.

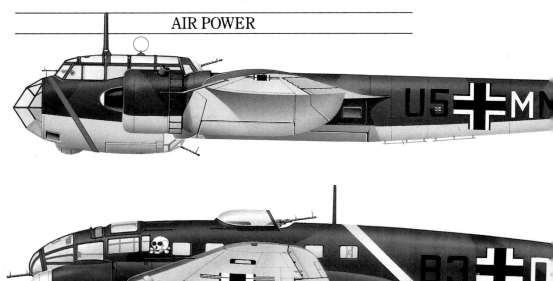

German fighters. Both the Ju88 *(top)* and the He111 *(bottom)* were prominent in the daylight bombing attacks on Britain in 1940 and later. The measure of a successful warplane is in its ability to be converted to quite different roles. With the Spitfire the Ju88 was such an aircraft, being a fighter in one mark, a bomber in another, and there were some in-between roles. It carried formidable armament in the fighter variant, having three 7.9mm machine guns and three 20mm cannons. The first He111 appeared as a civil transport and mailplane in 1935, thus disguising its intended role with the Luftwaffe. Successful over Spain in the Civil War, it needed added armour when it met the stiffer opposition of the RAF during the Battle of Britain.

direct contradiction to one of the accepted principles of war – the maintenance of the aim. Instead of persisting with the attacks against the RAF fighter squadrons and their airfields, the Luftwaffe switched to attacking radar stations, having finally realized their value to the defenders. This had some success, but it had been foreseen and mobile stations and emergency repair crews were ready to move in and repair the damage or provide emergency cover which kept the protective screen in place. In one case, when a station on the Isle of Wight was seriously damaged, a deception transmitter was placed, sending out a spurious signal which resembled that of the radar station, so that German interception radio in France reported that the radar was functioning. Again failing to maintain their aim, the Luftwaffe now shifted back to attacks on airfields.

The attacks continued daily, and by the end of August the situation was beginning to look serious for the RAF; put simply, they were losing fighters faster than industry could supply them, but what was worse was the attrition of the most highly-skilled pilots. Between 24th August and 6th September, for example, 103 pilots were killed and 128 hospitalized, a rate of loss which could not be countered by replacements. Moreover the replacements were not battlewise and were thus a near-liability on their first few missions.

"London can take it"
What saved the situation was an action by Bomber Command. On 24th August a German force had raided London by night; this was against orders – they had been specifically instructed not to attack London – but during raids on various airfields some had failed to find their targets and had scattered bombs indiscriminately across south London. By way of retaliation, Bomber Command raided Berlin four times during the next 10 days. Hitler forthwith ordered Goering to change his daylight strategy and mount retaliatory counterattacks on London. Fieldmarshal Sperrle, one of Goering's commanders, opposed the idea, sure that a few more days would break the RAF – and, in retrospect, one can see that he was probably right. FM Kesselring, Goering's other commander, was of the opinion that attacks on London would lead the RAF to throw every fighter they possessed into defending the capital city, making them prey to the German escort fighters. Goering agreed, and the policy changed from day attacks against airfields and associated targets to an all-out attack on London. The RAF had won, at the price of London's agony.

The bombing attacks which now began upon London and other towns and cities in Britain appeared to be the opportunity to prove the contentions of the strategic bombing school. Tons of bombs rained down, and once the night attacks began the defenders were limited in their response, since although radar could guide defenders to the approximate area of the bombers, once there they had to rely entirely upon their own unaided eyesight to find and destroy them. As a result the score

London's East End bombed
Photographed from another German bomber an He111 flies over London's Thames, apparently without opposition, even as low as the 8000ft or so here. When the RAF began to make daylight raids prohibitively expensive Hitler turned to night bombing. The daylight raids had resulted in severe damage to property and sad loss of life, but they had not broken the will of the population, which was Goering's intent.

against the night bombers was poor, and the damage sustained by the targets was immense. In spite of this, though, the morale of the population held up and production of essential munitions was rarely affected for more than a day or two. Indeed, looking back it seems that Britain was lucky; to quote but one example, the entire production of Bren light machine guns for the army was carried out in a single factory on the outskirts of London. One raid on that factory would have had immeasurable repercussions for the Army, but by pure luck no attack ever took place. In spite of this evidence of the ineffectiveness of bombing to affect the nation's will and its productive capacity, the desire to retaliate in kind against Germany, which was understandable in the man in the street, was still uppermost in the minds of the higher echelons of the RAF.

The blitz spreads

During the winter of 1940/41 the German raiders moved further afield; Coventry, Birmingham, Swansea, Hull, Plymouth, Bath, Exeter, Bristol, Southampton – almost every major city was attacked at some time, many more than once. Although London is invariably cited as the prime target, many cities suffered far greater damage: the centre of Hull was obliterated: the centre of Portsmouth

was simply an acreage of rubble. But for all this damage the spirit of the inhabitants never broke, production in factories was only impaired by a direct hit on the plant, and the general level of war production was scarcely affected. The policy of strategic bombing in order to break the will of the civilian population failed completely.

At the same time, the defensive system began to improve. Radar was now developed which could be carried in night fighters, so that they could be guided by ground radar to the general area of the attack, and then use their own radar to pick up a target and open fire. The radar was fitted into a new machine, the Beaufighter, a powerful and heavy twin-engined fighter armed with four 20mm cannon and six .303 machine guns, and with this in use the odds began to turn in the RAF's favour. The first radar-aimed kill was made on the night of 19 September 1940. It is amusing to recall the dilemma facing the public relations department at that time; they were anxious to publicize the fact that they were mastering the night raiders, but could not disclose the use of radar – which was still secret. The result was a remarkable tale of special diets – carrots were said to be vital for improving the pilots' night vision.

On the night of 19 April 1940 the Germans threw a last major raid against London, and lost 24 bombers to night fighters. A few days later they began to withdraw from their bases in France, moving east to prepare for the forthcoming invasion of Russia.

The German occupation of Europe had at least freed the RAF Bomber Command from its politically-imposed fetters. From the late summer of 1940, almost every night saw the Hampdens, Whitleys and Wellingtons making the journey across the North Sea to targets in Germany. The German defences were a mixture of guns and fighters working in a manner which was unco-ordinated in comparison to the centralized British defence, but nevertheless they managed to take a slow toll of the raiders.

On 12 December 1940, an attack was made on Mannheim which broke new ground. For the first time this was not carefully directed against a specified factory, rail junction or refinery, but simply at the city of Mannheim. It had been ordered by Winston Churchill as retaliation for the attack on Coventry; the principal difference was that where 400 German aircraft had devastated Coventry, 10 RAF bombers attacked Mannheim with relatively little result.

However, as was becoming apparent in 1941, few of Bomber Command's raids were having much effect on German industry, for the very basic reason that few of the bombs ever found their designated targets. The problems were cumulative; firstly the pilot and navigator had to get the bomber to the right place; then the bomb-aimer had to identify the target; then he had to aim the bombs and drop them; and finally the pilot had to find his way home again. Night navigation had rarely been practised in peacetime, and moreover, in peacetime the lights on the ground were a help to navigation.

Würzburg radar dish The secrets of the German radar installations were laid bare by a combination of Enigma decipherment and the brilliant intuition of Dr R V Jones, Head of Scientific Intelligence at the time. After being briefed by Dr Jones, a photo reconnaissance Spitfire pilot brought back photographs which showed an installation at Bruneval. Following this, a commando raid was launched, which resulted in most of the secret equipment being brought back to England – along with one of the startled German *Würzburg* operators.

In wartime, with Europe rigorously blacked out, navigation became a priority; but navigation by the stars only worked when the right stars were visible, and navigation by dead reckoning – calculating mileage and bearing from the start point, correcting for wind drift, adjusting when something identifiable was seen and starting the calculation again, was shot through with variables which added up to formidable errors over a flight of several hundred miles. And once the bomber was over the assumed target, the bomb sights were primitive and inaccurate, so that even if the pilot got to the correct town and the bomb-aimer identified the correct target, there was still a considerable chance that the bombs would miss.

Navigational aids

It would be unfair to suggest that this defect was solely to be found in the RAF; every air force had the same problem, since every air force was faced with the same task and had roughly the same technical expertise with which to solve it. It needed something radically different to the accepted methods of navigation, and the first air force to find an answer was the Luftwaffe. Once in possession of the major part of the Continent they could erect radio beacon stations in widely separated places and from them could direct radio beams of considerable precision across Britain. By directing the beams so that they intersected over their chosen target, it was then a fairly routine matter to fly the bomber force along one beam, using special radio equipment to detect the beam and keep the aircraft aligned with it. When the radio receivers detected the second beam, crossing the first at an angle, this indicated the proximity of the target and the bomb-aimers took

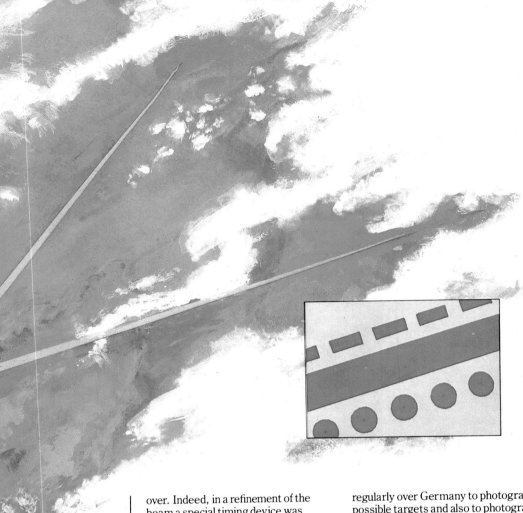

Knickerbein beams The Germans had devised a means of directing pilots to within 370m (400yd) of their targets by a system of beams called *Knickerbein* ("Dog-leg"). The aircraft flew along a beam that was aimed to pass over the target. Another beam, sent from a transmitter some distance away, intersected the first over the target. When the pilot's visual or aural equipment gave the required signal he dropped his bombs. To keep on-beam the pilot listened for a continuous tone; if he strayed to starboard the signal became dashes and if he went to port off the beam he heard dots. He was able therefore to maintain a correct course to the target.

over. Indeed, in a refinement of the beam a special timing device was triggered by the radio signal and instructed the bomber when to release its load.

The Royal Air Force Technical Intelligence department detected these beams eventually and by using various electronic measures managed to jam them – not "bend" them as has often been stated – so that they were no longer an accurate guide. Moreover some astute analysis of the beams, when they were heard, frequently suggested the general area of the target and allowed the defenders to be deployed accordingly.

The British were unable to adopt this beam system; firstly it would have been rapidly detected, since, after all, the Germans had originated the idea and would doubtless be watching for it; and secondly the necessary wide separation of the transmitters was impossible within the British Isles. As a result, therefore, the bombers used sextants and pencils for their navigation, and by the middle of 1941 it was becoming apparent that the desired results were not being achieved.

By this time the RAF had a useful number of photographic reconnaissance aircraft which flew regularly over Germany to photograph possible targets and also to photograph targets after attack. In the late summer of 1941, Lord Cherwell, the Prime Minister's personal scientific adviser, instructed a Mr. Butt of the Cabinet office to obtain as many photographs as he could, together with Bomber Command's records of attacks, and compare the two to provide an analysis of the effectiveness of the bombing campaign. In August 1941 Butt produced his report, which caused consternation. It became apparent that overall only about one-third of the aircraft reached their appointed target and bombed it; in some areas the success rate was as low as one-tenth. On moonlit nights 20 percent of crews found their targets; on dark night the proportion fell to about 7 percent.

The senior figures in Bomber Command shrugged the report off; wrong analyses, the man had picked a time of bad weather, the photographic interpretation was poor. But Churchill was in no mood to have it shrugged off; he demanded explanations and action from the Air Staff.

The Air Staff reiterated their confidence in the effectiveness of bombing. The only trouble, they suggested, was that there were not enough bombers – with 4000 bombers, they could obtain decisive results in 6 months. Churchill was less confident: "Everything is being done to create the bombing force on the largest possible scale, and there is no intention of changing this policy. I deprecate, however, placing unbounded confidence in the means of attack, and still more expressing that confidence in terms of arithmetic... One has to do the best one can, but he is an unwise man who thinks there is any certain method of winning this war...."

Blanket bombing

And so the policy gradually changed; since it appeared that the bombers could guarantee to hit nothing smaller than a city, cities would therefore become the targets. The briefing given to crews before raids still specified particular targets and aiming points within the cities, but this was no more than a token; once over the target city the bombs would be unloaded without too much reference to the aiming point. During the winter of 1941/42 the bombing effort was reduced, largely because the German defences were beginning to take an excessive toll of raiders, and because Bomber Command wished to husband its resources in order to build up an

impressive force with which to start a fresh campaign in the spring of 1942 when the weather improved. By that time the factories would be turning out four-engined bombers in quantity and, most important, a variety of modern radar navigation devices would be available. The first of these, known as Gee, had been tested on operations in 1941 and had since been perfected and put into production. This used radio signals to provide a grid over Europe by means of which any aircraft could rapidly determine its position. Like all radio methods it was open to jamming, but it was assumed that it would take the Germans six months to discover its parameters and set up suitable countermeasures, during which time the RAF would make the most of it.

What was needed to build up confidence in the bomber offensive was some spectacular coup, and in February 1942 Air Marshal Arthur Harris was put in charge of Bomber Command. Harris was a fervent believer in the strategic bombing theory. In an interview given some days after his appointment, he is on record as having said "There are a lot of people who say that bombing cannot win the war. My reply to that is that it has never been tried yet...." Unfortunately, Harris was totally unrealistic in his appreciation of the abilities of the force. He was convinced that immense damage had already been done to Germany and that the bombing being carried out was accurate; so accurate that he was scornful of radio navigational assistance when it was first offered. Blind to all reason, Harris also looked with disdain upon any attempt to direct the bombing offensive against targets such as oil, ballbearings, chemicals or any other sensitive spot in the German economy, calling these "panacea targets".

The thousand bomber raid

Harris now looked at his new command and considered how best to revitalize it. What was needed, he saw, was a string of spectacular successes and he set about ensuring these by directing the heaviest possible raids against targets which were easy to find, relatively thinly defended, and preferably had never been attacked before. On 9th March, 235 bombers raided the Renault works on the outskirts of Paris, employing a new technique. First came a wave of aircraft dropping flares, then a wave carrying nothing but incendiary bombs and, finally, the main body

Short Stirling World War II's first four-engined heavy bomber, the Stirling was described as "a magnificently conceived flying and fighting machine...put together by semi-skilled builders and watered down by beaurocracy and circumstance". In spite of its shortcomings in the air, 100 were ordered even before the prototype had been built. It carried 14,000lb of bombs, had a crew'of six, but needed 56 ground-crew to keep it flying. In the photograph a petrol bowser is refuelling the bomber while the armourers deliver 500lb bombs for the night's operation.

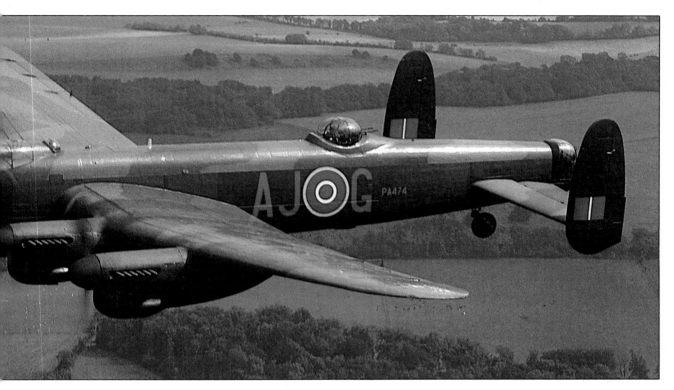

Avro Lancaster Beloved by aircrews for its magnificent flying characteristics and reliability, the "Lanc" was the best heavy bomber of the war. It was developed from the twin-engined Manchester, and with four engines the Lancaster could carry the 22,000lb "Grand Slam" bomb, which created a local mini-earthquake when it exploded. This massive bomb was used to shatter large concrete structures that had withstood conventional bombs.

loaded with high explosives. Four-hundred and seventy tons of bombs were dropped and the post-raid damage reports were ecstatic; the final assessment, based on agents' reports and other intelligence, some weeks later, was less enthusiastic, suggesting that perhaps six or eight weeks' production might have been lost, but by that time Renault was in the past.

On 28th March, Lubeck was attacked by 234 aircraft. Lubeck, a mediaeval town on the Baltic was easily found, and weakly defended since it had little industrial importance. What was important to Harris was that the closely packed streets of half-timbered buildings would burn well. The old heart of Lubeck was totally destroyed. This was followed up by an attack on Rostock, another mediaeval Hanseatic town on the Baltic, equally vulnerable and equally unimportant. This time the raiding was spread over four nights, a tactical error because by the third night the Germans had mustered every mobile anti-aircraft gun they could in order to thicken up the defences. In spite of losses, though, Rostock was thoroughly devastated.

On the night of 30th May, Harris played his masterstroke of publicity for Bomber Command; by scraping aircraft together from operational squadrons

and training units, he put together a force of 1046 bombers of all types and directed them against Cologne. Attacking in waves, in just under two hours over 3000 houses were totally destroyed and 9000 damaged, 36 factories destroyed and almost 300 damaged in varying degrees, 469 people killed, 5000 injured and 45000 homeless. Forty British bombers were lost on the raid.

The British newspapers headlined the "Thousand Bomber Raid" next morning, and to keep up the impetus Harris managed to mount two more raids of almost equal strength, on Essen and Bremen before the artificial force had to be dismantled, the training aircraft returned to their proper role and the service squadrons allowed to devote their attention to smaller raids. But the publicity was invaluable; it must be remembered that in the middle of a hard war the British population, having suffered from German air raids, were in no mood to contemplate humanitarian arguments. Their credo was simple; they had been bombed, now it was the turn of the opposition to suffer. And the thousand-bomber raids gave Bomber Command a popular image of retribution which they retained in the mind of the man in the street until the war ended and long afterward.

TECHNICAL DEVELOPMENT

The pace of war sows the seeds for the air wars of the future

Meanwhile, in other theatres of war, air power was being applied in different ways. In the North African desert, where the British and Commonwealth forces faced the Italian and German armies, there was relatively little scope for strategic bombing, since the sinews of war were manufactured far away and imported into the theatre. The first air priority was therefore to stop the flow of supplies; the British attacked Italian and later German convoys crossing to North Africa, while the Italian and German air forces did the same to the British convoys which were sailing the length of the Mediterranean to supply the Egyptian base. The island of Malta was a vitally important British base in the middle of the sea, and became the focus of the air war, being a base for British aircraft attacking enemy convoys and protecting friendly ones, and a target for Axis air attacks directed at the supply ships and the defending aircraft. In addition the Royal Navy's Fleet Air Arm, which had returned to Naval control in 1938, mounted attacks against shipping and also made bombing attacks against land targets.

At the same time as this battle for domination of the sea took place, the land-based armies were fighting it out supported by tactical air forces. The Germans were using their Luftwaffe in the same manner as they had used in in Europe, but for the British it was a time of trial as the RAF worked out the most effective method of supporting ground operations. Fortunately, in Air Marshal Sir Arthur Coningham, the Desert Air Force had a commander who saw his prime task as assisting the land forces in their battles, and the desert war was the cradle of effective British army-air cooperation and the use of the RAF in the tactical role to support the ground troops. Coningham's headquarters accompanied that of the army commander so that the air forces were fully in the picture about military intentions and plans could be harmonized with the least possible delay and without inter-service friction. In this desert battle the British learned and perfected the techniques so long practised by the Luftwaffe and the Wehrmacht, techniques which were to prove vital in the years to come.

Birth of the jet

The spur of battle also led to an acceleration of technical development. The air forces of the combatants demanded fighters which were faster and more manoeuvrable, bombers that flew higher and farther and carried greater loads, all in the hope of putting an aircraft into battle, which was better than the opposition. The prime requirement, of course, was engines which would deliver more power, and this meant developing something entirely new. The conventional piston engine was well understood, and there was little hope of extracting more power other than by building bigger engines, and the conventional engine was nearing its limit by the early 1940s.

In 1941, for example, the principal American engine was the Pratt & Whitney Double-Row Wasp, a massive 18-cylinder radial engine which developed over 2000 horsepower; when put into the Republic Thunderbolt fighter the machine weighed over 4.7 tons. The Supermarine Spitfire Mark V used the Rolls-Royce Merlin V12 engine developing 1440 horsepower and weighed about 2.75 tons. The two had roughly the same speed, and any improvement in performance would mean a disproportionate increase in engine size.

P47 Thunderbolt A 4.5-ton US fighter which used 100gal of high octane an hour and had a range of only 850 miles. Efforts were made to reduce its weight to make it a match for the German lookalike FW190.

Me262 Germany had the distinction of having the Me262 as the world's first operational jet. At first take-off was assisted by two Walter rocket boosters, but later improvements made them unnecessary. Aviation historians claim that the 262 could have gained air supremacy for the Luftwaffe, but Hitler's uncertainty whether it should operate in the fighter or bomber role prevented it.

Gloster E28/39 Having designed the Whittle gas turbine engine, an airframe was needed to see if it worked as part of an airplane. The result was this early jet which flew for the first time in May 1941 at RAF Cranwell. A second version was built which crashed after a few months of test flying.

remained slow. In Britain there was an understandable reluctance to change horses in the middle of a war; far better to continue making engines which everyone understood until there was a sufficient stock of aircraft, after which it might be feasible to begin production of the new idea. In Germany the air force saw the need for a new machine, and had developed the Me 262 jet fighter by the middle of 1942, but Hitler saw it as a "defensive" weapon, which he abhorred. Production was therefore deferred, and work went into developing a bomber version. A jet bomber, the Arado 234, finally appeared in September 1944 and saw some combat use. Also in 1944 the Allied air raids on Germany finally persuaded Hitler to order the mass-productioin of the Me 262 for production in its original fighter form. The first Allied jet fighter, the British Gloster Meteor went into service on 12 July 1944, eight days before the first Me 262s went into service.

Focke-Wulfs and Typhoons

But in 1941 all this was in the future and the designers were more concerned with using existing technology, pushed to its limits. By this time the Luftwaffe were fielding the Focke-Wulf Fw 190; this first flew in June 1939, but was unknown to the Allies until 1941, when it suddenly became a very embarrassing opponent. Far superior to the current Spitfire, it was faster than any Allied fighter, had heavier armament (two 13mm machine guns and four 20mm cannon), was exceptionally strong and highly manoeuvrable, and generally gave the impression that the RAF had fallen behind in the technical race. A specimen of this machine was captured in June 1942, as a result of which Britain developed an equivalent, the Hawker Fury, though it was not ready for service before the war ended. More timely was another Hawker design, the Typhoon, which had first flown in October 1939, but thereafter went into a decline since the chosen engine, the 24-cylinder Napier Sabre, was untried

This conclusion had been reached as far back as 1930 by an RAF officer, Frank Whittle. He sent a memorandum to the Air Ministry pointing out that the reciprocating engine was a power-wasting device and that it would very soon reach practical limits, and that a far more efficient and powerful system would be to thrust the aircraft forward by the jet reaction of burning fuel in an enclosed chamber. The idea was ignored, but Whittle persisted and eventually, in May 1941, the first British jet aircraft, the Gloster E 28/39 flew. But the same idea had occurred to people elsewhere; two German scientists, Hahn and Ohain, suggested a similar idea to the German authorities at much the same time as Whittle, but the Germans reacted more positively with the result that their first jet aircraft flew in August 1939, a few days before the outbreak of war.

Both countries saw the advantages of the new engine, but progress

Arado 234 The huge increase in power when the jet engine came into being gave airframe designers different kinds of problems and the chance to evolve into another flying dimension. One of the results was the Arado, the world's first jet bomber, but it was not available in sufficient numbers to make an impression by the time the war ended. The prototypes were mounted with skids for landing and three-wheeled trolleys for take-off. Production models had a conventional tricycle undercarriage. It had something of the look of an aircraft five years into the future.

and required a great deal of work to make it serviceable. Production aircraft began to appear late in 1941, but these were plagued with mechanical problems, and in was not until late 1942 that the Typhoon suddenly "came right" and demonstrated that it could be a high-speed fighter and catch the fastest German machines then raiding England, and also act as a ground attack machine and scourge German troops in France and the Low Countries.

One facet of army cooperation which had been thoroughly explored in the Western Desert was the employment of fighter aircraft to attack tanks, and a number of Hurricane fighters were fitted with 40mm cannon for this purpose. Then came the use of solid-fuel rockets with solid steel warheads, no more than a different method of propelling the standard antitank artillery projectile of the day. These rockets were also applied to anti-submarine warfare by RAF Coastal Command and Fleet Air Arms machines and proved to be highly effective. The Typhoon, a heavy and strong machine, was well suited to the carriage of rockets and cannon, and it was to become one of the premier "tank-busting" aircraft of the war.

"The Yanks are coming"
In December 1941 the United States was pitchforked into the war, and by the summer of 1942 their 8th Air Force was assembling in Britain to throw its weight into the bombing attack on Germany. The Americans had developed the Boeing B17 Flying Fortress as their strategic bomber,

together with the legendary Norden bombsight. The Fortress took its name from the multiplicity of defensive machine guns it carried, the theory being that a formation could put up a pattern of interlocking fire which would prevent any fighter ever getting close enough to do them damage. This, coupled with the accuracy of the Norden sight, convinced the US commanders that their forte was daylight raiding. Nevertheless, they were intelligent enough to spend the remaining months of 1942 on attacking targets in Northern France and the Low Countries which could be reached accompanied by Spitfire fighter escorts. The commanders of the first US bombing squadrons were smart enough to realize that they were coming late to the war, and that those who had been fighting for some time might have some useful experience to offer them. Moreover, most of the bombers being shipped out from the USA were going to support the North African campaign, and less than 100 were available for work in Europe.

He162 Called the *Volksjäger* ("People's Fighter"), the 162 looked as if it were designed by a committee of vacuum salesmen. Strangely, in December 1944, a mere 90 days after the project was formulated the prototype was flying. Only three bolts held the BMW turbojet to the light metal airframe, and confidence in it staying with the aircraft must have been minimal. A few 162s were removed by the Allies at the end of the war for testing and evaluation.

Gloster Meteor The first British jet to go operational, it was delivered to the RAF in July 1944 and immediately flew sorties against the V1 flying bombs. The original plan was to call it the Thunderbolt, but American objections prevailed since the name had already been given to their P47 fighter.

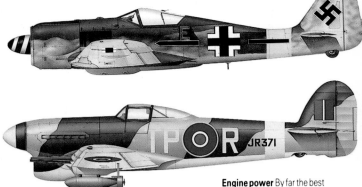

In January 1943, the Casablanca Conference gave a directive to Harris and his American counterpart General Ira C. Eaker: "Your primary aim will be the progressive destruction and dislocation of the German military, industrial and economic system, and the undermining of the morale of the German people...." In practical terms, the USAF were to bomb by day and the RAF by night until Germany collapsed. The Americans would precision-bomb selected strategic targets – their first stated priority was the German aircraft industry – while the British would area-bomb cities and industrial complexes.

The Americans were soon disabused of any ideas that the Flying Fortress was invulnerable or that the Norden bombsight could guarantee precision. Trials of a bombsight in cloudless American skies with the aircraft flying straight and slow were one thing; using it in combat in the foul weather which frequently shrouded Europe, with the aircraft weaving and dodging the defences was something different. And theoretical drawings of arcs of fire of a perfectly-aligned formation bore little resemblance to the actual arcs of fire delineated by hard-pressed gunners in ragged formations trying to cope with two, three and four oncoming targets at once. With much practice, some accurate bombing was achieved, but at a terrible price, and it was not until the development of the Mustang and Thunderbolt long-range fighters which could escort the bombers to their targets and back that the Fortress formations could hope to make raids without being severely mauled.

The battle over Germany

The RAF were also taking punishment. The German defences had been overhauled and improved, with radar detection of oncoming attacks, radar control of fighters, and a solid belt of gun and fighter defences – the "Kammhuber Line" – stretching from Denmark to the French frontier over which every incursion had to fly. Nevertheless, between the two forces German cities and German industries were put under attack with ever-increasing frequency and ever-increasing weights of bombs. Yet in spite of this, German productivity actually rose during 1942-44.

While all this was in progress, the technicians were busy at something new. The growing power of defensive measures, and the resulting attrition of

trained aircrews led to contemplation of remotely-controlled aerial weapons which could be simply pointed in the desired direction, launched, and left to look after themselves.

The concept of remotely-controlled, or even automatically-controlled, bombing machines had arisen during the First World War and had been toyed with from time to time. Generally, the imagination of the inventors went no further than a conventional aeroplane with some form of automatic pilot; this theory might be said to have reached its zenith in the "Weary Willy" bombers developed by the American air force in 1944. These were war-weary – i.e. nearly worn out – heavy bombers which were fitted with automatic pilots, stripped of defensive armament and stuffed with high explosive. They were flown off the ground by a pilot and skeleton crew who aligned the aircraft on a course which would fly it to some selected German target, set an automatic pilot and a timing device, and then parachuted out just as the machine was about to cross the English coastline. The whole affair was extremely hazardous, and after one or two of these flying mines had detonated in mid-air before the crew had completed their preparations and left, the idea was abandoned.

The rocket arrives

In Germany, though, far more advanced ideas were under development. The rocket had gripped German military imagination in the late 1920s and early 1930s; the Army had seen that the rocket gave them the possibility of developing a long-range bombardment weapon which was not proscribed by the Versailles Treaty, simply because it had never been considered. By the time the war broke out a massive research establishment had been set up at Peenemünde, on an island in the Baltic, and two weapons

Engine power By far the best German fighter the war produced, the Focke Wulf 190 *(top)* was also their first radial-engined monoplane, the power coming from a BMW 8011D. A prototype flew as early as 1939, the first clash with the RAF coming in August 1941. A late model, the Tu152, had a speed of over 460mph at 35,000ft. The airframe of the Hawker Typhoon *(above)* was designed to fit around a new and powerful 24-cylinder Napier engine. There were some engine failures and structural weaknesses which plagued its initial squadron service life in 1941, but once these had been cured the "Tiffy" became a real killer, for some reason particularly of trains, at least 150 a month being destroyed in 1943. On D-Day 1944, 26 squadrons of Typhoons assisted the ground troops, carring 2000lb bomb loads or eight high-explosive rockets.

THE FLYING FORTRESS

With the entry of America into the war in 1941, the strategic bombing of Europe took on new and awesome proportions.

In order to achieve the pinpoint accuracy needed to hit the specialist industrial targets, aircraft of the American 8th Air Force flew by day. High in the rarified air, massed formations of B-17 Flying Fortresses and B24 Liberators flew in streams over 20 miles long. They flew in tight box formations of six aircraft, enabling the formidable firepower of each aircraft to be directed at defending its neighbour.

The raids met with terrible resistance from the German Luftwaffe, desperately defending their home soil. The early raids proved costly in men and materials and it wasn't until the range of the fighter escorts was improved with the addition of long-range, disposable fuel tanks that the losses could be cut.

The effectiveness of the daylight raids on German industry is still a matter of debate, but the fact that towards the end of the war the full available strength of the Luftwaffe had to be thrown against them meant that in other theatres of operations the Allies had better control of the skies.

Focke Wulf 190 One of the finest fighters the Germans produced, the FW190 was a match for all the Allied fighters. Armed with 20mm cannon, the pilots attacked head-on, raking the vulnerable cockpit and engines of the American bombers with lethal fire.

FW190 versus B17 The view from the cockpit of an FW190 as it attacks a B17 head-on, the best angle from which to achieve a kill. The first picture shows the B17 at a range of 730m (800yd). Just over a second later, the fighter opens fire at a range of 460m (500yd) (3) and ceases firing at 370m (400yd) (4). The fighter would have to begin moving out of the way by 275m (300yd) (5) otherwise collision is inevitable within half a second at 180m (200yd) (6).

The fighter escort Several types of aircraft were used at various times to escort the bombers. Flying faster than the bombers, the fighters would zigzag above the stream, keeping a watch out for approaching enemy fighters.

P51 Mustang When re-engined with a Packard built Rolls Royce Merlin engine, the American-built Mustang became a superlative fighter aircraft. With a maximum speed of 440mph at 30,000ft the Mustang's slightly meagre armament of four 0.5in machine guns was more than compensated for by its strength and manoeuverability. With the introduction of long-range tanks the Mustang was able to provide fighter cover for bombers all the way to targets deep in the heart of Germany.

B17 Flying Fortress The B17 got its name from the heavy defensive armament it carried. Turrets at the tail, nose, above the cockpit and below the centre of the fuselage housed pairs of 0.5in heavy machine guns while single machine guns were fired from the waist position of the fuselage, in front and from below and behind the cockpit, making a total of 13 guns. Against a target such as Berlin, the B17 would carry a crew of 10 and a bombload of 5000lbs, while cruising at 180mph at up to 28,000ft.

were under development. The FZG-76 was a pilotless, winged aircraft powered by a primitive jet motor and carrying a warhead of 1870lbs of high explosive. The A4 was a pure rocket, fin-stabilised, carrying a one-ton high explosive warhead. The FZG-76 had a range of about 130 miles, while the A4 could reach to about 180 miles. Their accuracy, though, was not comparable with bombing aircraft; about 80 percent of FZG-76 would land inside an eight mile circle at maximum range, while the A4 could expect to fall somewhere inside a rectangle 16 miles long and 13 miles wide around the target point. To put it bluntly, these were simply methods of conducting area-bombing without involving bombers; they could hit nothing smaller than a large city.

Once these offensive weapons were into the prototype stage, the scientists turned their attention to defensive applications of their new technology and began devising rockets which could be fired into the air and steered against aerial targets. They also applied rocket technology to aircraft, developing the Me 163 fighters, capable of enormous speeds for a short period and provided with highly destructive weapons, so that they could be flown through a formation of bombers, protected from danger by their speed, and firing their

weapons as they passed. An example of the weapons proposed was "Jägerfaust", a bank of thirty 50mm gun barrels mounted vertically behind the pilot of the Messerschmitt Me 262 jetfighter. These were fitted at divergent angles so that when fired the projectiles would spread out, covering a greater area. The pilot attacked from ahead and as he passed beneath the bomber a photo-electric cell triggered the firing circuit to fire barrels in pairs as two-millisecond intervals. As the shell was launched upwards, so the gun barrel was ejected downwards, balancing the recoil and removing stress from the aircraft. A flight of 12 Me 163 rocket fighters were fitted with six-barrel Jägerfaust units in March 1945 and flew from Brandeis airfield near Leipzig; according to some sources an Allied bomber was actually shot down with this weapon, but this has never been definitely confirmed. A similar device, called "Bombersage" used a battery of 30mm barrels, firing shells upwards and discharging the propellant gas downwards to give a recoilless effect.

V1 and V2

By various intelligence methods the British had become aware of the threat of the two German bombardment weapons, the FZG-76 and the A4 rocket, though their knowledge was rudimentary. Nevertheless, some

V2 rocket *(Below left)* in German the *Aggregat 2*. The underground assembly plant at Nordhausen, Germany, was a V2 production line. Below, the transporter/erector conveyance carrying a test rocket, identifiable by its chequered markings.

Me163 Komet The pilots of this stubby monster had a mere three seconds in which to fire at enemy aircraft, then they were many miles away. But a successful mission didn't signal the end of danger, for the Komet's engine had a nasty habit of catching fire on landing. The first Allied aircraft to meet the Komet were B17s on 28 July 1944 when five of the strange, bulky jets attacked them.

defensive schemes were formed, and when the attack finally came, on 13 June 1944, the defences were ready. In fact the initial launch of FZG-76 missiles was premature; Colonel Wachtel, commanding the firing organization, was under orders that the attack must begin on that date. He knew full well that he was not ready, but he was a clever enough soldier to know that as long as he managed to get a token number of missiles away, honour would be satisfied and he could then close down to perfect his arrangements while his superiors reported up the chain of command that the missile campaign had begun on time. And so at 3.30a.m. on 13th June, the first V1 was launched; nine followed in quick succession, of which five crashed immediately, one flew off never to be seen again, and four crossed the English Channel. Three landed in the countryside but one penetrated into the suburbs of London and, by pure luck, landed on a mass of railway lines.

On the 15th June launching began from 55 separate locations scattered around France and the Low Countries, some 255 missiles being launched against London and 50 against Southampton. Of these 144 crossed the English coast; 14 were shot down by guns, 7 by fighters before they reached London. Seventy-three crossed into Greater London and 11 were shot down by London gun defences. One or two reached Southampton, and one went wildly astray and ended up in Norfolk.

The bombardment by the FZG-76 – now known as V1 for *Vergeltungswaffen Ein* (Vengeance Weapon No. 1), having been so-named by Hitler – was to continue with varying intensity until 23 March 1945. Two-thousand four-hundred and nineteen missiles reached London to cause 5500 deaths and injure about 16,000 people; 3957 were shot down by the defences. But before this campaign finished, a second had begun; on 8 September 1944 the A4 rocket was thrown into the battle.

Hitler called this the V2, and it posed a terrible problem for the defences. The rocket was launched vertically from a small portable pad which could be quickly emplaced and even more quickly removed after firing, so that detecting the firing sites was almost impossible. Once fired it ascended rapidly into the stratosphere, tilted over to assume a ballistic trajectory, shut off its rocket motor at a radio signal, and then coasted at supersonic speed towards its target. As a result there was absolutely no warning at the target; the first indication was the detonation of one ton of high explosive, followed a few seconds later by the noise of its approach. No gunnery in existence could hope to shoot the device down, no aircraft could catch it. The only countermeasure was to set up observation stations to pick up the faint trail of vapour and smoke as it rose or to track it by radar, after which a blanket warning could be given to London to take to the shelters. In short, there was no effective form of defence whatever. A total of 1359 V2 rockets were aimed at London, of which 517 arrived on target, killing about 2400 people and injuring 1850. The last rocket fell on 27 March 1945, simply because the Allied advance in Europe had overrun the launch areas within range of London and forced the German missile-operating regiment to retire.

The German missile attack had been a last furious riposte, an attempt to deal out to Britain what Britain had, through 1944 and early 1945, been dealing out to Germany. For by this time the bombing campaign had acquired an almost self-sustaining momentum. It had been interrupted for a short time in order to become subservient to the Allied invasion plans, though much against the wishes of the two commanders, Harris and Eakers. In spite of their objections the bombing force had been placed under Eisenhower's orders and had been directed to attack the railway and fuel supply systems sustaining the German Army in France and Germany, and in this they had performed an invaluable role. By cutting the railway communications, German reinforcements were effectively stopped from mustering to throw back the invasion forces before they could get themselves established. By damaging the fuel supply organization tanks, trucks and aircraft were brought to a halt. But just as soon as could be managed, the bomber commanders got back their autonomy and began their general bombardment of Germany once more. Although they were loath to admit it, their efforts on behalf of the invasion had also paid off to their benefit, since the fuel shortage now crippling Germany meant that fighter opposition was negligible, and the bombers were able to range far and wide with relatively few casualties. But even with this virtual freedom of the air, and with the ability to bring cities into piles of ruin in a single night, the morale of the German populace was not significantly effected, nor was their ability to turn out munitions. It was the Russian, American and British armies tightening like a noose around Germany which finally brought about the end of the war.

Tactical air power

These armies had been assisted in their advance by the application of tactical air power. The British armies which invaded Normandy in 1944 were accompanied by the 2nd Tactical Air Force, commanded by Coningham, the man who had perfected air-ground co-operation in the Western Desert and had later carried it forward to the invasions of Sicily and Italy. Brought

back to England to take command of the invasion air support, his force ranged far and wide ahead of the advancing British and destroyed tanks, supply lines and troop concentrations, trains, bridges and power stations with total impartiality. Anything which moved and much that didn't fell victim to the rocket-firing Typhoon fighters of 2 TAF. One of the most notable innovations of this time was the perfecting of the cab-rank system of air support, in which a standing patrol of fighter-bombers flew gently back and forth behind the Allied lines. Ground observers, usually pilots who could appreciate the airmen's problems, were attached to the forward troops and were in radio contact with a controller. As soon as one of the observers saw a target he informed the controller, who immediately despatched the first aircraft on the cab-rank. As it approached its target area it

B29 Superfortress this giant USJ bomber could fly over 3000 miles at speeds of 350mph while carrying 20,000lb of bombs. It went into action against the Japanese mainland in 1944 from bases in India. On 6 August 1945, the B29 *Enola Gay* obliterated Hiroshima with "Little Boy", the first atomic bomb; three days later another B29, *Bock's Car*, dropped "Fat Man" on Nagasaki. These two bombs were the catalyst which led to the Japanese surrender. The B29 bomber dropped 167,000 tons of bombs on Korea in three years, but could not win the war. Then, true to form, the Russians, using three B29s that had to land in their country, made almost exact copies and later introduced them as Tupolev 4s.

was contacted by the ground observer by direct radio and by verbal messages and assisted by coloured smoke or flares fired by the ground troops, the precise target was clearly indicated. The aircraft attacked, and then returned to its base to refuel and rearm, then flew back to take up its place in the cab-rank once again. Once this system was running properly, air support for ground troops was guaranteed in a matter of minutes. A similar system was operated by the US Army Air Force in support of US ground troops. The only restriction on the system was, of course, that imposed by weather – as the Battle of the Bulge showed. The Germans were able to form up and make their advance under the cover of weather which made flying impossible, and the Allied troops, who were by now accustomed to a high quality of air support, were hamstrung without it. The tide of battle began to turn in a decisive manner only when the weather improved and the cab-ranks were able to resume operation.

The blitz on Japan
In the Pacific theatre of war the Americans had applied their bombing techniques to the Japanese cities with devastating effect, once they had developed aircraft capable of covering the immense distances and once they had captured islands which could provide them with bases within reach of Japan. A sortie against Tokyo had been made in April 1942 by flying 18 twin-engined bombers off an aircraft carrier, overflying Japan to land at friendly bases in China, but this was a major undertaking, suffered losses, and was more in the nature of a propaganda exercise than an operation which could be repeated at will. Only when Okinawa, Saipan, Tinian, Guam and similar islands were in American hands, and when the Boeing B29 Superfortress, with its 3250 mile range, became available, did the attacks on the Japanese homeland begin in earnest. When they did, they revealed the inadequacy of the Japanese defences – since the Japanese had been safe in their long-distance isolation and had paid small heed to the lessons they might have learned from Germany. The effect of incendiary bombs on Japan's closely-packed and highly inflammable cities was worse than the effects obtained in Germany; although much has been said about the death toll from the atomic bombs dropped on Hiroshima and Nagasaki, the fact remains that a single fire raid on Tokyo on 9 March 1945, killed an estimated 120,000 people, destroyed thousands of homes and did more short-term damage than did the Hiroshima bomb.

POST-WAR

The final years of the bomber, the birth of the multi-role aircraft

After the war, when the analyses of bombing effectiveness were made, doubts began to be expressed about the value of the immense sacrifices which had been made in men and material. According to some analysts the RAF's Bomber Command absorbed as much of the national resources as the whole of the British Army; it had suffered the loss of 55,573 officers and men killed and 9784 shot down and imprisoned. Post-war German calculations determined that 593,000 civilians had been killed, 3,370,000 dwellings destroyed, five million people rendered homeless, and all the major city centres of Germany were razed to the ground. But between 1941 and 1944 German production of armoured vehicles increased five-fold, of military aircraft three-fold, of artillery weapons eight-fold.

The bomber barons
These figures, of course, took a long time to appear. And in the interim the bomber ethos had become firmly established as the world's air forces continued to build bigger and better bombers, notably for carrying the new nuclear weapon but also for conventional bombing if necessary. The huge propeller-driven machines were replaced by huge jet-propelled machines, leading to the Boeing B-52 Stratofortress – 630 mph, 12,500-mile range, 35 tons of bombs; the Hawker-Siddeley Vulcan – 620 mph, 4600-mile range, 12 tons of bombs; or the Tupolev Tu-20 – 540 mph, 7800-mile range, 12 tons of bombs.

Avro Vulcan One-third of the trio of V-bombers, the Vulcan, Victor and Valiant, Britain's post-war nuclear bomber force, the Vulcan entered service in May 1958 as a delta-winged strike bomber. The B2 version could carry Blue Steel stand-off bombs or 21 1000lb HE bombs.

B52 Stratofortress A billion dollars has been spent building just over 300 of these awesome bombers. One variant, the B52D, is coded as BUFF, standing for "Big Ugly Fat Fella"; but ugly or not, plans are that it will still be operational by the year 2000. However, the many advances in missile technology may preclude this possibility.

At the same time the improvements in missile technology led, in the middle 1950s, to the adoption of air defence missile systems which could deal very effectively with these huge machines at high altitudes, and this led to a change in strategic policy, to the development of stand-off bombs which were self-propelled and could be released well before reaching the danger area around the target and guided to their destination while the carrier aircraft turned back to its base. And finally came the perfection of intercontinental ballistic missiles which, in an extension of the German A-4 rocket policy, permitted the bombardment of distant countries to an unprecedented degree of accuracy without employing aircraft at all. So far as major warfare between major powers went, the bomber was now obsolete in its primary role. But like the battleship of earlier days, its owners were reluctant to part with it since it was the outward and visible sign of their power.

Nevertheless, under the influence of tactical and strategic facts, the world's air forces have gradually been brought to realize that their principal role must be the tactical support of the land armies if they are to find a role at all. In consequence, the designers of the 1970s and 1980s have thrown away their ideas of huge aircraft and have concentrated upon multi-role fighter-bombers, aircraft which by slight modification during manufacture can be structured for the interceptor role or for the ground attack role.

The other imperative facing aircraft designers is the enormous cost of developing a modern aircraft, a cost so daunting that more and more designs are being shared between like-minded nations so as to spread the expense and increase the production. An example of these two tendencies can be seen in the Panavia Tornado, developed by Britain, West Germany and Italy as a collaborative venture between 1967 and 1972. Carefully designed to be all things to all users, the Tornado can be employed as a close air support and battlefield interdiction machine, a long-range strike aircraft, a naval strike

aircraft, an air defence interceptor, a reconnaissance machine or a trainer. With the ability to fly at Mach 2 (1320 mph), climb to 50,000 feet, range to 1000 miles on its internal fuel and carry a bombload of 15,000 lbs, and armed with two 27mm Mauser cannon, there are very few tasks which the Tornado cannot perform. The comparable Soviet aircraft, the Sukhoi Su-19, is somewhat faster, is armed with a twin-barrel 23mm cannon, carries about the same load of bombs or missiles, but has a range of little more than 500 miles.

From Korea to Vietnam
This, though, is the major war scenario. Where smaller wars are concerned the belief that air power applied in the grand strategic manner will solve all the problems has been a long time dying. In 1950, the North Korean Army rolled across the 38th Parallel and attacked South Korea, leading to the prolonged Korean War in which various United Nations forces opposed first the North Koreans and latterly the Chinese Army. In order to interdict the supply lines running south from Manchuria the US Air Force mounted massive bombing raids, using Superfortresses, from Okinawa and from bases in Japan. Using radar navigation aids they were able to drop immense bombloads quite close to the UN front line, as well as striking at important rail and road junctions, reservoirs, power stations

and other strategic targets in North Korea. From the viewpoint of the UN soldiers on the ground, they might as well have stayed at home. There was no diminution in the supply of ammunition, weapons, men or rations on the other side; indeed as the war went on things seemed to get worse, with more artillery, bigger rockets, more troops appearing daily. The Chinese, using manpower on feet rather than relying on trains or trucks, built up unbreakable supply lines which stretched for hundreds of miles and delivered their simple requirements in ample proportion, and no matter how many tons of bombs rained down on some vital rail junction in North Korea, several thousand labourers simply walked around the damaged area with the supplies on their backs.

Where air support worked superbly was in the immediate provision of support to the front-line soldiers. Artillery observation posts across the UN front invariably held an observer from one of the Allied air forces who was in radio contact with an air strike controller, and just behind the front line a cab-rank of fighter-bombers was on continuous patrol. As soon as anything of importance – a gun, a tank, even a suspicious cluster of men – was seen, the first fighter off the cab-rank would immediately fly to the target and, under the direction of the ground observer, open up with rockets and machine guns.

Tornado This fine aircraft is probably the only successful weapon to come from the decisions of a committee, that body in this case being three Western Powers, Britain, West Germany and Italy. With wings that can be swept forward and back in flight for different flying characteristics, the air defence version seen here has an extra 1.37m (4½ft) added to take the advanced technology instrumentation needed to operate four Sky Flash and two Sidewinder air-to-air missiles; it also carries a 27mm Mauser cannon. The ground attack version can fly at great speed at very low level with the help of its terrain following radar. This method of attack enables the aircraft to fly under enemy radar so avoiding detection. The Tornado would probably be the main weapon thrown against enemy armoured forces attacking Nato.

If a UN patrol was caught out in no-man's land, a fighter could be brought up to shepherd them back to the safety of their own lines. American F-80 "Shooting Star" jets, or British Naval Sea Fury propeller-driven fighters were always on call and invariably on target.

The helicopter at war
The war in Korea, however, did introduce a new machine to battle – the helicopter. This had made its first serious appearance during the early years of the Second World War but at that time was not entirely reliable nor held in much esteem, and it was principally used as a liaison machine in rear areas. By the time of the Korean War its reliability had improved significantly and it found considerable application in the evacuation of wounded from points immediately behind the front line. This did immeasurable good to the morale of the soldiers, and before the war ended it was commonly said that a man wounded in the line would be safely tucked up in a base hospital in Japan within six hours, having been helicoptered back to an American air-base where hospital planes were flying a regular shuttle service between Korea and Japan.

From this service, the use of the helicopter spread to observation and artillery spotting, moving bodies of troops and mounting raids, but these latter missions were in the nature of trials since the machines of the period were not capable of carrying heavy loads for long distances. One remarkable fact was the ability of the helicopter to survive above the battlefield. While the North Korean and Chinese anti-aircraft machine gunners in the front line appeared quite capable of shooting down high speed fighter bombers making strikes, they rarely managed to shoot down a helicopter. This was probably due to its unconventional appearance and manoeuvering, which made it a difficult target to gunners accustomed to more conventional speeds and courses.

In Vietnam, in the 1960s, the same

Bell Iroquois and Aerospatiale/Westland Puma The official name Iroquois was soon replaced by the nickname Huey (from its military designation HU1, for helicopter utility 1). It was used extensively in Vietnam for transport and casualty evacuation and was one of the first "Gunships" when heavy machine guns were mounted either side in the doors. As a medium transport helicopter the Puma *(below left)* can carry 16-20 fully armed troops for 355 miles to points where they are needed fast. In the photograph it is seen hovering above a 105mm light gun at the British Army training ground in Canada.

Fairchild A10 Thunderbolt
This is an unconventional
USAF tank-buster with no
frills. Designed to take heavy
battlefield damage and still
fly, it carries a General Electric
Gatling gun in the nose, not
the old-fashioned American
Civil War weapon, but a
fearsome monster with
seven rotating barrels which
fire 30mm shells at up to 4200
rounds per minute. In a single
second 70 explosive shells
will strike the target at 3650m
(4000yd) range.

lesson was re-learned. Massive air bombardments of North Vietnamese targets entirely failed to prevent the build-up of troops and supplies in the south, opposing the American and South Vietnamese forces. Remarkable feats were performed in bombing isolated targets which, the intelligence experts assured the airmen, would immediately result in the North Vietnamese war effort coming to a dead stop. The targets – bridges, dams, power houses, railroads – were duly bombed. But it made no difference to the soldiers in the front line. All they were concerned with was the availability of close support aircraft, operated on a system similar to that used in Korea and virtually guaranteeing massive fire support at a moment's notice.

By this time, also, the helicopter had made enormous strides in technology and for the first time made an impact on the conduct of battle. It was now possible to supply isolated posts, move fighting patrols, rescue downed pilots and recover wounded troops under fire all by the use of helicopters. The US forces developed their Air Cavalry, highly mobile troops capable of being placed into combat by helicopter – "vertical containment" was one phrase which became common – enabling Vietcong guerilla bands to be rapidly surrounded or have their lines of retreat blocked while conventional ground forces moved against their front. Bigger helicopters allowed artillery and even light vehicles to be ferried from point to point for faster and more

effective deployment of resources. Against this was the fact that by this time, with the helicopter becoming a more common sight, it had lost its novelty and had become an easier target for air defence weapons.

The helicopter also assumed great importance in naval air operations. Since its earliest days it had been appreciated that its slow speed and excellent field of view would make it useful as a submarine-hunter, though the post-war development of deeper and faster submarines tended to reduce this factor. But as a method of moving underwater sensing devices and as a platform for the discharge of anti-submarine weapons, the helicopter soon became indispensable for naval operations.

Looking for a rule
In the years since the end of the Second World War much money and effort has been poured into air forces all over the world, and particularly into navigational and bomb-aiming equipment. When the British Army was given the task of regaining the Falkland Islands in 1982, after their annexation by Argentina, it was an obvious task for the RAF to use their strategic bombing ability to fly the immense distance, firstly to Ascension Island and then to East Falkland, so as to destroy Stanley airfield, Argentina's sole supply link. Vulcan bombers were deployed, and some 40 heavy bombs were dropped in the face of relatively negligible defences. One bomb clipped the edge of the runway, but the airfield remained in use throughout the

campaign, supplies being flown in until shortly before the final Argentine collapse. Carrier-borne fighter-bombers, however, performed valuable close-support attacks in appalling weather, and helicopters allowed the British force to move rapidly and deploy effectively, even though the helicopter strength was seriously depleted by Argentine action against their transporting ship. The lessons had been relearned yet again.

Shortly after the conclusion of the Falklands campaign it was announced that the Vulcan bombers would finally be retired. The US and Soviet air forces still maintain bomber fleets, but one is entitled to wonder how much of their retention is due to honest belief in their value or to the battleship complex mentioned previously. The lesson of history is clear: air forces deployed to support the action of ground forces will assist the conduct of war. Air forces acting in a vacuum, as an independent force, contribute little.

The Harrier The only V/STOL operational fighter in service in the western world. The ground attack version *(top)* can be sited close to the battle area on a makeshift launching pad. The Sea Harrier *(left)* made its mark very effectively by taking on the Mirages of the Argentine Air Force during the retaking of the Falkland Islands. There, the Sea Harrier operating from carriers provided air cover for the fleet and ground troops, using an impressive weapon array backed by the latest technology.

AIR MOBILITY

The advent of the helicopter brought a new and important tool to the battlefield. Used in the transport mode, it proved highly effective in bringing troops and materials to the heart of the action and evacuating casualties quickly and with a degree of comfort not possible before. In answer to the problem of ground fire around the landing zone, the "gun ship" evolved. Initially a transport helicopter with heavy machine guns mounted at the doors on either side, the modern development, the "attack" helicopter, has a chin turret with rapid firing machine gun and can carry rocket pods or antitank guided missiles.

Bell Huey Cobra There are two versions of this helicopter, the Huey and the Sea Cobra, both being heavily armed with various missiles depending on the tactical role. The chain gun is available, as are Hellfire and TOW missiles and rockets, all of which are linked by avionics to laser trackers, laser rangefinders, thermal detectors, and a digital fire control computer. There is a crew of two sitting tandem.

Hughes 500 This helicopter, well known in civilian guise, is used in the battle zone as a forward observation post. Its speed and agility are enough to keep it out of trouble, though later developments are now appearing armed with antitank missiles and sophisticated sighting systems enabling it to spot targets from behind cover and at night.

Boeing Chinook The workhorse of the helicopter league, the Chinook is used in the transport and heavy-lift role. It can carry over 40 fully equipped troops or heavy loads internally while further equipment is carried slung beneath. The Chinook can airlift an artillery piece straight to the battle zone and keep it well supplied with ammunition.

Sikorsky Black Hawk A relatively new helicopter on the inventories of the world's forces, the Black Hawk is a great advance in aviation technology. In its primary role as troop transport, it can carry an 11-man infantry squad with all their equipment along with its three man crew. Yet it has many other roles, including special communications jamming and the attack role when it is armed with missiles, mine dispensers and machine guns.

IN CONCLUSION

The influence of the technologies of today on the warfare of tomorrow

In the 1930s, it occurred to a handful of scientists that if it were possible to split an atom, the energy realeased could be utilized. That this was achieved is now a matter of history, and the first manifestations of the harnessing of nuclear power are still a subject of controversy.

The first atomic bomb was dropped on the Japanese city of Hiroshima on 5 August 1945; the second was dropped four days later on Nagasaki. The first bomb, called "Little Boy", contained a central tube which carried a charge of explosive and a quantity of Uranium-235. When the bomb fuze functioned at the designated altitude the explosive fired, launching the U-235 down the gun tube to come into contact with another portion of U-235. The two separate portions were each below the "critical mass" necessary to initiate the atomic reaction; once brought rapidly together they exceeded this mass and detonation automatically followed.

The second bomb, "Fat Boy" took its descriptive name from being much larger than "Little Boy" since it used a somewhat different system of initiation and a different critical material, Plutonium-239. The power of each bomb was roughly equivalent to 20,000 tons of TNT, i.e. 20 kilotons.

This demonstration of power brought the war to a rapid close – and a new dimension to warfare. Meanwhile the Soviets had acquired the technical information to enable them to build their own bomb, as a result of which an armaments race began, and it has continued to this day.

The Soviets exploded their first atomic bomb in September 1949, but by that time American scientists were developing something far more powerful: the thermonuclear bomb.

Known also as the "fission-fusion" bomb or the hydrogen bomb, this was a more complex design relying upon a simple atomic bomb which, by nuclear fission, developed intense heat and pressure which caused fusion of the atoms of a quantity of deuterium which formed the core of the bomb. The high-energy neutrons released by this fusion then reacted with a charge of U-238 to provide the ultimate detonation. Bombs of this type, first fired in 1952, develop detonations measured in the megaton range (i.e. millions of tons of TNT), with wide-ranging destructive effect. Five years later, the Soviets were able to detonate their own thermonuclear device – the age of the nuclear superpowers had begun.

In that same year, the Soviets launched Sputnik I, the first orbiting space vehicle. Instead of, as the USA and Britain, developing fleets of long-range bombing aircraft to carry free-fall nuclear bombs, the Soviets had, while still developing a small air fleet, gone straight to the development of intercontinental rocket-propelled missiles capable of carrying nuclear warheads enormous distances. Both the USA and the USSR had benefited from the wartime German research into rockets and had deployed various medium-range missiles on either side of the German border in the 1950s. At the same time, under the drive of Admiral Gorschkov, the Soviet Navy was beginning to expand and experiments were already under way on launching rocket missiles from submarines.

By the late 1950s, it was clear that the Soviets were rapidly approaching a point where their offensive capability would be considerably greater than that of the USA.

Atomic bombs The first A-weapons were man's most advanced instruments of destruction in 1945. "Fat Man" *(top)* obliterated much of Nagasaki in August 1945, "Little Boy" *(above)* had destroyed Hiroshima and most of its population in seconds three days previously. We have today made great improvements on these crude weapons, which only had the effect of 20,000 tons of HE. Now, we talk of megaton warheads.

Mutual MADness

During the 1960s, under the Kennedy administration, American policy changed to the "Mutually Assured Destruction" (MAD) theorem. This was initially based on the principle of targetting missiles not on cities but more accurately on Soviet missile launching areas, the presumption being that if the Soviets essayed a first strike, then a retaliatory firing would destroy their ability to follow up. Or, if the USA tried the first strike, then the Soviets would, by destroying all the USA launch sites, be in a similar position. Hence "mutually assured destruction". However, Soviet strength became so overwhelming that the USA was no longer capable of dealing with all the possible launch sites with one salvo of missiles, and therefore the targetting policy changed back to "city-busting", the threat of devastating every Society city in response to any attack.

By the end of the 1960s the nature of the game had changed once more, this time due to the development of "multiple independently-targetted re-entry vehicles" (MIRVs). These were complex warheads which, after re-entering the earth's atmosphere from their stratospheric flight, would break open and dispense a number of smaller warheads, each with a thermonuclear bomb and each with rockets and pre-programmed guidance mechanisms so that they would disperse to attack different targets. By this means the USA gained two advantages: firstly the ability to strike several targets from the launch of a single missile; and secondly the ability to deceive the Soviets as to where the weapon might be aimed.

The MIRV came about because of advances in anti-missile technology. The ability to provide very accurate guidance, and the high speed of which modern missiles were capable, meant that, provided the approaching enemy missile could be detected, then it was theoretically possible to launch a small, fast missile to intercept it well outside the earth's atmosphere and detonate it where the nuclear explosion would be relatively harmless. This led to the deployment of enormous early-warning radar screens across the Northern Hemisphere so that missiles could be detected as they rose from their launching pads.

The drawback to this, it transpired, was the staggering cost of attempting to defend an entire continent with batteries of anti-missile systems, and eventually both the USA and the USSR gave up the attempt.

Search for the clean bomb

In the 1970s technology made some advances in bomb design. During the 1960s the "cobalt bomb" had been devised; this used cobalt as part of the fission-fusion process and, due to the peculiar qualities of cobalt, resulted in a very "dirty" bomb, one which scattered huge quantities of radio-active dust and radiation. Calculations soon showed that the cobalt bomb would be a two-edged weapon, since the cloud of radio-active fallout would, in all probability, linger long enough to drift across the country which had fired the missile and thus wreak as much destruction there as it had on the target. The accent therefore changed to research into a "clean" bomb, one which would destroy but with limited after-effects.

One result of this was the so-called "neutron bomb" devised in the late 1970s. The effect was to produce a limited nuclear detonation of quite small power but throwing off intense short-range radiation which would have extremely rapid effects against the human body. The object in view was to provide short-range missiles with neutron warheads to be fired against Soviet armoured vehicles. The limited detonation would do little material

B52 missile launch The gigantic USAF B52 can launch a number of missiles as well as carry conventional bombs. Perhaps the most controversial armament is the "cruise" missile, seen here in a test launch over the Nevada desert. Carrying a nuclear warhead, it flies at aircraft speeds at very low level avoiding detection by radar. Its pre-programmed guidance computer will direct it to a chosen target.

damage, but the intense radiation would kill or severely injure the tank crews.

The Soviets promoted a vast "peace" campaign to counter the neutron threat. The Americans promised to stop development of the neutron device, and the campaign stopped overnight. The Soviets had won their point – and had been given a breathing space in which to develop their own neutron weapon. With a new American administration, the neutron weapon idea was revived; but by that time, the Soviets had got their programme into working order and their objections were relatively small.

From control to Star Wars
Interspersed with all this activity, there were repeated attempts to limit the spread of nuclear weapons. The Strategic Arms Limitation Talks (SALT) began in 1969 between the USA and the USSR, and by 1972 some agreements had been reached. These included a Treaty on the Limitation of Anti-Ballistic Missile Systems, an Interim Agreement on Limitation of Strategic Offensive Arms, and a "Statement on Basic Principles of Mutual Relations". Then, in 1974, came an agreement which established a common ceiling on the number of all strategic delivery vehicles and a maximum of 150 kilotons for underground nuclear testing. Since that time the discussions and arguments have continued; SALT 2 was to be

negotiated within five years of SALT 1, but though discussions were held the US Senate refused to ratify the agreement, and after the Soviet invasion of Afghanistan the whole question of SALT agreements was put to one side. Then President Reagan took office and, after the period of detente under the Carter regime, the Americans began to look to re-armament and a re-statement of the MAD theory.

In 1983, President Reagan stunned the world by making a broadcast in which he spoke of embarking on "a programme to counter the awesome Soviet missile threat with measures that are defensive". The aim, he said, was two-fold: to strengthen deterrence and to make nuclear weapons "impotent and obsolete".

Officially called the "Strategic Defense Initiative" (SDI), though nicknamed "Star Wars", the programme has since been studied in depth; President Reagan, in a later interview, expanded on his ideas: "Effective defences against ballistic missiles have the potential for enhancing deterrence by increasing an aggressor's uncertainty and helping reduce or eliminate the apparent military value of nuclear attack to an aggressor. In our SDI research we seek to reduce the incentives – now or in the future – for Soviet aggression, and thereby to ensure effective deterrence for the long-term."

The SDI programme is currently only a paper assembly of several lines of high-technology research, many of which have yet to be brought to fruition. The general aim is to place in space a number of orbiting stations provided with high-technology weapons which will be able to strike at missiles. These weapons include high-energy lasers, chemical lasers, gas-dynamic lasers, particle beams, hyper-velocity electro-magnetic guns, radio-frequency weapons – and some of these technologies have been proved feasible in limited tests.

In 1984 another programme, the "Homing Overlay Experiment" demonstrated that an ICBM could be intercepted and destroyed more than 160km (100mi) above the earth by an infrared guided missile fired over 6540km (4000mi) away. In 1985 a laser beam was fired from the earth to strike a target no more than 15cm (6in) across, which was deployed by the Space Shuttle some 350km (220mi) up. Also in 1985 the US Army demonstrated their ability to acquire and track a missile in space by means of a laser, and lasers have already shown their ability to shoot down remotely-controlled targets in flight. Congress approved the Pentagon's plans and has set aside $26 billion for the programme's operation until 1990.

It is interesting to review the past century of military endeavour and note how the aim has changed. In the 1880s, weapons were developed for offence, the object being to acquire territory and dominion. The last 50 years has demonstrated to the democracies that territory and dominion are little more than a nuisance, and an expensive nuisance at that. As a result the accent in the West is now turning to weapons of defence, simply to keep potential aggressors away.

INDEX

ACKNOWLEDGEMENTS

7 Robert Hunt Library; **8t,c** Ann Ronan Picture Library; **9, 11c** Mary Evans Picture Library; **11r** Ann Ronan Picture Library; **12, 13c,t** Mary Evans Picture Library; **13b** Ann Ronan Picture Library; **14, 15, 16/17, 18, 19t** Mary Evans Picture Library; **19b, 20** Ian Hogg; **22, 23c,b** Mary Evans Picture Library; **23t** Ann Ronan Picture Library; **24tl,b** Mary Evans Picture Library; **24tr, 25, 27t** Ann Ronan Picture Library; **27b, 28** The Trustees of the Imperial War Museum; **29b** Ann Ronan Picture Library; **29t** Mary Evans Picture Library; **30, 31t** Ian Hogg; **31b, 34r** Mary Evans Picture Library; **34l, 35, 36b, 37** The Trustees of the Imperial War Museum; **36t, 40** Ian Hogg; **41, 42** Robert Hunt Library; **43** Ian Hogg; **41, 42** Robert Hunt Library; **43** Ian Hogg; **44, 45** Robert Hunt Library; **48** Ian Hogg; **50l** The Trustees of the Imperial War Museum; **50r, 51** Robert Hunt Library; **52t,b, 53, 54t,b, 55** Ian Hogg; **57** Mary Evans Picture Library; **58** Ian Hogg; **59, 60** Mary Evans Picture Library; **61, 62l, 63l** Robert Hunt Library; **62r, 63l** Mary Evans Picture Library; **64, 65l** Ian Hogg; **65r, 66** The Trustees of the Imperial War Museum; **67** Ian Hogg; **68, 69t** Mary Evans Picture Library; **69b, 70, 71b** Ian Hogg; **71t** Mary Evans Picture Library; **72, 73** Ian Hogg; **74, 75** Mary Evans Picture Library; **76, 77t** Robert Hunt Library; **77b, 78/79** Mary Evans Picture Library; **80r,l** The Trustees of the Imperial War Museum; **81, 82t,b, 83, 85, 86/87t, 87b** Mary Evans Picture Library; **88, 89** Robert Hunt Library; **90** The Trustees of the Imperial War Museum; **92/93** John Hamilton; **94, 95, 96** The Trustees of the Imperial War Museum; **98, 99** John Hamilton, The Trustees of the Imperial War Museum; **102** Ian Hogg; **103, 104l** The Trustees of the Imperial War Museum; **104, 105t** Beken of Cowes Ltd; **105b** Ian Hogg; **107, 108b** Mary Evans Picture Library; **108t, 109t** Pilot Press; **109b** Ian Hogg; **110, 111r,l** Mary Evans Picture Library; **112** Pilot Press; **113, 114** Mary Evans Picture Library; **115** Pilot Press; **116, 117t** Mary Evans Picture Library; **117b** RAF Museum; **118** Barnaby's Library; **119t,b** The Trustees of the Imperial War Museum; **120l** Mary Evans Picture Library; **120, 121** RAF Museum; **122t** Pilot Press; **122b** Jeremy Flack Aviation International; **123, 124b** The Trustees of the Imperial War Museum; ; **124t** Pilot Press; **125** RAF Museum; **126, 126/127t,b** Barnaby's Picture Library; **128t,b** Pilot Press; **129** The Trustees of the Imperial War Museum; **130, 133** Jeremy Flack Aviation International; **132** The Trustees of the Imperial War Museum; **134, 135t** Pilot Press; **135c,b, 136t,c,b** The Trustees of the Imperial War Museum; **137** Pilot Press; **140l,r, 141, 142/143t** The Trustees of the Imperial War Museum; **142b** Pilot Press; **144, 145** Barnaby's Picture Library; **146** Jeremy Flack Aviation International; **147t,b** Barnaby's Picture Library; **148, 149t** Jeremy Flack Aviation International; **149b** Barnaby's Picture Library; **153t,b** The Trustees of the Imperial War Museum; **154, 155** Barnaby's Picture Library

KEY: t=top   c=centre   b=below   r=right   l=left

A full list of titles published by Photographers' Institute Press is available by visiting our website, www.pipress.com

All titles are avail   specialist retailers.

                                                            ct:

PIP, Castle   ed Kingdom

                                                            om